My Father, My Monster

My Father, My Monster

McIntosh Polela

JACANA

First published by Jacana Media (Pty) Ltd in 2011
Second, third and fourth impression 2011

10 Orange Street
Sunnyside
Auckland Park 2092
South Africa
+2711 628 3200
www.jacana.co.za
Job No. 001652

ISBN 978-1-4314-0160-4

Cover design Shawn Paikin and Maggie Davey
Set in Sabon 11/15pt
Printed by Ultra Litho (Pty) Limited, Johannesburg

See a complete list of Jacana titles at www.jacana.co.za

Acknowledgements

I dedicate this story to my mom, Delisile Edista Shezi. The moments we shared will forever be special.

To my beloved sister Zinhle, I know that reading this book will bring back bitter memories, but at the same time I hope you will find in it some release and healing.

Saying thank you seems so inadequate, but I offer my heartfelt gratitude to the following people: to Auntie Zinto for clothing my sister and I and caring for us after losing our mom; to the McNamaras for rescuing my sister from abuse, and giving the two of us so much love and our sister Tita (Laurelle); to Sister Margaret Von Ohr for taking me under your wing, without which this story would probably never have been told; to Cheryl Wood for treating me as your own son at high school, and teaching me the value of forgiveness so I could begin to live; and to Gogo Mambizane, to whom I am forever indebted for your help during my first year at technikon.

How can I ever thank you, Father Lindani Madela, Mike and Janet Maxwell, and the Konrad Adenauer Stiftung Foundation for your kindness and help through technikon? I am also grateful to the British Council for opening the doors to the world to me.

Thank you, Aunt Sibongile, for helping me take the first steps into my life journey, and my stepmother, for helping me through this journey despite your own hardships.

To my love, Tebogo, thank you for supporting me throughout this project and wiping my tears when grief overcame me.

Thank you, Janet van Heerden Harrison and Susanna Coleman, for guiding me through the first few chapters of my work, and Gwen Hewett, my editor, for breathing so much life into this book while staying true to the storyline.

Lastly, a big fat thank you to Jacana Media, my publishers, and finally to you, for taking the time to read my life story.

One

I was just five years old when my sister Zinhle and I arrived in Underberg in the middle of 1982. Just a two-hour drive from South Africa's east coast, the tiny town nestles beneath a majestic mountain range, known as the Drakensberg for its spiny outcrops that resemble a dragon's back. Streams carve their way among the contours, swelling into rivers that explode into waterfalls when they run out of mountainside. And everywhere, grand cliffs stare back implacably, the knowledge of ages etched deep into their faces.

In summer a blue sky smiles down on the lush vegetation; by late winter snowfalls carpet the land in white. Apart from year-round tourism, farming is the mainstay of the economy here. And there is no shortage of labour, for many small villages surround Underberg.

Without a word, our babysitter had simply packed our belongings and put us on a bus that wound noisily along the tranquil country roads to the little village of Pevensey. We didn't object; we were used to being bounced from one babysitter to the next.

When we arrived we were introduced to the people we were to live with: our extended family, we were told. An old woman called Gogo, Grandma, was to look after the two of us, along with the many other children she cared for.

Our hut was made of wattle and daub with a thatched roof. It smelt of woodsmoke, musty grass, dried cow dung and dried mealies. The floor was of dried dung, but unlike the hut of our previous babysitter, it was cracked, dusty and littered with food scraps, discarded bones and fallen thatch. The paint was cracked and peeling from the mud-plastered walls, and there were holes where the rain had softened the mud so that it fell away from the sticks. Dried mealie cobs and onions hung in bunches from rough wooden beams. The thatch was draped with cobwebs and alive with spiders and cockroaches.

Gogo was strong and as musty and dusty as the hut. She wore multilayered skirts under a dirty cotton apron, and an old olive-green jersey with unravelling cuffs was all that protected her from the cold. Covering every hair on her head was a *doek*, a twisted piece of fabric tied and pinned in place. Gogo smelled of woodsmoke from endlessly coaxing the indoor fire. Wrinkles webbed her eyes and deep lines bracketed her mouth, like an old potato left too long in the dark. Her hands were creased and dry, the veins strained with effort, her fingernails broken short. Her fingertips were fissured and engrained with dirt, her feet bare and caked from the fields, their soles cracked and horny.

How could Gogo be related to our beautiful mother who always smelt so good and dressed so smartly, even when she was in her maid's uniform? When would we see her again, and why were we here? These were questions I couldn't answer for Zinhle or myself.

There seemed to be so many children living in the hut, all dressed in filthy, ragged clothes. Most were bigger than us. The only two who were smaller didn't even wear pants. All the children had snotty noses, and some even crusty eyes. Wasn't the family ashamed to let their children look like this?

The children stared at us in our clean clothes and "new" shoes. When our little suitcase was opened and more clothes were found, Gogo snatched them away. At church a few days later other children appeared wearing them. They were *our* clothes, I wanted to say. But I was too timid. At church we were introduced to another old lady, our step-grandmother, we were told. We were to call her Khulu. She worked at the Catholic mission three kilometres away.

For the first few days people streamed in to meet us. In Pevensey, everyone knew everyone else. We had many new faces to get used to. It was difficult to keep up with all their names and titles and how they were related to us. But there was no one to ask. We were too small to talk back to adults. We simply had to accept what we were told.

It wasn't long before I was expected to join the older boys driving the cattle to the pastures along the Polela River. All children had their tasks, and it was made clear that we were also to take part in the family chores. My job was to herd the cattle each day, along with the other boys of more or less my age.

This was my first encounter with cattle. They were as big as motor cars but with sharp horns. Overnight they were kept in an old kraal made of thick poles and thorny branches, and I had to be careful going in or out to avoid getting scratched by the long, white thorns. We had to pull open a gate hung on wires to let the cattle out. The first to emerge was always the big bull with a mean look in his eye. He liked to swing his head to try to catch us with his long, hooked yellow horns. Then the three cows would follow, each with a calf at her side. Last came the two ploughing oxen, even bigger than the bull but not as mean.

On my first day out, we reached the foothills where the cattle began to graze peacefully. My fellow herd boys then made a fire. As the morning wore on, the number of cattle grew as other homesteads released their livestock to graze in the pastures along with ours. Steadily, more boys joined us around the fire. One had a tin of water which he put on the fire. One by one the boys took eggs out of their pockets and put them in the tin to boil. "I only managed to get one egg today," said a boy. "My mother's starting to notice that eggs are disappearing." That was when I realised that each boy had raided a chicken's nest before coming here. The eggs were shared equally, though.

As a five-year-old who had spent most of my time in the city, such a vast open space was liberating. I made friends quickly, I thought, as I spoke to the other boys around me. Sitting in the shade of a thorn tree, surrounded by mountains and eating a boiled egg, I decided I was going to love it here. I began planning how I would raid the chicken coop back at the homestead.

Then a couple of boys got up and left the group. They returned moments later in high spirits. Then I began to notice that the focus of the group was directed towards me. The boys who had briefly disappeared told me they'd found something exciting, a special egg of some sort called *iqanda lenjelwane*. I was curious. "What sort of egg?" I asked. "Come," they said, "we'll show you."

Eagerly I followed them to what they explained was the nest of a creature I'd never heard of. One boy, a great storyteller, eagerly filled me in on the details. It was a rare creature that dug a small hole and then carefully laid an egg in it – a very rare event – before leaving again to look for food. Once the nest was found, it had to be raided quickly because the egg had a habit of vanishing as if by magic.

We reached the spot and they told me to approach the nest slowly, shove my hands into the soft soil around the nest and pull out the egg as fast as I could. Cautiously I crept through the grass, taking care not to make any sound. I was so keen to learn the ways of the pastures that my heart was beating wildly. As soon as I was near enough, I thrust my hands into the sand, grabbed with both hands and withdrew it excitedly. My prize, I discovered, was a fresh, stinking human turd.

The boys were rolling around the grass with laughter, delighted by my distress.

"It's not funny," I said as I ran to the river to wash my hands, trying not to show my tears.

Afterwards, they told me that the prank was a sort of initiation into the grazing fields, and made it clear that I would be expected to participate in future when unsuspecting newcomers arrived. I wasn't impressed. When I got home just before sunset I told Gogo about the prank. She just laughed and said boys didn't talk about what happened in the pastures.

At home there seemed to be endless work to do. It was relentless. Even when the schools opened we had to carry on with our chores. We'd wake at first light every morning to milk the cows before driving the cattle into the pastures to graze. After school, each child in the family carried a container to fetch water in the stream over a kilometre away.

The five-litre container I had to carry was heavy for my size. Zinhle's container held two litres. It took several trips to the stream before the small water drum at home was full. We were always relieved when it was filled. There was little time for the two of us to chat or have fun. The cattle had to be back in the kraal by sunset. After doing my part to fill the water drum, I had to leave to help with the cattle once again.

The hut where we ate had a hearth in the centre where a fire burnt all day. There was only one door and two small windows. Everyone crowded in and sat on the floor, except for two crooked old benches for the men. Women sat on reed mats. Even when we sat in the thatched hut around the fire in the evenings, females were separated from males. The girls had to sit on the left of the hut and boys on the right. Zinhle and I weren't used to such strict social segregation. It was hard not to be able to sit and talk together.

I hated being separated from my sister, but our chores were clearly defined. Girls did girls' work and boys had their own tasks. During ploughing and planting seasons we were especially busy. Only boys could enter the kraal and work with the cattle. Girls weren't allowed there at all. Instead they had to help Gogo sweep, wash, cook and replenish the firewood. They also had to hoe the mealie and vegetable patches for weeds and collect the wild plants to make *imifino*, the spinach dish we ate with our mealiemeal porridge. Although I hated the endless work, I soon grew to prefer it to idling at home.

It all started one day when Gogo was away. That day, all the kids were sitting around the galvinised stove in the main four-roomed mud house. It can rain heavily in the southern Drakensberg. The thunder and lightning can be very loud, and sometimes the hailstones were so big we likened them to chickens' eggs. That day the skies had opened and the rain was falling so heavily we could barely hear each other as it pounded the corrugated-iron roof above us. Suddenly the older children instructed Zinhle and me to get up and stand together. To teach us something, they said. They told us to march like soldiers around the kitchen.

It began innocently enough. I stole glances at Zinhle and smiled as she marched diligently behind me. She smiled back. We were enjoying ourselves. But the older children started to pick on Zinhle, and things began to take a nasty turn. They began to smack her whenever her marching wasn't good enough. Our smiles started to fade. We marched and marched and it seemed we'd never be allowed to stop. Tears rolled down our cheeks but our instructors just laughed, thoroughly enjoying our torment.

At first I didn't know what to think. But soon teasing us became the prime source of amusement for the other children. They were all bigger than us and they'd grown up rough. Their skinny arms and legs were strong and muscled from the constant work they had to do. We were nothing more than toys to entertain them.

The eldest boy, Zozi, was about twelve then. He was dark skinned with small eyes that he made even narrower to look mean. He was the boss and all the children knew it. We had to listen to him or he would get nasty. Sometimes it was just a hard pinch; at other times he would smack us on the head, or push a cow so that she stepped on you.

Everyone was wary of him. We also knew to please him at times. If you did something for him, he might give you some extra sour milk or an extra spoon of sugar.

The two older boys liked to prove their toughness by kicking the dogs that came with us when we herded cattle. They also liked to kill the chickens when Gogo needed one for the pot. Then they would get a little extra when it was cooked, or maybe one of the claws to chew on. It was these two who had engineered my memorable introduction to cattle herding.

After what seemed like an eternal march, these boys told Zinhle to sit on a large wooden bench in the kitchen. Her legs weren't long enough and her feet dangled in the air. They instructed her to keep moving her legs up and down so that the bottom of her thighs thumped against the bench with every movement. She had to carry on until the skin on her thighs turned bright red, and still they wouldn't let her stop. Zozi threatened to come and pinch her or hit her with Gogo's wooden spoon.

Eventually, she started to complain of pins and needles. And all the time I was forced to watch. But I couldn't take it when she started to cry. "Please stop," I said as I went forward to pull her away.

The bigger boys pushed me back and ordered her to continue. No matter how loud she cried, they didn't seem to care. Eventually I crawled to the corner of the kitchen, where I crouched on the floor, crying and begging them to stop. But they wouldn't. The more my sister cried and said her legs were numb, the more they laughed. "Carry on!" they ordered. She and I both knew that worse would follow if she stopped.

Eventually they relented and let her stop. I was so relieved. She retreated to my corner and we cried together while the rain continued to thunder down. All the time they were tormenting her I'd been praying, "Please, God, don't let them hurt us again." But my prayers didn't seem to help.

They grabbed Zinhle again. I tried to hold on to her, to pull her back, but they smacked me so hard I had to let go. I knew then that something was terribly wrong. They'd never hit me that hard before. "Please let her go," I begged, but they laughed and ignored me.

Our tormentors had been steadily feeding wood into the iron stove in the room. Now it was red-hot. One of them suddenly shoved Zinhle towards it. It all happened so quickly. I remember the blisters popping up on the palms of her hands. They'd forced her onto the fiery stove.

It was too much for me. Without a thought, I dashed out into the raging downpour. Feeling my powerlessness as a five-year-old, I leaned against the wall, whimpering in the pouring rain. I didn't care about the lightning and thunder. I wanted to die. I felt I deserved it for failing to protect my sister. I stood there, drenched and shivering, glad to be cold, hoping I would freeze to death. I deserved to.

There was no question of challenging the ringleader. Sometimes his younger brother grew uncomfortable at his sadistic games and asked him to stop. In those rare moments I prayed that he would listen. But he simply ignored these appeals or gave his brother a warning smack. I fantasised about growing bigger and challenging him, of having the strength of my TV heroes, the A-Team, to turn the tables and beat him up, to protect my sister and save us both from this torture.

Anything would have been better than watching Zinhle suffer. I wondered desperately why Mom and Dad didn't come to visit so I could tell them what was happening. Why didn't they fetch us and take us back to Durban?

"I'll tell my mother when she comes," I would sometimes say.

"She's not coming back," the ringleader would reply, and he would laugh as he said it. I thought he was just saying it to be cruel.

As time went on we soon realised that crying didn't help. We hated our daily chores, but when it was raining or too cold to go outside, it meant another onslaught of misery as we were confined with our abusers.

When they weren't tormenting us physically, they loved to tell us scary stories. When I first arrived I was fearless to venture outside at night. But the bigger children started to tell us ghost stories. They told us how those who'd died after a life of sin would leave the vast cemetery behind the Catholic church and wander around at night, terrorising anyone they came across. They would elaborate on each horrific detail until Zinhle and I were terrified. I stopped being carefree, and grew too scared to walk alone from one house to another at night.

To scare us even more, they told us the myth of Maphasela, a drifter who raided local farms for food and stole anything portable he could find. If he bumped into children, he chased them and cast evil spells on them. You could hear Maphasela coming because he carried a portable radio wherever he went. Whenever he was caught stealing or walking through farms, he simply turned into a horse and grazed peacefully. That's how he could always escape. No one paid much attention to just another grazing horse on a farm. But as soon as his pursuers left, he'd turn back into a man and walk off listening to his radio.

What scared me most was that Maphasela always walked

through the fields where we grazed the cattle on his way to his forest home nearby. When it was my turn to herd the cattle home, I would scurry along, looking over my shoulder for a grazing horse or a man with a radio. With the rains, the pastures soon grew taller than me, and I couldn't see more than a few metres. I spent every moment terrified that Maphasela would appear out of nowhere.

When the boys wearied of scaring us with stories, they resumed the physical abuse. It was a vicious cycle. I couldn't work out how to rescue my sister or escape myself from this ongoing ordeal.

One night our tormenters made my sister strip half naked and lie on a reed mat. One of the children sprayed insect poison over her bare back and lit a match repeatedly, which exploded into balls of purple fire. Zinhle was incredibly brave. She didn't cry at the time, so I thought they weren't hurting her. Only when she showed me her burns the next day and shared the pain of their torment did she cry. I cried too.

The torture grew even worse when they forced me to participate in their assaults on my own sister. Joining in their humiliation of her left me wracked with guilt. She was my own blood, the person I loved more than anyone in my small world. We were usually abused together, but they picked on her more often, perhaps because she was smaller, or because she was a girl. I didn't know why, but we had to live through it together. I can't imagine how hard it must have been for her when her own brother joined in the cruel games. Even though I cried about it, she must have felt betrayed.

When they stopped, I would sit with her, away from the eyes of our tormentors. We'd cry again together. "I'm sorry. I had no choice," I would tell her. "They were going to beat me up again if I didn't."

"I know. I understand," she would answer.

"Do you forgive me?" She always did.

Two

Our life in Pevensey formed a stark contrast to the life we'd led with Mom and Dad in Durban. Sometimes I got lost in daydreams and even convinced myself I was still back there, back in that house, back in a time when Zinhle and I were important, when we were loved and spent entire days playing and laughing.

Life in Durban was far from perfect, but at least we were allowed to be children. Back then, people around us let us be, and our parents showered us with gifts. They kept us clean, well-clothed and fed. Strangers often told us how beautiful we looked as Mom led us through the streets of the brand new township. And Dad loved driving his car with me on his lap. Adults in those days were a source of warmth. Of love and security.

Here in Pevensey, I was starting to feel that I didn't matter. I wasn't important enough to live. I started to reminisce increasingly about my parents. Zinhle and I talked about them constantly whenever we got a chance to be alone. These memories were our only source of comfort. Thoughts of my parents kept me strong even in the most difficult times, but I began to wonder if Mom didn't love us anymore. Why had she let us be brought to this village?

I was born in the late seventies. Mom and Dad were of a signature generation in the social fabric of black South Africa. They were both migrant labourers from rural parts of the country who had come to Durban in search of a better life. Like millions of other young people who flocked to South Africa's cities from every corner of the country, my parents believed they would find the better life they were searching for.

My mother, Delisile Shezi, was still a teenager when she arrived in Durban from Underberg. Her mother had died when she was a child and she grew up an orphan. Her father had remarried the woman called Khulu who now worked at the Catholic mission three kilometres from Pevensey. But when he passed away, my mother had no prospect of a decent education. Her best chance of improving her life was to go to Durban and become a housekeeper for a white family.

My mother always had a smile on her face. She was tall, pretty and light in complexion, with beautifully shiny, brownish hair. By contrast, my Dad was short, and wore an Afro and a long unkempt beard. It was common in the early eighties for men to be unshaven. Facial hair was a fashion statement at that time. He wasn't what you would call handsome, but he was eloquent, persuasive and deceptively charming, which made up for the shortcomings in his looks.

By the time Zinhle was born, two years after me, our parents had moved into a four-roomed brick house in Clermont, a black township just outside Durban. Our brick house was a sign that we were moving up in the world. Dad worked as a bus driver for the municipality. It was a prestigious job, considering the restrictions on which jobs black people could do.

None of the houses around us had electricity. Mom used a paraffin stove, and Zinhle and I used to watch her pump and coax the plate to life and then cook our meals in a shiny aluminium pot. Everything inside was clean and bright, from the floor to the windows, and the smells of paraffin and cooking and red floor polish made up the unique aroma of home.

Outside, just metres from the stairs, were showering facilities. I hated the shower. The water was always cold, and it took some coaxing from Mom to get us to wash. We would keep on using our bar of red Lifebuoy soap until it was just the thinnest sliver that slipped through your fingers under the icy spray. Then Mom would dry us and apply sweet oil or lotion before dressing us in clean pyjamas. Her hands were soft on us, despite the hard manual work she did every day.

In Pevensey no one encouraged us to wash, so we rarely bothered, especially during the holidays. I used to sleep covered in the dust of the pastures. Zinhle and I were always dirty. Our nails were long and filthy. We didn't even have toothbrushes. Our teeth were yellow. No one commented on how beautiful we were any more. In this tiny village no one cared about us, and I missed the cold shower from my mother and the smell of Lifebuoy soap.

Near the shower in Durban was a tap that my parents kindly shared with their neighbours. I used to watch the neighbours climbing the stairs from their houses below to fetch water or do their laundry.

Being clean was a priority for everyone. The little boxes of Surf powder and the soft green bars of Sunlight kept the evils of dirt at bay. To be dirty was to be truly poor, and the women took great pride in household cleanliness. Every morning they would sweep their steps and yards with grass brooms made by women in the rural areas. Clothes and floors would be scrubbed and pots and pans polished till they gleamed.

One day a neighbour who shared our tap left her little box of Surf behind. When I found it, I poured water into the powder and had fun squeezing it in my fingers and making it foam. When the neighbour discovered what I'd done, she was upset at the waste and complained bitterly to Mom. That was the only time I remembered her giving me a hiding.

Now, the life my sister and I had lived with our parents seemed like a fairy tale. They had showered us with love, and solved minor complaints with treats and endless supplies of peanuts and Coca-Cola, or sometimes Mellow Yellow, a drink that later disappeared from the shops.

Whenever there were treats, our parents made sure we each got an equal share. One day Mom brought home two balls. Mine was white with black dots; Zinhle's was a beautiful pink with cartoon drawings. Mom had a tough job persuading me that pink was for girls and my ball was just as beautiful.

Dad had a scooter and several cars. He loved lifting me on his scooter when we went to the shops. Sometimes we rode to watch football several blocks from our house. I would perch proudly on the base of the scooter as we made our way through the narrow dusty streets. Dad must have trusted his riding skills to be confident enough to do this. In his truck he sometimes put me on his lap, and I felt really special whenever he let me hold the steering wheel, though he always guided my steering.

While Dad was at work, we would walk to the nearby shop just to buy sweets. At other times we went for walks. Occasionally Mom would stop to chat with the other women in the neighbourhood. I loved hearing her friends ask, "Are these your children? They're so beautiful." Mom was so proud of me and Zinhle. She loved us completely and we loved her back.

The township men often sat outside their houses all day long, drinking traditional beer. At times they sang and danced, which made my sister and I curious. We would hear the melody of the music they sang and the rhythm of their shoes as they thumped to the music.

Their shoes fascinated me. They were shiny black, brown or red leather with round or pointed toes, and sometimes they were pierced with tiny holes in pretty patterns. Some of the older men wore homemade sandals made from old tyres. They usually had beards, and some still had earlobes that hung like looped strings from being pierced and stretched to hold big round wooden plugs. Because people mostly walked everywhere, shoes were important. The shoes a man wore told you something about him, just as the way he walked told you what he thought of himself.

Across the road from our house lived my friend. There was no preschool in the township, so we spent a lot of time playing together. When we weren't amusing ourselves in a disused car under a tree behind my house, we were sliding down an embankment on pieces of cardboard, racing each other. Sticks and stones be-

13

came anything our imagination wanted: we were stick fighters one minute, then warriors with *assegais* the next.

Across the hill to one side of our house were some newly built township houses, their yellow paint still fresh. I used to mimic the sounds of the tractors and bulldozers I saw working there, imagining the sound of my very own car when I got older. My favourite toy was the pedal car my dad had bought me. Though our yard was barely big enough, I would pedal round and round in circles with my sister on my lap, just the way Dad held me on his lap in his truck.

Mom and her friends sometimes gave me and my friend a handful of coins to go to the nearby shop and buy Mellow Yellow and Coca-Cola. Sometimes we arrived at the shop and found we were short of money. On our way back we'd find the coins we'd dropped and return to the shop, hoping this time we had enough for what we had been sent to buy. We were such regulars, I'm sure the shopkeepers sometimes gave us the drinks even when we were a few cents short.

Zinhle and I had everything a child could ask for in Durban: parents who loved us, new clothes, balls to kick around. Dad would sometimes drive us to town in one of his cars just to buy cool drinks if we wanted them, or to replenish the supply of peanuts he kept in his bedside drawer. It was a happy childhood.

But once, while I was playing outside with my sister, I saw Dad through the open doorway whipping Mom with a *sjambok*, a whip made of hippo skin. Zinhle and I kept on playing. We became accustomed to my father beating my mother, and assumed it was normal. I thought maybe Mom was being punished for being naughty. Like me, I'm sure Zinhle had no idea that anything serious was happening to our mother.

But our happy days as a family in Clermont were shortlived. Soon I found myself alone with Dad. Mom and Zinhle had moved out, and I didn't know where they now lived. Days would pass without seeing either Zinhle or Mom. As a kid I adapted quickly, barely noticing the change. The only time I sensed something wrong was one day when we met Mom and Zinhle on a street in Westville where Mom worked. Zinhle and I sat in Dad's car while our parents stood outside talking. It was clear that they were having an argument. But my sister and I were too happy at seeing each other to pay much attention to the adults. We were playing with an orange and an apple that Dad had bought me. Suddenly Mom walked over, grabbed my sister from the car and walked away. I tried to pass Zinhle the apple, but Dad shouted "No!" and we sped off in the car.

After that I barely saw my mom. With no one to look after me, Dad sometimes left me with strangers when he went to drive buses. Whenever he was around, though, Dad and I were almost always on the move. I would be with him on the sidelines of a football field watching football, or in his truck when he visited friends. Sometimes he even took me along when he worked as a driver.

One day we drove to a nearby location. I sat in the car while Dad spoke with several women outside a flat. I remember him suddenly grabbing one of the women by the arm. He snatched the watch from her wrist, dropped it on the concrete and stomped on it until it was shattered. Then he strode to the car and we sped off in a fury.

Another day we were out shopping together, Dad humming and bobbing as the radio blasted out the hit song *Make That Move*. We stopped at a shop, and emerged to find a man taking a leak against our tyre. Dad was so livid that he grabbed his *knobkerrie*, a stick with a solid wooden ball on one end, and chased the poor man, who hadn't even finished relieving himself.

I don't remember Dad getting angry with me. I adored him. Whenever we drove through the busy city streets, I thought he was so clever to understand how traffic lights worked: he knew exactly when to stop and when to go. I wondered if I would ever be as clever as he was.

Months later I was reunited with Mom. But that meant being alone most days, in the outside room where she now lived behind the house where she worked. My sister was nowhere to be seen. Sometimes I played with the employer's cats, who had a woven reed basket with a blanket to keep them warm. I would stare through the fence as the neighbour's kids played tennis. Now and then my mom would pop in and chat to me. I guess she was checking if I was okay.

Many weeks after moving in with Mom, I was reunited with Zinhle. We were sent to a distant relative of Mom's called Dala, who lived in the large rural village of Nkwezela in Bulwer, roughly forty kilometres from Pevensey where my mother originally came from.

Bulwer was nothing like Durban. There was no endless supply of sweets, cookies, peanuts and cool drinks. But Dala treated us as her own, and let us to do what every child loves: to play. Later I realised that this was where Zinhle had been all the time while I was alone in the outside room with only the cats for company.

It was wonderful to be with my sister again, although I missed my toys, especially my pedal car, and the big juicy apples Dad used to buy me. But Dala was a good nanny, and the care she gave us made up for the luxuries we had to do without. Dala dressed me in my uniform for my first day of school, with a raincoat because it was raining. She handed me a black slate with a wooden frame and matchsticks to scratch on it, because paper and pencils were scarce. Our school was a derelict mud room beside the church.

Sometimes Mom came from Durban to visit us. Then she would shower us with toys, sweets and other treats that reminded us of Durban. Once she arrived after Dala had just covered the floor with fresh cow dung, and her high heels left little holes behind her in the floor. Another time she arrived with Dad, whose untidy beard now almost covered his face.

Mom always sneaked off while we were sleeping without saying goodbye. I suppose she wanted to spare us the pain of watching her leave. She knew we'd cry and want to go with her. And we might have asked questions she couldn't answer.

Now, in the dusty village of Pevensey, these thoughts of my

parents kept me going through the most difficult of times. I wished so badly for them to show up again. I had so many things to tell them, so much pain to share. Hopefully, they would take us home with them if we told them about our abuse and humiliation. But weeks turned to months and still there was no sign of them. So I daydreamed even more. It was my only respite.

But daydreaming could only stave off reality for so long. Most of my time was spent hating Pevensey, loathing the people I lived with and longing to leave. But time marched on, and still Mom and Dad didn't come. The abuse continued daily, and I clung doggedly to the hope that one day, no matter how long it took, our parents would come for us. We would not be left to endure this forever.

Three

We learnt to trust no one. We spoke to no one in the family about our frequent abuse, for they showed us no love. In fact, the adults punished all the children, our abusers included, for the slightest of mistakes. Every misdemeanor, no matter how small, was met with a severe whipping. The beatings were disproportionate to our offences, and as bad as any we received when they weren't around or weren't looking.

On my first day of school in Pevensey, it rained just before we walked home. I splashed through the mud puddles with the other boys, and then slipped and fell on my backside. I tried in vain to get the mud off my shorts. As I walked in through the kitchen past Gogo, I used my bag of books to try to cover my back.

"*Ufihlani*?" she demanded. "What are you hiding?" She saw, and I knew what was coming. In her rage she grabbed the wire that strung the curtains across the window, ripping it right off the wall, and delivered one vicious stinging blow after another. I'd never known such pain.

"I'm sorry!" I kept wailing. But by the time she had finished with me I was mute. Later, as I washed the blood from my legs, arms and back, the pain made me cry out again.

It was the first time she'd punished me. From then on I feared her. It was as if all the kindness and softness she might have once had had been hammered out of her. There were just too many children, too many chores, and too little money and food.

Gogo's favourite tool of punishment was *isitilobho*, a whip made of leather thongs twisted together. Its primary purpose was to attach the ox yoke during ploughing, but all adults used it to punish children. Whenever Gogo said *"ngizokufaka isitolobho,"* I was instantly on my best behaviour. But at least her punishments were brief. If I couldn't take any more, I could make a dash for it and outrun her. Later, she wouldn't bother me much, she'd just shout at me while giving me my sour milk with mealiemeal.

We stayed clear of Gogo as much as we could, for she offered us no warmth or love. But she did make sure we were fed before going to school. There was precious little food, but she did her best. If it wasn't sour milk and mealiemeal, it was tea and a sliver of bread. The few times there was butter she gave us lots of it, perhaps to compensate for the meagreness of the bread. She also made sure we left in time to get to school early. She had never gone to school herself, and couldn't read or write, but she made it her mission to ensure that we never missed school.

I developed a strange relationship with Gogo. I feared her, yet I still preferred her to the other adults in the family. Even when it came to punishment, I preferred to be punished by her, perhaps because it was brief and I could at least escape her.

But when her sons came home from the goldmines in Johannesburg, I lived in terror. They must have been in their twenties at that time, strutting in smart suits and shiny shoes to show how successful they were. Beneath their suits were powerful muscles, honed by the backbreaking sweat of deep-level mining. At home they expected us to wait on them and obey their every whim.

It was strange to have men in the house. Even Zozi who bullied us was careful around them, although he liked to hang around them and listen to their talk. He was determined to work in the mines one day just like them, and then buy lots of nice things.

But Gogo's sons always seemed angry at something or someone. Every night they drank cheap brandy, bottled beer or the yeasty homemade sorghum beer Gogo brewed them. And beating us seemed to be their favourite hobby, so all the children in the family did their best to avoid them. Unfortunately, it wasn't always possible.

One Sunday after a night of heavy drinking, one of her sons

woke late and found me and my cousin in the yard. Why weren't we in church, he demanded, and ordered me to fetch a sjambok. The viciousness of his whipping that day left permanent scars on my thigh. Even Gogo was shocked to discover how harshly he had beaten us. It was the first time I'd ever heard her raise her voice in our defence.

Yet even harsher beatings followed whenever any of the cattle strayed and we failed to return them to the kraal by sunset. We'd scour kilometres for hours on end, searching vainly for the animals, often long after dark. We knew what awaited us back home, so we'd keep on and on long after we knew it was futile, just to delay the inevitable.

The adults would strike with anything they could grab in the moment. They threw cans at our heads, firewood, even burning wood plucked from the fire. Other kids in the neighbourhood were probably punished just as severely as we were. Certainly, there were adults in other homesteads with reputations for delivering the most vicious beatings. But to me it seemed that we were the only ones being overworked and beaten up. Cleaning the blood off myself after a beating was something of a ritual.

I especially hated the sjambok. It always reminded me of Dad whipping Mom in Durban while I played outside with Zinhle. Each time I was struck with a sjambok, I felt Mom's pain. Now that I had experienced such cruelty myself, I began to grasp the gravity of the beatings my father had given my mother. Was Dad a bad person, I started to wonder? As bad as these people we lived with? Or worse? Were we brought here to get us away from him? But there was no one to answer my questions. Only in the unfriendly atmosphere of Pevensey did I begin to realise that there hadn't been much peace in my family.

To reach the pastures we had to herd the cattle across a railway line. We were always warned to drive them well past the tracks to discourage them from straying back and being struck by the goods train that ran three times a week. And mostly the cattle stayed well away from the railway line while we were at school. But on occasions one or more of them would graze their way right back and end up on the track.

Once we spent most of the night looking for a missing cow. As usual we were punished. Early the next morning, after a sleepless night, we resumed our search. Hours later we found her bloated body down an embankment alongside the railway track. Her left hind leg was snapped, and it was clear she'd tried to outrun the train before being knocked down the side of the tracks.

We went back home to get the oxen and a wagon, then loaded her up and took her back home, where she was cut up and eaten. The meat wasn't very tasty, and all the time we were eating we were being shouted at for failing to look after the cow.

We didn't realise then just how valuable a cow was. She provided us with the milk we ate soured with stiff porridge, our staple family diet. Her dung was used to build and repair walls and floors, and to fertilise the crops in the fields. For some villages the cattle were also a link between the family and their ancestors. It was extremely rare for a beast to be slaughtered for its meat.

At six years old I learnt how to put a yoke over the necks of the oxen. The oxen were much taller than me and the yoke heavy and awkward. It was extremely difficult to get the yoke on without the oxen moving from side to side or pulling forward before the yoke was in place. Once the yoke was on I still had to fasten it with the *isitilobho*. Sometimes a knot would pull loose and the yoke be dragged to one side. Then the animals got nervous and kicked out with their sharp, dirty hooves. There were lots of near misses under their hooves when one of us missed a step. I once watched a cousin break his arm during such an encounter. But I had no choice. I had to be brave.

I learnt to lead the oxen to pull the plough back and forth in the blazing heat. I would pull on the leather reins or *riempies* to try to guide the oxen in a straight line. But I was so small that when they lifted their heads I would often fall or be yanked up. It was scary. Sometimes the oxen were temperamental. Another boy would walk behind them, flicking a long whip to keep them moving, while an older boy was responsible for pushing the plough deep into the soil to dig up the rows for planting.

Ploughing was a man's job, but there were hardly any adult men in Pevensey during the year. Most worked in the towns or the mines in Johannesburg. Only the old *madalas*, the pensioners, were around all the time, many weakened by TB or other illnesses. Our household had no men at all; we were a homestead of old women and children. So the work of the men became the work of the boys, and although we were many, we were all as thin and stringy as whipcords.

I learnt to milk cows by hand. I had to squeeze very hard and pull down on the cow's teats to get the milk to flow into the bucket. At times we milked as many as three cows every morning. This meant a decent supply of sour milk, which we liked much better than dry mealiemeal porridge with tea. Sometimes we even got a sprinkling of sugar.

In the kraal where we did the milking, the floor was thick with dung. When it rained the kraal became a slippery soup of mud and dung. Then it was very difficult to keep the milk in the bucket clean. When the cows were restless during the milking process, we had to guard against them jumping and kicking their hooves into the bucket, which would spoil the whole bucket of milk. And any mistake would cost us a hiding.

One cow was notorious for kicking over the bucket when it was half full. She'd be restless from the moment you put a rope around her horns. With less excitable cows you simply got close enough to reach with your arms through and around the hind legs. Then you grabbed the other end of the rope before tying the legs. But not with this one. That would just bring on a paralysing kick. Because of her restlessness she constantly had sores on her hind legs caused by the rope.

It took two boys to get a rope around her hind legs. One would throw the rope under her and the other would catch it on the far side before securing her legs. One of the older boys had a habit of running off and leaving the bucket under her hooves. I was lucky, perhaps, or stupid, but I always managed to grab the bucket and make a run for it. It seemed better to lose a bit of milk as I dashed away than to get a lashing.

Lacking electricity, all households in the village used galvanised stoves. I hated Saturdays when the neat pile of firewood was about to run out. We'd walk six kilometres to the Qoyintaba Forest, where we'd spend the entire day chopping wattle trees. It took four backbreaking Saturdays to replenish the dwindling stocks.

The walk to the forest was tiring enough. But then we had to cut down the trees with a blunt saw, which took a tremendous effort. Then we used a bush knife for the tedious business of removing the branches. The blazing sun didn't help. Porridge was all we'd had to ward off hunger before the hard manual labour.

Once the trees were stripped of branches we had to tie them in bundles as big as we could wrap our arms around. Then came the labour of lugging them back home, balanced on our heads, after a full day's labour with no lunch to sustain us. In the beginning it was especially difficult for me because I wasn't used to carrying things this way. My bundle would fall every few metres, often scratching me on the way down.

What made it even worse was the shame of it. This was women's work. But with only Gogo and small girls who couldn't walk this far or carry such heavy loads, it became the job of the boys in our family. In a deeply traditional village like ours, this marked us out as different, and subjected us to mockery from other boys.

In Pevensey my childhood ended abruptly. In place of endless time to play there were endless chores. And at the end of the day no one tucked me into bed with a soft mattress and pillow. There was just a reed mat on the floor and a flimsy blanket, through winter and summer alike. I missed Durban's subtropical warmth. Winter in Pevensey brought ice and snow, and I learnt to sleep with my jersey on, curled in a ball. There were no warm clothes to replace those I wore out or outgrew.

Year round there was no let up. If we weren't milking, we were ploughing, then hoeing weeds and finally harvesting the dry, scratchy mealie cobs. There was no love to be had. Just work, shouting, being called a fool, punishments and yet more work.

Unless it was too cold to work, the only rest time was at church on Sundays. I would put off going home after church by joining the other boys raiding pigeon nests up the church tower. The wooden ladders we climbed were old and wobbly, but it was so much fun. When we weren't climbing the tower, we might play with a lift in the disused mill a short walk from the church. When we tired of this, there was the waterfall. We climbed down the cliffs and spent hours chucking stones into the river. Staying too long meant punishment for getting home late. But these were my only moments of fun, so I was prepared to risk another beating. I got beaten anyway, so once in a while it seemed worth doing something to deserve it.

Four

The guilt I felt for failing to protect Zinhle gave me many sleepless nights trying to think of ways to rescue us. I didn't trust adults, even if one was nice to me. Many people probably meant well when they smiled at me, but mostly I looked away. I doubted their intentions. And so I told no one in my village what Zinhle and I were going through. I couldn't. I was too ashamed that I had allowed our abusers to treat my sister badly. I felt it was all my fault.

I detested myself for my weakness. I wanted so badly to be grown up, big enough to take on those who picked on my sister. At night I fantasised about challenging them to fight and whipping them into submission. I dreamt of revenge. I so much wanted to get us away from this suffering. I dreamt of having enough money to get us onto a bus to Durban to find our mom and dad.

It seemed too much to bear. My heart ached to let it out. I longed to tell someone. But every night fatigue got the better of me, and I fell asleep without a solution. I just couldn't work out what to do or who to tell. There was no one I could trust. But I had to do something, because it looked like our parents weren't coming to rescue us. At school, I found it hard to concentrate. Escaping Pevensey began to occupy my mind all the time.

I thought about telling my teachers. But I was sure they would do nothing about it. After all, they also beat us. Sometimes they lined up all the kids in the class and told us to take off our shirts so they could check us for hygiene. They saw the marks on my back from the whippings with the sjambok and *isitilobho*. They were there for all to see. The kids in the queue behind me would say, "*Ubani obekubhala kangaka?* Who beat you so badly?" But the teachers said nothing. All they did was whip me again for being dirty and unhygienic.

I thought about telling Khulu, my step-grandmother who I saw on Sundays at church. But from the start, she never seemed to acknowledge us. She would never smile at us. Although the Catholic mission where she worked was just three kilometres away, she rarely came to the village. The few times she did, she was no different from the other adults in the family who beat us at every opportunity. She seemed to regard us as an additional burden on the limited family resources. I could have told Auntie Zinto, Mom's younger sister, but she worked in Durban. And I just couldn't think of anyone else to confide in.

Then, one Sunday in church, the perfect solution came to me. Finally, I realised that there *was* someone I could trust, the only person, apart from my sister, who listened when I talked, who seemed to care what I said.

After church, I stood in the queue and waited my turn at the confession box. When my chance finally came, I knew exactly what to say: "Forgive me, Father, I have sinned. I participated in humiliating my sister. But I didn't mean to do it, Father, I was forced to. If I didn't do it they would beat me up. They always do."

Father Sebastian was German and spoke broken Zulu. I didn't know if he had understood what I was trying to tell him. He promised to pray to the Lord to forgive me. I needed more. I needed him to realise we were being abused. I was desperate for him to take action. Fast.

Every Sunday after that I went to the confession box. I looked at Father Sebastian through the holes in the partition, and told him stories. Sometimes tears poured down my face as I related the latest instalment of abuse. Each time, he promised to pray for me. He told me the Lord would forgive my sins.

Each Sunday, I hoped he would ask me to wait for him outside the confession box and tell me to relate my stories. I hoped he would pay attention and help me. It was months before I realised that he hadn't understood a word I was trying to say.

I was shattered. I began to pray for a miracle. I prayed that one day I would be delivered from this hell to a place where my sister and I could be kids again. Where there were people who loved and cared for us. I prayed that the two of us could have time together, just the two of us. To play and laugh together like we did back in the brick house in Durban.

At the same time, I continued to lie awake at night devising rescue plans. We had learnt from the elders in Pevensey that if we had coins, we could bury them and they would multiply. One day I found a two-cent coin. I wrapped it in a piece of paper, dug a hole while no one was watching, and buried it.

I spent weeks and months going back to inspect my investment. But every inspection brought the same result. The coin was still there, alone. In the end, I realised that this was a lot of nonsense.

It dawned on me at last that nothing was going to save my sister and me. Father Sebastian had failed to understand my cry for help; the coins had failed to multiply. It was time for drastic measures. I had had enough of this village and the people I lived with. We had to go. I didn't dare tell my sister about my plans, in case she said something during one of our moments of humiliation. I waited for the right moment.

When the time came, it was swift. It was a hot day. The other kids in the family, our tormentors included, had gone to do work that didn't include us. The two of us were playing in the yard with a couple of small cousins, one Zinhle's age and the other younger. They could do nothing to stop me. Gogo was no problem. I could outrun her. Before she realised we were gone, we would be on the bus to Bulwer.

I dashed to where I had buried my coin, dug it up and ran for my sister. Our cousins were startled as I grabbed Zinhle by the arm. As she looked at me, I knew she understood what I had in mind.

We could hear our cousins screaming as we rocketed through the gate, onto the dusty street on our way to the bus stop.

My aim was to use the two-cent coin to board the same bus Dala had used to bring us to Pevensey. Every day the bus passed along the gravel road about fifteen minutes' walk from our homestead. I saw it every day, yet it had only recently occurred to me that it was our one chance of escape.

We were about a kilometre down the dust road when I heard Gogo yelling, "*Vimbani bo*, stop them."

"*Asigijime kakhulu, Zinhle*," I told my sister. "Run faster." I planned to tell Dala our plight the moment we reached Bulwer. I knew she would listen, and take us back to Mom and Dad.

But Zinhle was getting tired. She couldn't keep up the pace. Villagers were coming from every direction in pursuit, bearing down on us. Kids, adults, everyone; it seemed as if the whole village was after us. When some of the older kids who ran faster got even closer, I started to despair. "Run, Zinhle, please," I begged.

But she was too tired. She let go of my hand. I continued to run for a moment. But when our pursuers caught up with my sister, I couldn't leave her behind. I sat down, panting, and burst into tears.

We cried all that day. By now it was clear to both of us that nothing and no one was ever going to save us. We were destined for abuse for the rest of our lives. There was no more hope of escape.

Five

For some time, my attempt at escape made me the butt of jokes in the pastures and at school. Every kid in the village picked on me for being a softy. It was common while we were herding cattle for the bigger boys to amuse themselves by staging fights between the smaller boys. They made us tease and insult each other, and then fight. Sometimes you were forced to fight your best friend or get a hiding from the older boys. Or the others would call you a coward.

After my attempt to escape, I was the one they all picked on. Boys lined up to choose me every time fights were staged. They hurled abuse. And whenever the abuse involved my mom they got to me. It triggered instant rage. I would immediately tangle with my opponent to earn back my respect. The older boys made us believe that staging such fights was a good thing. It would toughen us up for the future.

I became just as vitriolic in the insults I hurled at fellow herd boys. I learnt to give as good as I got. I learnt to fight and to defend myself, to start a fight and refuse to back down. And I learnt to take the bruising that came with it all. I didn't win all my fights, but I learnt to survive in the grazing fields, to live to fight another day. Which was usually every other day.

While older boys sometimes chose our opponents, they mostly let us choose who we wanted to fight. There was a boy a year older than me from a neighbouring homestead who always picked me and always won. He was tough and fought well, and most boys

29

were scared of him. I lay awake many nights thinking of ways to defeat him.

I was getting desperate. This boy had turned his winning streak into an opportunity to bully me at school. I badly wanted this to stop. But I just couldn't figure out a technique to turn my fortune around. Whenever we fought, he simply wrapped his arms around me, lifted me up and tossed me to the ground. Then he sat on me and had a fine time punching me in the torso. I was small for my age, and all I was good at was exchanging blows while ducking my opponent's. He had worked this out, so he avoided exchanging blows.

One of our rewards for herding the cattle came whenever a beast died or was slaughtered. The family who owned the beast invited the village boys to eat *iphaphu,* the lungs. It was exciting to leave home as the night set in to go and eat this treat. Only elders were allowed to venture out of home after dark, so we felt very special.

When one such invitation came to eat *iphaphu* at a neighbour, I took the opportunity to get my revenge on my bully. When we went to collect wood, I dug up a young tree and made myself a knobkerrie, with the base of the roots forming the knob. It was common for us young boys to carry one. As we walked home in a group after eating the meat, I searched out my enemy in the darkness, and hit him as hard as I could on the head. He collapsed.

In the ensuing chaos, as he was helped from the ground, I wasted no time challenging him to a fight. The other boys were excited, and immediately agreed. For once he was less than enthusiastic. That night I won my fight, and he never bothered me again.

Unfortunately, outfoxing and defeating my bully didn't stop the bigger boys from picking on me. I dreaded going for a swim while watching the herds. The biggest boy in our group had a habit of using me to stage a show in the water. By now I was a good swimmer. But it didn't save me the pain that came with his show. He would grab me and throw me into the river. The Polela River was deep, but that was the least of my problems.

I would try to outswim him, but he was strong and well built and he swam fast. He would quickly catch up with me and hold me beneath the surface for what seemed like forever. I would choke and yell and plead for him to leave me. It was unbearable. But he simply held me down. Up. And down again. Repeatedly. He gave me as little time to breathe as possible. It was difficult to gasp air while crying at the top of my lungs. All the while, other boys stood along the river and laughed. My abusers from the extended family were always there, as if I was a just prop for the water show. They never once came to my rescue, and only laughed along with the others.

By the time the star of the show let go of me, my stomach would be bloated with water. As I swam for the safety of the river bank, I would be nauseous from the near drowning, my eyes bloodshot and stinging. I usually vomited when I reached the bank.

I hated everything about this village. I hated every day I woke up. I hated every season of the year. And I hated my extended family. I wished them dead.

During the frosty winter months, my toes were always numb. Sometimes the skies unleashed so much snow, we spent most of our time around the fire trying to keep warm. The first time I woke up to see a thick white blanket, I was intrigued. It had never snowed in Durban. But in no time I hated it. Snow or no snow, we still had to take the cattle from the kraal. When there was snow, we had to get it off the haystacks so that the cattle had grass to eat. The snow got into my mud boots. It was so cold I sometimes went beyond feeling cold. I went completely numb.

When there was no snow, I learnt other ways of getting warm while watching the cattle. Sometimes the animals settled down on the grass to take a break from grazing. The spot where they settled would soon get warm, and I would walk around shooing them off and curling up in in the warmth they left behind. But it was always brief. When it grew cold again, I would chase away another animal.

In Durban I had hardly noticed the weather. Durban was always warm. But in Pevensey, it felt like even the weather was out to make me miserable. The wind in July and August was merciless.

It would rise to a crescendo, sweeping dust along its path, and it came so hard you could taste the dust it carried. I gave up trying to keep the dust out of my ears.

In summer, the skies unleashed torrents of rain. Sometimes the rain and wind came together, making it bitterly cold. The rain would bombard me like a deluge of nails as I walked through the pastures. At such times the cows always stood together, backs to the rain. Sometimes it was so cold I peed in my pants just to feel its brief warmth.

Lightening was frequent, and so loud it made me say my prayers. The skies would crackle in sheets, followed by a reverberating thunderclap that echoed off the mountains nearby. When cattle wandered off in summer, I got used to getting drenched. Sometimes a hard downpour was followed by sunshine, and I would get soaked and then dried out while traipsing the land looking for the animals.

After the harvest, we drove the cattle into the fields to eat the mealie stalks. I hated walking through the fields at these times, because I had no shoes. In the fields my feet were under constant attack from thorns. When I wasn't battling the elements, there was always someone picking on me. Life was a constant battle.

Six

I craved love. I longed desperately for someone to take care of my sister and me. I yearned for the day Mom would come and take us back to Durban. I wanted so much to taste sweets and peanuts, to gulp down a Coca-Cola. I sometimes prayed for childless strangers to adopt us and treat us as their own. I dreamt of someone who would feed us generous meals and clothe us. Anyone. But time kept passing, and my angel never showed up.

Whenever I found an old magazine, I would stare at advertisements showing happy families. I loved the tile advert with a mother and her two children. I fantasised about the perfect life I saw there. I wanted the woman in the picture to be my mom, and the kids to be Zinhle and me. I loved the beautiful clean clothes they wore in the advertisement. I envied their smiling faces.

In the virtual world of my daydreams, I pictured myself as an adult. I owned a big beautiful house and lots of cattle. My cows produced plenty of milk, and my employees milked them every morning before driving them to the pastures.

There was lots to eat, plenty of sour milk with the mealiemeal and plenty of meat. My sister lived happily with me, and we drove around in my car. Sometimes we drove to visit Dala in Bulwer, and sometimes we drove to Durban to visit Mom.

It didn't look like I was ever going to have a decent upbringing, so I rolled the clock forward and saw Zinhle and me as adults. But my dreams were flawed: they didn't include growing up. There was no getting an education. I wanted to reach the finishing line without ever running towards it. As the rural life had become my world, I saw myself as a farmer. I didn't consider other options. My social horizon was too narrow.

One of my great hardships was going hungry and eating bad food. I wished I could somehow get the mealiemeal and tea into my stomach without eating it. I wished I could swallow it whole without tasting it. I hated the shabby food when it was available, but craved it when I went hungry.

The craving was so intense that I would imagine myself as a grown-up completely immersing myself in food. Lots and lots of good food. I fantasised about large juicy steaks, rice, chicken and an endless supply of ice cream. I thought so much about food I could almost taste it.

Reality would quickly jolt me out of my daydreams. It was going to take years before I could get hold of the good food I dreamt of. And I wasn't so optimistic about the future. Sometimes I doubted there would ever be good food again. Whenever we went to church, I would envy the other kids their new clothes and shoes they showed off.

In place of new clothes, Zinhle and I were getting used to wearing rags. We went to school with our toes showing through our shoes. Or with no shoes at all. We no longer bathed each morning. We were dirty kids, so dirty that I had cracks in my feet from a lack of cleaning myself. The only clothing or shoes we occasionally received were secondhand items donated by neighbours or villagers.

Sometimes Auntie Zinto came from Durban. She crossed the river from her house on the hill, and brought us clothes and shoes. It was after one of her visits that I walked her home afterwards. I started to cry as she took her shoes off to cross the river.

"*Ungakhali mfana wami, indoda ayikhali*," she said. "Don't cry, my boy. A man shouldn't cry." She must have thought I was crying because I was sad to say goodbye.

"I'm not a man, Auntie," I told her. "When is Mom coming back? Zinhle and I miss her so much. We don't want to stay here any more. We want to go back to Mom in Durban."

Auntie put down her shoes, walked a short distance away and started to cry. I didn't know what to do. After what must have been three years with no mention of Mom from anyone, I had finally summoned the courage to ask about her.

"Let's trust in the power of the Lord," Auntie said when she calmed down. "The Lord will look after you and nurture you until you grow up to be a man. Some day we'll talk about your mom. But for now I want you to be strong and look after your sister. I know how hard it is for you to stay with your relatives. Whenever you feel down, please pray. Okay?"

I nodded. Then I watched in despair as she crossed the river. It would be months, maybe a year, before she would be back.

And her tears had confused me when I mentioned my mom. Had something terrible happened to her? I asked myself. But there was no one to answer me. I could only return to my misery.

In the weeks after Auntie Zinto returned to Durban, I was kept busy. It was common for kids in my grade at school to start preparing to take communion at church. I was in a Catholic school, and the responsibility of preparing the kids for communion was left to the teachers. We had to learn to recite prayers. Teachers had to be satisfied that these were engrained in us. That we could say them confidently, before they passed us.

Very few kids failed. To do so was a great shame. The day of the ceremony was always a big deal. Every kid wanted to be a part of it. I got stuck into the preparations, and recited my prayers day and night to make sure I was ready. The ceremony was to be a day of pomp, pride and pageantry.

Soon the kids were abuzz about the brand new suits and beautiful white dresses their parents were buying them to wear on the day. I kept quiet. What would I wear? Gogo must have spoken to the neighbours about this, because one after another they came around and summoned me to try on their kids' old suits. I finally had to settle for one that was dowdy and oversized.

I forced a smile as those who watched me try it on assured me I looked good in it. Then I went out to play, knowing that every kid would laugh at me that Sunday.

When we went to fetch the cattle, the boys in my grade kept boasting about the outfits their parents had bought them for the big day. It was smiles all round. I had nothing to say and nothing to smile about. I was resigned, but I wanted to hide. Not even Zinhle's assurance that I was going to be fine made me feel better.

"Mom would have bought me a suit," I told my sister. "But she doesn't love us any more."

Just two days before the big day, Auntie Zinto appeared from Durban with a brand new brown suit and matching shoes for me. Suddenly, I was able to talk with the other boys about what I would be wearing on the day.

But on the day of the ceremony, as we went from house to house to share cakes and good food, I felt no joy. I was preoccupied with my own thoughts. Why had it been Auntie Zinto, not Mom, who bought me the suit? I was desperate for someone to tell me where Mom was.

At school, the teachers sometimes asked us to write essays about our parents. I wrote about the good things Mom used to do for my sister and me in Durban, the new clothes she used to buy us, the toys. I wrote about how beautiful and loving my mom was, and that one day she was going to come and visit us and bring us new clothes. Whenever I read out my essays in class, the teacher would give me a strange look. But I was too young to understand, and too scared to ask questions.

No one sat us down to explain why Mom and Dad had abandoned us. My sister and I talked only between ourselves, wondering why they stayed on in Durban while we endured all the beatings and abuse. We yearned for what could be, caught up in our game of "if only". If Mom came to visit us, we wouldn't be abused. If she came home regularly, those who beat us would be nice to us. But life went on. Years passed, and still they failed to show up.

In Pevensey the hierarchy was very stark between kids, teens, young men and women, and older members of the household. You never sat with the elders while they were chatting with their equals, let alone asked pertinent questions. As kids you sat or played with other kids and kept your distance, preferably in another room.

The only time kids and adults huddled together was around the fire when it was cold, raining or snowing. Even then they ignored us. They expected us to keep quiet and feed wood into the fire. During this time the only communication between the kids was through body language and whispering. We held our elders in awe.

We couldn't ask about such things as why our mom wasn't coming home. There could be no discussion of anything serious with adults, no conversation. We could only reply to questions they asked; otherwise we had to keep quiet. So Zinhle and I waited, wondered and speculated about what might have happened to our beloved mother.

We couldn't seek answers to why the gifts we longed for never appeared, why the other kids laughed at us for wearing torn, ill-fitting secondhand clothing and shoes that showed our toes.

Some villagers treated us with pity. More and more we heard the words "*musani ukudlala ngabo ngoba bengenabani,* don't ill-treat them; they have no one to defend them", usually when we were wailing from another beating, or when other kids were bullying us. I didn't know what they meant. After all, we had our parents. And one day they would come for us.

Seven

Another Christmas approached, and we still had no information. I especially loved the December holidays. I looked forward to Christmas Day when we ate rice and meat. I loved being invited to parties where I stuffed myself with cookies and cool drinks. There were so many cookies that we would use them to hit one another as we made our playful way home in the late afternoon.

The best day of the year was New Year's Eve. We looked forward to *ukushaya amathini*, the drum beating to greet the new year. As young boys, we made sure we stayed awake, and ridiculed those who fell asleep.

To prepare for New Year's Eve we collected as many tyres as we could from the dumpsite of the Catholic mission farm. When the big night finally came, we collected dried grass and plastic bags to light the tyres. As night set in, the young men on holiday from the mines showed up with their shiny portable radios. They put on cassettes of the latest releases of disco and bubblegum music.

As some of the tyres burnt out, we collected the wire that was left behind and sneaked away. Each homestead in our village was fenced, so that neighbouring houses were separated by two fences, creating passages between the homesteads. The young men from the mines liked to walk along these passages to drink with their friends or join other groups around a burning tyre. So we tied our pieces of wire across the passageways at ankle height, and then a couple of metres away at neck height.

As they strode to their next destination, their ankles would get caught up in the wire, and they would fall flat on their faces. As they dusted themselves off, cursing and rushing onward, the next trap would catch them by their necks. Sometimes we hid in the undergrowth to laugh and enjoy hearing them stumble into our traps, but mostly we sneaked back to our groups around the burning tyres, grinning from ear to ear with anticipation. It was our way of getting back at them for beating us up.

We knew they had got caught when they came with their sjamboks, demanding to know who had set the traps. They went from one group to another looking for the culprits. Sometimes they didn't even bother to ask who the guilty parties were, and simply drew their belts or sjamboks and beat every boy in the group. But we were always prepared after setting our traps. We stayed on the lookout, and scattered as the young men emerged, dragging our burning tyre with a wire as we made a run for it. You could tell boys were in trouble when you saw a burning tyre rocketing through the dark. When it was our turn to run, we usually led our pursuers to the next set of traps. It was fun watching them get caught as they charged towards us.

During one December holiday, nearly six years after I arrived in Pevensey, I sat around the fire with Mom's cousins who worked in the mines. They were knocking back whisky until late at night, talking all the while about their work in the mines and the squalor of the men's hostels. I always felt safe from the sjambok when my uncles were drinking; for some reason the bottle seemed to calm them. Then they would be nice to the kids in the family.

That night, as they grew increasingly drunk, the conversation took a different turn. They started to talk about my mom. They became tearful as they related how kind she had been to them while they were still at school. She always brought them clothes from Durban, they told me. And she gave them pocket money for school.

They spoke about Mom in the past tense. Then one said,

"*Ubaba wakho usiphule inhliziyo ngokusithathela usisi.* Your Dad broke our hearts by taking away our big sister."

I was puzzled.

"Your mom was everything to us," one told me. "Your dad didn't just rob you and Zinhle of a loving mother when he killed her. He robbed the whole family of their favourite daughter. Your father's a monster!"

They wanted revenge, they said. They swore they would kill him if they ever found him.

Even though so many years had passed, I had clung to the hope that one day she would walk into the house and apologise for disappearing, and give Zinhle and I a good reason for abandoning us. All would be forgiven and we would instantly be a family again, rescued at last from this hellish home.

I couldn't accept that my mom could be dead. The whisky was making my uncles hallucinate, I told myself. It was impossible that my dad could have killed my mom. It didn't make sense. A part of me had started to believe that Dad was probably a bad person, but I couldn't believe he was capable of taking my mom's life.

The next day I told my sister what I had heard. She believed it, she said. People had called her *intandane*, orphan, more than once. She had thought nothing of it, but now my story made it clear to her. Our mother was dead.

Zinhle was just three when she had last seen our mom. She hardly had any real memories of her. For her, Mom was more of a fable than a person, so I guess it was easier for her to accept what we were being told. For me it was different. Mom was no myth. She was flesh. I remembered her voice, her smile. I had felt her hug, her love and warmth. How could I possibly believe without proof that she was dead? There had to be another explanation. It simply wasn't possible.

Then I remembered the day Auntie Zinto had cried when I asked her when Mom was coming to fetch us. I remembered the looks my teachers gave me when I recited essays about Mom. I remembered the people's words when we cried, that we had no one to defend us.

And still I hoped it was all a mistake.

I couldn't see myself enduring the rest of my childhood under these circumstances. I didn't feel I could get through high school still living like we didn't matter. And I couldn't cope with the responsibility of looking after and protecting my sister. I had already failed her too many times. If Mom was never coming back, I wasn't sure I had the strength to continue.

Eight

After this first piece of information suggesting that my mom might be dead, people in the village seemed to talk about it more openly and frequently. Now people started to refer to me, too, as an orphan. Whenever something sad happened, they told me that I was special, that my mom's soul would guide us. Villagers offered to pray for us.

But some references to my mother's death were not so kindly meant. Whenever villagers shouted at me for being naughty, my mom's name was often mixed in with the insults they flung at me.

I had made a friend, and during the winter holidays the two of us spent plenty of time in the harvested mealie fields while the cows fed on the wilted corn stems. We passed the time trapping rats. They were small rats with brown streaks along their spines. I was disgusted at first when the other boys showed me how to trap, roast and eat these rats. But as time went on I stopped being squeamish and trapped them myself, although I never warmed to the idea of eating them. Instead, I caught as many as I could and prepared them for Zinhle, who found them a delicacy. In truth, she simply ate them to ward off hunger.

My friend was shunned by the other boys as a softy, because he ran to his grandma whenever the boys staged fights. One day while we were setting our traps together, we had a bitter argument. I felt he had been nasty to me and I wanted to get him back.

I knew where his traps were, so I sneaked back, disarmed them and put a stone in each one instead. The rats could now feed safely on the corn he had set as bait, and then run off. It was a good prank, and it had other boys rolling around in delight. I was pleased with myself.

But his grandma wasn't laughing when we got home that evening. She was livid, and her words burnt like acid.

"You are as ruthless, as heartless as your father!" she raged. "This is the attitude that killed your mother. You're becoming just like him, you son of a monster!"

One day, two older boys and I yoked the family oxen and set off with them to fetch sand from the river bank. As usual, I held the rope and led the oxen. We spent the entire morning digging and loading the sand into bags. On our way back, the animals were temperamental. They were hungry and stubborn from the lack of proper grazing. They kept reaching for the grass as I led them back home. No amount of pulling would help.

I was getting frustrated, while my two older cousins fumed at the lack of pace. We were all ravenous and keen to get home to fill our stomachs. They turned on me, blaming me for failing to control the oxen. I tried my best to tug the animals from the grass, but they shook their heads so hard they just yanked me right back. I was too small to be a match for the brute power of the cattle. They simply swung me back and almost tossed me onto my side.

In the end, the elder of the two lost his temper, and started whipping me with a piece of carpet he had picked up on the way. As I rolled on the ground in pain, he whipped me even more. I screamed at the top of my lungs.

I was in so much pain that I refused to lead the oxen any more. I simply walked away. I didn't even run as he came after me to deliver more punishment. I didn't care anymore.

As he delivered another blow, a woman's voice stopped him in his tracks. It was a woman from the neighbourhood who had seen the whipping as she walked along the railway line and rushed to my rescue. She took me home and sat me beside her fire to warm up while she fed me biscuits. She told me he was victimising me because I had nowhere to turn for support. He was wrong, she said, to pick on an orphan.

Suddenly the biscuits became tasteless. I wanted to stop being called an orphan. It didn't make sense. There was no proof that Mom was dead. I hadn't seen her body, there hadn't been a funeral. As far as I was concerned, they were all wrong.

Neighbouring kids were also starting to latch on to the story, probably hearing it from their parents. But I refused to entertain one bit of it. Everyone else was wrong, including my sister who now believed the story.

Life went on, and our priorities were simple. We woke up, herded the cattle to the pastures and returned as quickly as we could to prepare for school. When there was a young calf, we woke early to do the milking before releasing the cattle. Yet I had so much emotion to deal with. My sister was still being abused, and I was fighting a losing battle trying to protect her. I hated myself more than ever, and wished that I would die.

When Auntie Zinto returned to Pevensey during the holidays, I crossed the river to visit her. She was happy to see me. As usual, she had bought secondhand clothing for Zinhle and me. She handed me a plastic bag of clothes and asked me to open it. Among the items was a beautiful blue T-shirt and some blue jeans I really liked.

I thanked her.

"Do you like your clothes?" she asked.

I assured her I did, and thanked her again.

"But you don't look happy," she insisted. "Come on, give me a smile."

"I can't, Auntie," I told her. By now I was in my early teens, and becoming confident enough to speak to adults, although I still avoided eye contact.

"Why can't you smile my boy? What did they do to you this time?"

"Nothing, Auntie." I hesitated. "I just need to ask you something."

"You can ask me anything, my boy."

"Is Mom dead?" I blurted. "Are Zinhle and I orphans? Everyone keeps telling us this. I don't believe them. I've been waiting to hear from you because you live in Durban. When last did you see Mom? Has something happened to her? Why did you cry last time I spoke to you about Mom?" I couldn't stop my torrent of questions.

All the while, Auntie Zinto looked down, her hands over her face. Now she got up, and went silently to another room, then returned with a piece of paper.

Finally she spoke. "Your father killed her, my boy."

I felt like a knife had been driven through my heart.

She took a deep breath. "Your mom disappeared around June of 1982. Her body was found in the Lions River area, outside Pietermaritzburg. That monster, your father, was arrested for her murder, and received a six-year sentence. But he only spent a couple of weeks in prison."

"But why weren't we invited to her funeral, Auntie?" I cried.

"The police couldn't locate our family, my boy, so they had her buried by the state. Later I found my sister's grave, and marked it with a stone. A few months later, I went back to put in a cross with your mom's name on it, but the grass and the vegetation had grown. I spent the whole day looking for it. Eventually I had to give up."

"Isn't there some way of finding it, Auntie?"

"I've tried several times, my boy. Even with the help of the police I couldn't find it. I don't think we'll ever find your mom's resting place again. We just have to pray that she's with God. But I love you and Zinhle, and I pray for you all the time. The Lord is looking after you very well." She smiled at me. "Look at you, growing up so fast! Soon you'll be a man!"

"Now that I've told you about your mother," she added, "I need to give you this to keep." She handed over my mom's death certificate. "Look after it."

I read it out loud. "Provisional death certificate in respect of a person who presumably died from other than natural causes. Edista Delisile Shezi. District of death: Boston Road, Lions River. Age: ±30 years."

When my father managed to avoid going to prison, Auntie Zinto told me, the family was heartbroken.

"Why didn't he go to jail?" I asked.

"I guess a black person's life isn't important in this country," she answered.

I didn't ask what she meant. I was too young to understand.

Now there was no denying it. My mother was dead. Zinhle and I were orphans, with no prospect of a decent upbringing. No chance of making it in life.

"I know it's difficult for you," Auntie tried to console me. "I understand the conditions under which you live. But I need you to listen to me. Whatever those you live with say to you, let it go in one ear and out the other. Understand?"

"Yes, Auntie."

"I want you to be strong for your sister. Look after her. Okay, my boy?"

"Okay, Auntie. I'll look after her."

Nine

It tore me apart to learn that Mom was truly dead. And it was equally devastating to know that my dad, my own blood, had taken her life. From this point on, I no longer questioned those who referred to him as a monster. And I accepted them calling me an orphan. Instead, I started hating my father. My reminiscing about the good old days with Dad were over, about those times he had held me on his lap and let me hold the steering wheel as we rolled through the streets.

He didn't even deserve to be called my father. It was his fault I went to school with no shoes and had to grow up wearing rags, I realised. He was to blame for the abuse being meted out to us. Everything bad that happened to us was his fault. This would never happen if Mom was alive, I started saying to myself, over and over again.

At home, I started to disobey and rebel. I no longer cared about the punishments I received. I told my punishers to beat me to death if they wanted. I had no reason to go on living. I saw no meaning in going through so much hell.

And now I also began to court trouble.

Not long afterwards, the Polela River started to swell after a few days of heavy rains at its source in the Drakensberg; it was one of the river's annual tantrums. Against the rules, I managed to convince two other boys to join me in an illegal hunt on farmland across the river. The boys were a neighbour three years younger than me and one of my cousins who was four years younger. I knew I was flirting with danger. But by now nothing in my life made sense. I didn't care about rules anymore, as long as no one found out.

The boys hesitated on the river bank. I was a little nervous myself. But once I had tossed my hunting stick across the river, there was no turning back. The two boys and our dogs followed suit, and together we jumped into the river. Immediately the current began to sweep us all downstream. The dogs managed fine but the youngest boy panicked and began to scream.

"Keep swimming," I yelled. "There are trees to grab onto down there."

After a mighty struggle we made it across the river. The current had swept us well downstream, far from where we had thrown our hunting sticks. "We made it," I reassured them. Their eyes were still popping from the horror of being caught up in the powerful current.

We covered kilometres without sighting any game, and were just about to give up and cross back to where our cattle were grazing when we spotted a porcupine. But the porcupine saw us and dashed for the nearest burrow. We spent hours trying to coax the dogs to enter the burrow. They did so for a couple of metres. But each time the porcupine made a thundering noise, they would back off, barking. It was nearly sunset before I realised we were wasting our time, and we set off back towards the river.

The ground was unbearably hot beneath our feet, which slowed us down, as we had to avoid the rocks and bare earth, and try to stay on the grass instead. At some point, I looked back to find that we had company. A game ranger with a rifle in his hand was stalking us. By now he was just a short distance away.

"*Nanti iphoyisa lentaba*," I warned the boys, and we rocketed downhill at full speed. The dogs, startled by the suddenness, started barking and following us. My mind was racing. Things would be very bad if we got caught. The ranger would hand us over to the farmer, who would shoot all our dogs. Then I would be in deep, deep trouble at home.

We ran on for a short while, before my cousin and I suddenly realised that our companion was no longer with us. Glancing back, we were shocked to see him in the distance, standing with the ranger. It was clear that the ranger had caught up with him. After a moment's hesitation, I decided it was best to keep running to save the dogs.

We were terrified that our friend would identify our home. Then the farmer might come for the dogs. As a result, I ran past our home, and only returned after sunset.

Predictably, we were in serious trouble. As the eldest, I was responsible, so I avoided going inside, knowing I was going to be whipped.

Zinhle came out to keep me company. The look on her face told me just how much trouble I was in. Crying together, she told me that Khulu, who was spending her leave days at home, was waiting up to punish me before she went to bed. "*Ngizomshaya impela!*" I could hear her yelling. "I'm going to give him such a hiding!"

We tried to devise a way for me to avoid punishment. I suggested sleeping outside, but it was cold and Zinhle was concerned I would freeze. She was also scared I wouldn't be safe. In the end, we couldn't find a solution. We decided that I had to face the punishment.

"It *will* pass," I told Zinhle as we walked into the house. Khulu was busy feeding wood into the stove. As she saw me her face changed, and I knew in that instant that my punishment would be brutal.

She started hitting me with the firewood. By now I had learnt not to run away from punishment. Some called me stupid, but I had learnt to take the flogging and get it over with. When it became clear that I was going to be punished, I sometimes began to daydream about when the beating would be over. I developed the attitude that it would pass. And it always did.

Only after my beating, as I nursed my wounds from the firewood, did Khulu tell me what had happened to the friend we left behind. I was horrified when she told me that the ranger had only caught our friend after shooting him in the head with a light calibre rifle. It struck me then just how much danger we had been in.

The mischief I had caused refused to die down. The friend's family opened a case against the ranger for shooting at us. My extended family and the neighbours met to prepare us to testify in court. It was only when we told them that we hadn't heard the sound of gunfire that they decided to settle with the ranger. He footed the medical costs for my friend.

No one was certain if my friend had really been shot. The ranger insisted he had hurt his head falling on the rocks while running. But he paid the medical bill nonetheless. At last it was all over, and I was off the hook.

Or so I thought. That was until I came across a village elder who warned my cousin and me to be careful on the grazing lands. He said the rangers were going around looking for a boy with big eyes who had run away after being caught hunting illegally. The details they gave fitted my profile exactly.

For a long time afterwards I was terrified when herding the cattle, especially when it meant venturing near the river. It took time for my fear to ebb away.

Ten

Even though the news of my mom's murder wrecked me emotionally and made me drift, there was no problem with my schoolwork. I always passed my tests and exams. But at night I began fantasising about taking revenge on my father. After so many years had passed, I didn't know where he was but I assumed he still worked as a bus driver in Durban.

I pictured myself putting him in handcuffs, dousing him with petrol and lighting a match. I would watch him scream and cry for help as he died a slow, painful death. Some nights I cuffed him, and made him kneel in front of me and confess his sins. I made him tell me he was sorry for killing my mom and turning my life into a misery.

Then, as he begged me to stop, I would cut off each of his ears and watch him bleed. And no matter how much he begged for mercy, it always ended the same: he wound up dead. I never once thought about the consequences of such actions. I never imagined myself paying for killing him. Going to prison never crossed my mind. I was convinced that revenge was just. And nothing less would satisfy my anger. It was all he deserved for what he had done to my mom. And to my sister and me.

As time went on, I started to think about turning my fantasies into reality. After all, there would be no justice if night after night all I did was think. I was tired of just imagining my revenge. I had to devise a way for my father to actually pay for what he had done. It was time to turn thought into action.

I would need a knife to cut off my father's ears. So I began making knives. I started collecting scrap metal from a farm dumpsite and laying it on the railway line that ran past the village. The train came through on Mondays, Wednesdays and Fridays, and its wheels would flatten my pieces of steel into blades. Then I would neaten and sharpen them with a chisel into fancy knives with nicely carved handles.

With the train coming three times a week, I had plenty of time to practise and get the shape and design right. I would hide in the undergrowth while the train passed, and then rush to inspect my latest attempt. For weeks I was disappointed. The wheels mostly damaged the steel. They cut it into pieces instead of flattening it into the long blades I desired. But I kept on going back.

My growing collection of knives didn't impress me. I needed something larger, I decided, more vicious. So I started collecting longer pieces of steel from the dumpsite near the Catholic mission. A sword would be the perfect weapon to kill my father.

Eventually my patience paid off, and I had a long flat blade with which to work. I spent days chiselling it into shape. After designing and fitting a wooden handle, I got red and white insulation tape from one of my classmates and covered the handle with it. Finally I was satisfied. This was the weapon with which I would end my father's life. Now, I just had to raise the money to get to Durban to find him.

I was so proud of my sword. I spent nights admiring it. Soon I took it to school to show off. My classmates were impressed when I revealed it during first break. Some even asked if I would sell it to them. But the answer was no. They all wanted to handle it. Mbongi, one of my schoolmates, was having fun chasing after his friends with my sword when a teacher noticed it. When confronted, he didn't hesitate to say that it was mine.

Whenever students were caught breaking serious rules at high school, we were immediately sent to the principal for caning. But the teacher felt this transgression required a more drastic response. He called a special student assembly, and announced that every one of us was to tell our parents and guardians to attend a meeting the following Friday.

The teacher didn't tell us what the meeting would be about. But I knew. I didn't dare tell Gogo or Khulu about the meeting. But other kids in the family did. For days I hardly ate. I kept hoping for time to stop. I prayed that the meeting day would never come. But it did.

I was just inside the classroom door as the parents started walking in for the meeting. As I leaned with my hands against the wall, my heart was beating hard and fast. Every parent looked intently at my schoolmate and I. I didn't dare look back. Then I caught a glimpse of Khulu entering, and I knew I was in serious trouble.

My sword was on display on the table in front of the meeting. The parents were horrified. Khulu started to cry. She told the meeting she hadn't known what the gathering would be about. "He didn't tell me," she said. "I was surprised to see him when I walked in. He has brought shame to the family!"

Parent after parent got up to speak. But no matter how hard they interrogated me about the weapon, I refused to take responsibility. I insisted I had picked it up among the trees behind the school and showed it to my schoolmates. But no one bought my story.

After several excruciating hours, the parents started to debate an appropriate punishment for me and the boy caught chasing schoolmates with the sword. They decided to make an example of us. The teachers called for a special assembly where we were to be lashed in front of the entire school. Five lashes for each of us, as a lesson to other students.

Mbongi was called first. He was already screaming before the first lash. Then it was my turn. I scanned the meeting of parents who were there to witness the punishment, looking them straight in the eye. Then I squared my shoulders to receive my punishment as if it were an honour. I didn't care about being punished. I wished they could know my suffering, know how it felt to have your mother's life taken when you were only five. They just didn't understand. Instead, all they cared about was seeing me get another beating.

The teacher delivering the punishment must have noticed my contempt. He seemed to summon all his strength for each blow he delivered. It was so acute that I cracked at the third lash and started to cry. I walked around to absorb the pain. He looked triumphant, pleased that the boy who had always been stubborn was defeated at last. Seeing this, I looked the parents in the eye once again, then went back and bent over again. With tears running down my cheeks, I proudly accepted the rest of my lashing.

"That one will end up in prison," yelled a woman from the audience. I didn't care. A part of me was embarrassed that I had paused to cry instead of taking it all like a man. But I was glad it was over.

The punishment didn't change my behaviour. If anything, I grew angrier. I felt nothing but contempt for the teacher who had dared to flog me in front of the entire school community. And I simply made myself another sword. But this time, I kept it well hidden. I was determined to have my revenge against my father.

I spent a long time thinking of ways to raise money for the minibus taxi to Durban. Then a solution presented itself. Some of the boys at school smoked, and among them were those who smoked marijuana. Within weeks I had negotiated a deal with some labourers from Lesotho who did logging for a family in the village. The labourers brought in the drug from the Mountain Kingdom, and I started selling it on their behalf to the boys at school. I took a cut of the profit. The deal benefited us all.

Every evening I came back with money, took my cut from the day's sales, and got a new stash to sell. There were always enough customers. The boys, who were mostly older than me, followed me into a little copse of trees behind the school during break. They paid every time without asking too many questions, and never demanded a discount for being loyal customers. Nor did they bully me or rat me out to the teachers. I was never caught.

Selling marijuana forced me to mix with the wrong crowd, but I never got into trouble this time. Still, at one rand for each sale, raising the cash I needed to get to Durban and survive there for a couple of weeks was awfully slow. And I kept needing the money for other things, so I never got to save it properly. As the months passed, I realised I was wasting my time. It was going to take too long to raise the money. I didn't have the patience.

I was still determined to make the trip and carry out my revenge. Yet I wasn't prepared to live on the street in Durban while I looked for my father. I didn't know where I would stay, but it had to be decent enough. When it became clear that I was never going to raise enough money to last me a few weeks, I put my plan on hold. For now.

Eleven

By now I was nearly fourteen, and becoming ever so self-conscious. I had also started taking an interest in the girls in my school. But I hated myself. As far as I knew, there was nothing about me that any girl would notice or like.

I was desperately ashamed of my old shoes where one sole flapped loose like a flipper. They were so useless that I was better off barefoot, I decided. So I started hiding them in the undergrowth on the way to school and retrieving them on my way home. But this was high school, and we wore long pants, so I felt out of place walking barefoot. I wanted to hide.

This was all my dad's fault, I told myself. Mom would have bought me new shoes.

When I was lucky enough to have shoes donated to me, they were too big, and I had to tie the laces tight around my ankles to prevent them falling off. My hand-me-down uniform was no better. I had to pin up my pants to stop them falling down.

Everything just seemed to go wrong for me. Every Sunday when the bells jangled for mid-morning mass, I had to put on the same old pair of jeans, and make the three-kilometre walk to pray for a change in my fortune. Sometimes I prayed for my sister and me to be delivered from our misery. But mostly I asked nothing specific of the Lord. I just prayed, and hoped He knew what I needed. That He had a plan for me.

Eventually I gave up going to church. I felt hopeless. I was tired of watching my peers arrive in fancy clothes. Pepe Jeans were in fashion, and almost every teenager in the village had a pair except me. I was tired of being the subject of ridicule, of wearing the same tatty old jeans every Sunday.

I missed out on who was dating the hottest girls by staying away from church. But I didn't care. I retreated into myself and became a hermit. I was angry. On the surface, I was mostly polite. But inside I was deeply troubled. I felt helpless and scared of the future. What did it hold for me? The answer seemed clear. Nothing.

I hated everything in my small village. I hated fashion. I avoided parties. I was probably the only person in my class who never attempted to join the choir. When the choir went on school trips, I stayed at home. When they celebrated winning the national competition in Durban, I was unmoved. I didn't care.

Everyone was listening to the latest music, singing rap, hiphop and R&B and dancing to Kwaito music. Instead, I listened to reggae, rock and country, and became a big fan of Bruce Springsteen and Jamaican icon Peter Tosh. I never danced or sang. I shunned everything conventional about society, anything considered normal. I went against the tide.

My life was taking a downward slide. I constantly questioned the point of being alive. My thoughts were dark, and I started to fantasise about ending my life. I was overwhelmed with stress, and spent nights thinking about how I could die quickly without too much pain. I wanted it to be peaceful. My existence had no meaning, and I was tired, tired of everything. Getting by day by day was just too tough. I couldn't do it anymore.

Soon I came up with a plan. It probably wasn't going to be quick after all, nor peaceful, I realised. But I was certain it would do the trick.

I was up on the railway bridge over the Polela River, looking down into the swirling water. It was time. I was a strong swimmer, but I wasn't going to swim. Everything around me seemed so peaceful. So quiet. I could hear the sound of the water crashing onto the rocks below. My whole life started to replay itself through my mind. I remembered my mom, her smile. I heard her laugh and felt her warm hug. I watched the branches of the trees swaying from side to side in the breeze and listened to the hypnotic roar of the water below. But as it crashed again and again against the rocks, I started to have doubts.

I started to think of my sister, the person I loved more than anyone in the world. And then I began to realise that there probably was a purpose to my life. Zinhle needed me. I couldn't possibly do this. I couldn't betray her by committing suicide. I felt dread when I started to think about how her life would turn out without me. It happened so suddenly. In that moment, I felt the peacefulness of the river whispering to me that there really was a reason to live. Even through the harshest of times. I felt ashamed to think that I had almost broken the promise I'd made to Auntie Zinto, to protect my sister and always be there for her.

A few kilometres downstream, the Polela took a spectacular plunge to form a beautiful waterfall called Ingqubushe. On nights when the river was swollen, you could hear the water announcing itself as it tumbled onto the rocks below. If you went closer during the day, you could see the water rebounding from the power of the impact. The clash with the rocks caused the water to shoot into the air in fine white sheets. Sometimes I walked the three kilometres just to watch the spectacle of the waterfall.

One day as I stood there just after it had rained, I watched the sun peek out through the clouds. The sheets of water shooting into the air caught the reflection and formed a shimmering rainbow. The sight of these neatly stacked layers of colour made me fall in love with nature. All at once I became acutely aware of the beauty of the scenery, something I had never noticed in all my years in this small village. I felt suddenly at peace on my own, without friends. Nature was my friend. This was no longer just part of my surroundings. It was part of me.

As the river continued its endless journey, it took a sharp curve that gave rise to the myth of Kwasalukazi. Here the water slowed down and gathered deep. This was an area where as boys we would have been tempted to fish. But this was Kwasalukazi. Its myth, which was known to the whole village, dissuaded even the most ardent fishermen from venturing to its banks.

Deep below the belly of the water, myth had it, lived an old woman. Some claimed to have seen her at night drying her washing on the banks. Others said that when there was fog she sometimes emerged in the form of a white horse, or sometimes a bull, to graze on these banks. It was said that the fish in this pool were huge, for the benefit of its occupant. I had never thought to ask how people knew the size of the fish if they never dared fish there.

The river, its beauty and its many stories distracted me from my dark thoughts. Sometimes I found myself dreaming of a better future, even though my reality told a different story. My horizons were no wider than the valley I could see: from the mountains in the east where the sun rose to the hills in the west that swallowed it at night. It seemed I would never make it in life. I was doomed.

My trips to the waterfall triggered whispers that I was going mad. Villagers no longer knew what to make of me, as I had almost removed myself from society. Members of the extended family started to ask if I was okay. I assured them I was. When they asked what I was doing by the waterfall, I simply said I was killing time. So they stopped worrying and left me alone.

This place was so beautiful, even though it had given me nothing but misery. But from now on, I was determined to overcome my distress. I would not kill myself. If anyone needed to die, it wasn't going to be me. I became more determined than ever to protect my sister. I would do anything to ensure that she was not harmed. I had stopped going to church, yet I continued to pray.

Twelve

Zinhle and I had recently moved in with Khulu and her son and daughter to a four-roomed house left empty by a relative who had passed away some years earlier. Left neglected for several years, it was already in bad shape when we moved in. Khulu's eldest son had gone off to find work in Durban.

One wall had started to cave in because of the rain, and the roof leaked badly. Whenever it rained we had to lay out buckets in every room to prevent belongings from getting wet. The water leaked in every part of the house, even on the beds.

Half the windows were broken. You could literally see the fleas jumping on the couches and beds, and each morning I woke up covered in spots of blood. A formidable army of rats had also made the house their home; so many that we gave up setting traps, as these simply made things worse. A trapped rat caused a tremendous commotion as the other rats fought over its carcass.

It was hard to sleep at night while the rodents banged around, fighting and chasing one another in the cupboards. I learnt to cover my face as I slept, because they sometimes ran right over me. The cats belonging to one of the grannies in the homestead also caused havoc by chasing the rats and eating leftovers from the pots. They would get in through the broken windows and often fight and make a great racket.

After failing to convince the granny to lock in her cats at night, I grew so fed up that I decided to do something about them. I loved animals but I felt it was time to teach them a lesson. So I set up snares at all the broken windows, just as we did to trap buck, rabbits and porcupines in the forest.

The first cat that got caught coming in through the kitchen window caused a commotion as it tried to free itself. I reached for a sjambok to make it think twice before raiding the house again. But Khulu's son simply reached for a hammer and clobbered it over the head.

I was sickened. I was too traumatised to sleep the rest of that night. In the morning the granny was seething with anger and everyone was disgusted with us. I felt ashamed.

Soon afterwards, Khulu's second son left to work in Durban. By now I had had enough of the other cat raiding our house at night, and set up another snare. A couple of days later it got caught, and I whipped it for a couple of minutes until it managed to get free, with a piece of wire still around its neck. I was relieved to see it running around the homestead a couple of days later, but it never came inside our house again. Still, the rats continued to cause mayhem.

I hated it whenever it rained at night. When it was too damp to sleep on the couch in the lounge, I had to shift the bed somewhere dry. The house was a source of shame to me, and I never let any classmates visit. But I was such a hermit that it was seldom an issue.

Khulu's teenage daughter had recently given birth to a baby boy. When school reopened in 1991, Zinhle was told she couldn't go back to school. She had to stay home and take care of the new baby.

My sister was inconsolable. For days the two of us talked about nothing else but how to stop this from happening. She was determined to go to school, and I badly wanted to protect her from being exploited like this. It was my duty. But a week passed, and still Zinhle was stuck at home, babysitting.

After school the second week, on the pretence of going out to fetch the cattle, I crossed the river to Auntie Zinto's to tell her what was happening. I pleaded with her not to mention that she had heard it from me, because I knew it would get me into trouble. "I just want to see my sister back at school," I told her. Auntie Zinto assured me she would do something.

Before school the next morning, as I was warming the water on the iron stove, Auntie Zinto arrived. She hadn't even reached the door when she started yelling at Khulu.

"*Angeke ngivume nidlale ngengane kasisi*! I will not let anyone exploit my sister's child! Zinhle has no baby, and she is going to school *now*!"

I kept quiet during her tirade, pretending to be busy.

Eventually Auntie Zinto walked into the house, where she found Zinhle sitting on the old couch in a corner of the kitchen.

She told Zinhle to leave the baby on the couch. "*Geza uye esikoleni*," she said. "Wash and go to school immediately."

Auntie Zinto was renowned for her feistiness, and even Khulu couldn't stand up to her. In no time at all, Zinhle and I were off to school.

I felt such pride that I had managed to look out for my sister this time. I was more determined now than ever to protect her. I went around telling every adult in the extended family who would listen to me that Zinhle needed a place to stay. I didn't know where or with whom she could possibly live without being exploited again, but I felt that remaining in this house would be bad for her. I feared she would end up as disaffected as I was. I was afraid that she, too, would start to drift.

By now she had confided in me that she was also having thoughts of suicide. If she died I would have no reason left to live. It was only because of Zinhle that I could still summon the strength to get up every morning. She gave me a reason to pray every night. I had no hope at all for my future. But my sister's presence kept alive the hope that one day the Lord might answer my prayers. I didn't care about myself. My sole mission in life was to protect Zinhle, and to avenge my mother's death.

Thirteen

It was a blazing hot day. After a three-kilometre walk from the forest, I paused to rest at the Catholic mission shop where Zinhle had started helping out.

A couple called Edward and Eugenia McNamara had recently taken it over. I had never paid them much attention and only ever saw them when I came to buy something or charge the car battery that powered our hi-fi.

Eugenia was just walking into the shop as I arrived. She smiled warmly at me, and I saw her eyes travel down to the holes in my battered red boots. I looked away.

"I think we need to buy you some new shoes," she said cheerfully. "Otherwise those little toes of yours are going to freeze in winter!"

I ignored her as she accompanied me into the shop. I distrusted adults. I had come to associate them with verbal and physical abuse. They were a source of pain and humiliation. So I couldn't accept a smile or a gesture of friendliness at face value, and brushed aside all efforts at affection with hostility. I didn't smile until I saw my sister behind the counter.

Edward was also sitting behind the counter, stony faced, flyswatter in hand, his eyes seeking his next target. He whacked his swatter onto the counter, then slowly scraped the remains of the fly onto the floor. He was tall and massively built, with a pale face that was always deep in thought. The few remaining hairs on his head were grey. His fluency in Zulu amazed everyone, but as I sat there I began to notice that he was abrasive and moody with the shoppers, constantly cursing in Zulu. Eugenia was much younger than him, in her late thirties perhaps, and probably the warmest person I had ever met. They made an odd couple.

Eugenia seemed to read my mind. "*Ungamnaki ubaba wakho!*" she said to me, laughing. "*Udlala ukuguga.* Don't mind your dad, old age is catching up with him."

I stared at her in silence. My dad? What the hell was she talking about?

Later, when the shop was quiet, Eugenia sat me down for a chat by the veranda.

"Edward and I have decided to adopt Zinhle," she started. "We're your parents now," she said, "and Tita is your sister." She was referring to her little daughter, Laurelle.

I looked down without saying a word. Perhaps realising that she was going to get nothing out of me, Eugenia changed the subject.

"We need to do something about your shoes," she repeated.

I managed a shy smile, but said nothing. I was flustered and confused. To be offered a mother and father was both appealing and repulsive. Even as a teenager, I still sometimes fantasised about a normal life with parents. But I was almost past the point of being able to call anyone Mom or Dad. The only father I knew had murdered my mother and turned my world into a living hell. The very word "father" stirred feelings of pain, loss and disgust, and set me churning with thoughts of revenge.

It seemed like a lifetime since my dad had held me on his lap in those township streets. I had long since resigned myself to growing up without a father. Someone else might have been happy at this display of warmth and kindness from the McNamaras. But I hadn't had a decent or healthy upbringing. The years of pain and abuse had taken their toll.

I could only stare blankly at Eugenia.

I had prayed and prayed for Zinhle to find a family to look after her. But now that the McNamaras had taken her in, I had mixed feelings. Yes, I was happy that she'd met people who seemed to love her. I was sure they would treat her well. But a part of me

64

was very, very sad. I was losing her. I was terrified that the bond between us would dissolve.

Unbeknown to me, my warnings that my sister was being exploited had been taken very seriously by Mom's younger brother, who had just returned from the mines. He discussed this with the McNamaras, who agreed to take her in to live with the other poor and orphaned children they looked after.

Zinhle's new home was an old pigsty that the McNamaras had renovated, nestled under some tall oak trees. When I visited Zinhle here I found a hive of activity. Women were cooking in the kitchen while Zinhle played with other teenagers, mostly girls. The stone floor looked bitterly cold to sleep on in winter, but I soon discovered that they all had foam mattresses.

But I was still concerned. The Polela River flowed past just a hundred metres away. "You're going to freeze here in winter," I told her.

"No," she grinned, "we have plenty of blankets. What do you think of it here? I'm so happy. I wish we'd grown up here together. Come and stay with us."

I refused. "As long as you're happy, I'm fine," I said. "I'll come and visit."

For the first time ever, my sister had a beautiful smile. We sat chatting under the oaks in front of the care centre. I was happy for her. The McNamaras treated her just like one of their own. They had another house in Pevensey village, and commuted between it and their mission shop. They usually brought Zinhle with them when they came to Pevensey, which made it easier for me to visit her on weekends. It was only a ten-minute walk compared to the three kilometres to the mission. I could see how fond the McNamaras were of my sister; they gave her more attention than the other kids.

"The moment you enter this gate," Eugenia explained to me, "you have to switch to English. It's important that you and Zinhle become fluent in English. It'll give you a head start in life."

"Yes, ma'am."

"Not ma'am," she said gently. "Mom. Edward and I are your

parents. So you need to call us Mom and Dad."

I didn't answer.

Eugenia tried hard to get me closer to the McNamara family, but I resisted. No amount of counselling or encouragement could persuade me to confide in them or ask for help. I was used to being on my own and I was determined to stay that way. I knew they meant well. But I had finally resigned myself to being an orphan. It was too late.

The more the McNamaras offered me help and tried to talk me into sharing my pain with them, the more doggedly I resisted. No one could penetrate the fortress I'd built around myself. Yet I kept visiting my sister and the McNamaras, even though I couldn't bring myself to treat them as parents.

Fourteen

The following year, I passed the last grade in our local school, which went only as far as Grade 9. For further schooling, students had to move to neighbouring towns and villages. All my classmates were excited when the exams ended. Setting off from the tiny village of Pevensey to live in a larger village was like a rite of passage, a ticket to independence.

As usual, I had nothing to look forward to. Khulu and the extended family had said nothing about my future. Going to school in another village meant paying accommodation and school fees. It was out of reach for Khulu. Until now she had shouldered most of the burden of paying my fees. But she earned a meagre salary as a cleaner at a home for the disabled six kilometres away.

I was resigned to dropping out of school at this point and finding work in Underberg, probably on one of the surrounding farms. Anything would do. Or I could follow Khulu's two sons and look for work in Durban. As I had predicted, there wasn't much hope of a decent future.

But as it turned out, Khulu had a relative in a village in Bulwer. At the last minute, she told me to pack and try to find a place at one of the high schools in Gqumeni village.

It was a strange feeling. I had always hated living here in Pevensey, but now I felt a little sad to leave it behind. Despite being a hermit, I was going to miss the familiar people and surroundings.

Khulu's relative, known as Gogo Khathi in her village, had agreed to take me in, as long as Khulu paid forty rand a month.

Unlike my former school, the high school had a large population of students. And lots of girls. And nobody there knew about my poor background. I realised straight away that they were not going to judge me or look down on me. Gone were the boys who teased me about my clothes. I was off to a fresh start.

From the onset, schooling took a back seat. It was just too exciting to be getting so much attention from girls, something I'd never had at my previous school. And at last I had decent shoes. Khulu's sons had started working in a shoe factory. So now I had several pairs of stylish and very durable handmade leather hiking shoes. No one else had shoes like mine, and their thick soles left a signature tread as I strode along the dusty roads.

Within months I had already had several flings. Each time I fell madly in love and got plenty of love letters. But I also got dumped regularly. Then I met an amazing girl. This time I was convinced it was finally going to last. When a letter came with the bad news, I was inconsolable. Even Gogo Khathi noticed my misery.

"*Zikwalile yini intombi?* Have the girls dumped you?" She had found several love letters over the months, and warned Khulu that I wasn't doing much studying. "He loves girls too much," she told her. Knowing that I always passed at school, Khulu didn't fuss much, but she let me know what she'd heard, and told me to focus on my studies and not waste her hard-earned money.

But I couldn't be stopped. It felt so good to experience love. The girls were trying to outdo each other for my attention. It was the coolest thing ever. Meanwhile, I was failing my tests and assignments. It began to worry me, because it had never happened before. But it never occurred to me that I might actually fail the year.

We were in the middle of a lesson one day in May when the principal walked into our classroom and interrupted the teacher. Our principal was a short, burly man, and he was looking distinctly nervous. Behind him followed five or six men who looked so unkempt they might have crawled out of a cave.

Failing to hide his fear, the principal announced that these men had something to tell us. One of them stepped forward and introduced himself while the principal disappeared. He was a short young man with a scruffy beard, and he had come to tell us to join the Inkatha Freedom Party, or IFP. The very sound of the IFP terrified the class. This was a Zulu-dominated political party, which was currently embroiled in a bloody political conflict with the other main party, the ANC.

There were over forty of us in the class, and no one uttered a sound. Most of us were looking down. After pausing to survey our faces, the man announced that our silence was a sign that we had agreed to join the IFP. He thanked us and welcomed us into the party. He expected to see us all at the weekend meetings and rallies. Then they turned and left. They apparently repeated this process with every class in the school.

The following Saturday, I was sitting outside the house listening to the radio when a mob came charging up the dusty street chanting slogans. I watched curiously as they approached. I had never seen anything like it before. Suddenly some in the mob pointed their sticks at me and ordered me to join them. I got up and did as I was told, guessing that any sign of dissent would be met with a beating.

We marched through the village for a while, during which many more people were forced to leave their homes to join the march. Eventually we settled at a schoolyard. Here, there was a diligent effort to indoctrinate us with IFP ideology.

This was 1992. Elsewhere in the country, we heard on the radio, political leaders were in talks that would lead to South Africa's first democratic election. But here in the villages the talk was territorial. Leaders in both the ANC and the IFP were keen to establish and maintain their fiefdoms. Warlords were in the making. It was clear that political violence was inevitable.

Like other teenagers, I felt that being part of the IFP was uncool. I hated what these uneducated men were teaching us. I was clean and getting an education. These unemployed men felt like backward, stick-wielding bastards trying to impose an unwelcome ideology. I joined the groups of older boys during school breaks to

69

discuss how we were going to deal with being forced to march and attend political meetings.

During one meeting we decided that resisting would be futile. It would almost certainly lead to injury or even death. Among us were village boys familiar with the IFP slogans. It was best to lead from the front, we decided, and to fool the party into believing that we were with them. This way, there would be no trouble. So every Saturday we enthusiastically joined the marching mobs, singing and chanting in praise of the political party and its leadership, while insulting the rival ANC.

But with every weekend spent chanting slogans instead of playing football, we grew restless. Every Saturday, local men made us listen to more of the same. We started to loathe the IFP. Our loathing drew us closer together as schoolmates, and also closer to the ANC.

The mask was about to be pulled, and our cover was about to be blown.

In the rural village of Nkwezela in the Bulwer area, a plan was hatched to challenge the IFP head on. From this village, where I had started my schooling when we stayed with Dala, we would march into IFP territory and launch an ANC branch. It was a journey we all knew was fraught with danger. But we were young, foolhardy and self-righteous.

Common sense should have stopped us from going there. But there wasn't much thinking going on. We just trusted in our instincts. In such a large group of boys it was impossible to reason. None of us rose up to warn the others of the danger we were plunging into. We were naïve and full of energy, and we felt invincible.

As we marched the four kilometres to the village, a teenager next to me told me how he'd stormed out of his house when his parents tried to stop him. He was angry that they didn't understand that we were fighting for *their* freedom, too. I had doubts about what exactly we were fighting for. I knew that leaders were busy trying to work out a political settlement somewhere far away. But I sensed that ours was a fight for territorial control. An act that was going to trigger a senseless war.

A voice in my head constantly nagged me to turn back. There were others who backed out in fear, or from the realisation that this was foolish and dangerous. But I didn't. Instead, by the time we entered the IFP-dominated village an hour later, I was in front, jumping as high as I could and marching to ANC slogans into a village where this was alien, where such action was punishable by flogging or even death.

One of the local leaders tried to ram his car into us. He tried again and again, but we simply left the gravel road and scampered for the grass. As his car passed we reunited and surged forward.

"*Angeke kuphume noyedwa sizonibulala nonke!*" he yelled. "None of you will come out alive." But we laughed and surged onward. He left us forging ever deeper into enemy territory.

Virtually no one who marched with me lived in this village or went to school here. But I did. I should have thought about the fact that the following Monday I would have to return to school. I knew it, but I ignored my racing heart. We had come to conquer, to take over enemy territory, and announce our new status as the rulers of the fiefdom. Without a fight.

The villagers looked nervous as we pressed on deeper. Doors closed. People disappeared into passages. Others didn't bother trying to hide their fear or retain their dignity. They ran. We were headed for a playground deep in the village, where our leaders had told us we would be received by a group of young local comrades, all in their late teens. Here, we would officially launch an ANC branch.

We arrived at the playground to find several boys from my school. They were nervous. The plan had changed, they said. Our rivals, the IFP, were assembling, and they were armed with guns, machetes and pangas. They had pump guns but no multi-bullet magazines, they said. The details didn't mean much to me. Few in our group were armed, and those who were had only homemade guns, made of a plank with two iron pipes clamped together. They could shoot only one bullet at a time. That is, if they managed to shoot at all.

We were such a big crowd it would be difficult for our enemies to avoid hitting us if they opened fire. And if they used spray bullets, even a bad shot would hit target.

The enormity of what I had gotten myself into was beginning to dawn on me. What if I died today? Leave immediately, they advised us. They pointed the best way out, through a plantation, which would lead us back to the neighbouring village from which we had come. Hours of walking.

It was clear this was not just a goodbye-comrade-see-you-soon kind of dispersal. We needed to run: our enemies could appear at any moment. But we were reluctant, and marched away without running.

Suddenly, from nowhere, a mob came charging towards us. Now it was everyone for himself.

We rocketed away, crouching instinctively at every crack of gunfire, or throwing ourselves to the ground to dodge the bullets, then dashing off again. If the bullets hadn't hit anyone, no doubt they had already whizzed past by the time we crouched.

We split into small groups and just kept running, not stopping until we ran out of breath. By this time, fortunately, our pursuers appeared to have given up. I really hoped they had. But I still didn't know if the mob had managed to shoot, hack or capture anyone. All I knew was that my group of twelve or so was safe.

We walked kilometres across farms and through forests. We were tired and thirsty, but what mattered most was getting back to our own villages. To safety.

Bit by bit, we reunited with other groups and our numbers swelled. It was during this long march that I was introduced to guns and bullets. I held a homemade gun in my hand and inspected several bullets.

I was instantly hooked. I realised I had found the best solution for revenge against my father. I would make a gun. And no matter how long it took, I was going to find him and put a bullet through his brain. I told those who were flaunting their weapons that I could do a better job. They laughed and challenged me to prove it.

On we trudged, mouths dry and stomachs growling, for what seemed forever. We reached our destination as the hills swallowed the sun over to the west. Others who had run faster or managed to find a shortcut were waiting near a supermarket. But their mood was subdued. They should have been happy. We had survived! Then we learnt that one boy had caught a bullet in his spine. When he could no longer run, the mob had caught up with him and hacked him to pieces.

His name circulated through the crowd. His friends wept. But I had never known him. I was just happy to be alive. We were such a big group that we couldn't know everyone. What kept us together was the spirit of comradeship and our hatred of the IFP. Nothing more. But knowing that one of us had fallen to the enemy made me realise the enormity of what we had started. We had triggered political violence. We had started a war. There was no going back.

The group could speak of nothing but revenge. But that wasn't uppermost in my mind. How was I going to manage to make it to school the following Monday?

I decided to go to Dala's house. Everyone in her village now knew what had happened. "What about your schooling?" Dala asked as she gave me supper that night. I told her I had no choice but to go back. "They'll kill you," she said, fighting back tears. I forced a wry smile.

I was absolutely determined to go back to school. I wanted to see the girls there. And for the first time, I realised how important it was for me to finish the year and pass. I couldn't disappoint Khulu. I couldn't waste the money she had worked so hard for. I simply had to pass. She had spent money she didn't have so I could progress one more class, one more year. How could I look her in the eye if I failed?

Fifteen

On Monday morning, Dala gave me two rand to get to the village where school was. The ride to school cost one rand in the minibus taxi; the other rand was the return fare in case the IFP exiled me from the village.

I was nervous as I boarded the taxi. I prayed all the way that no one had seen me marching. But as I got to school, I realised that I was already unmasked. To the boys who supported the ANC, I was now a legend. To those on the side of the IFP, I was the enemy. Boys who had played football together just weeks earlier were now split along political lines. Friendships were torn apart by political loyalty.

Sitting in class, struggling to concentrate, I began to realise what our dangerous adventure into enemy heartland had done. Boys I used to hang around with now looked at me as an outcast, a piece of rubbish, simply because they sympathised with the IFP. For now they knew I was on the other side. I took comfort from those who shared my ideology. But I knew I wasn't safe.

It was a hot day. But as I passed the taxi stop on my way back from school, an IFP fanatic, Khelebane, was waiting there wearing a large coat, a sure sign that he was hiding a weapon – a spear, a machete, or maybe a panga. Just days earlier he had smashed the windows at the homestead of his closest relatives because he suspected them of ANC sympathies.

An icy chill came over me as I approached to pass Khelebane. I wanted to disappear. To get home. As I passed without looking at him I heard him shout: "*Uyakhuluma?* Did you say something?"

"No," I said quickly over my shoulder.

Walking as fast as I could, I kept looking back to see if he was following me. I felt relief. I knew he had meant to provoke me into saying something, to give him an excuse to attack. It unsettled me. In the village I was now notorious as an ANC member, a *qabane*. I couldn't sleep that night. I kept thinking that a mob would come for me.

I tried to study in the evenings. But life was hell. Gogo Khathi kept saying how stressful it was to have me in her house. Wherever she went the villagers accosted her for harbouring a *qabane*. I was a marked man. I now openly carried a large knife to protect myself. She advised me to redeem myself by attending a meeting the following Saturday, where all the boys who were known ANC sympathisers were to be flogged with a sjambok, and then forgiven and re-educated in the IFP ideology.

Saturday came. She prepared for the meeting and told me to come with her to receive my flogging and forgiveness. "I'll follow," I said. Uneasily, I made my journey through the passages to the dusty main road, to reach the school grounds where the flogging was to take place.

I had walked about two kilometres when I heard kids chanting: "*Kanti usekhona weQabane,* there's an ANC member around." The chant was used to intimidate those suspected of siding with the ANC.

I stopped to look across the valley. There on the hill beside the school, people were already gathered in numbers. I avoided looking towards the chanters, pretending I hadn't heard. They were seated in a group, now chanting IFP slogans. In front of the chanting crowd, a group of teenagers was already lined up, being prepared for their punishment.

Something told me I was handing myself over to certain danger. I now knew the hatred most villagers felt for me. I suspected my punishment was going to be different. Much more severe. Not just a flogging on the backside with a sjambok. Instinctively I sensed that I would be clobbered to death with a knobkerrie, or stabbed with a spear. I came to a dead halt. With one last look at the crowd gathered on top of the hill, I turned back.

Reaching the house, I gathered my belongings and flagged the first taxi that appeared. I had decided it was best to stay with Dala in the neighbouring village of Nkwezela, and commute to school. I needed to be out of the IFP's reach at night, when I was most at risk of attack.

Dala welcomed me with open arms, as always. She fed me and prayed for me. "I hope you're finally going to change your ways," she said. I hadn't given a thought to how she was going to raise my daily taxi fare to school.

Sixteen

Changing my ways was a lot harder than I had anticipated. By now I hardly thought or worried about Zinhle. I had entrusted my sister wholly to the care of the McNamaras. And they were doing a good job. Protecting her was no longer my priority. She no longer needed it.

Among my ANC mates in this village, the appetite for revenge was still strong. Within a few days they came to Dala's house to summon me. Soon a large group of teenagers was gathered at the house of our local leader, who was in his mid-twenties.

Before us were three young men, the eldest in his early twenties, the youngest my age or at most a few years older. My comrades had captured them at our local taxi stop, waiting for transport back to the school village, an IFP stronghold. That alone meant they were IFP members. As such, they needed to be dealt with. What were they doing here in our village? They had to be IFP spies.

The older boys were saying that after sunset, the captives would be dragged out to a clearing and killed. They said this right in front of the captives. Their sentence was decided even before the interrogation started.

I was easily the youngest in the group. For hours, starting at about midday, we interrogated them. I was actively involved, asking question after question as other boys assaulted them. I took the good cop role.

The assault was sometimes so severe that I couldn't suppress tears as I asked my questions. Yet even as I cried, I kept up the questioning. I had started out convinced of the guilt of our captives, but eventually I started trying to find them a way out. I couldn't take what I was witnessing. I despised the IFP, but I realised I wasn't cut out for this. I was still determined to kill my father, but these lads had done nothing to me. This wasn't my fight.

I didn't want our captives to meet a brutal end. But I proceeded with the interrogation, interjecting when fellow comrades questioned them, because most of their questions weren't genuine. They were just trying to set the captives up.

Sometimes one of our captives would ask to be taken outside to take a leak. I campaigned for them when their request was refused, and they were told they would be killed if they peed their pants or soiled themselves. I defended them several times, as each wanted to take a leak at different times.

During the ordeal, a small boy was brought in, having sneaked in to see what was happening. The more hardened teenagers were quick to suggest a punishment for the little boy, but in the end he was dismissed with only a shouting.

As the sun was about to set and the light starting to fade, the eldest captive asked to address our group. He was shouted down, but again I pleaded that we hear him. He might just confess. "Go on, talk then," he was told through a cacophony of voices.

"Like every one of you in this house," he said, "I fear and despise the IFP. They force my family and my community to attend weekend meetings."

Having just run away from his village myself, I knew what he was talking about. But my mates were unmoved. They wanted him to shut up because he was wasting our time.

"Let him finish," I insisted.

"*Noma ningangibulala bafowethu, angiyona Inkatha mina.* Brothers, I don't care if you kill me, but I'm not an IFP member."

I looked deep into his eyes. Right then and there, I knew he and his friends were innocent. I knew he was telling the truth. But he was tired of being beaten, and had accepted his fate. He wanted the pain to end. He had resigned himself to a brutal death. But he wasn't about to admit to something he was not.

Until that point I had been scared to stand up for the captives. I knew I would be called a traitor. Worse, I might have been punished along with them. But now I no longer cared. The truth was right there before me. And I wasn't going to be party to killing anyone.

"Let them go," I said. "We've punished them enough, and we have no evidence that they're linked to the IFP."

No one took me seriously. They looked at me as if I was mad.

It was starting to get dark when I realised I'd lost the fight to have the captives freed. As night set in, it was clearly a matter of time before the mob dragged them out and killed them. I couldn't watch. I wanted no part of this. It was time to go and leave the captives to their fate.

As I headed for the door, pretending to take a breather, there was a loud explosion, and flares illuminating the darkness. Suddenly, there was chaos. No one knew what was happening. We were all terrified, captors and captives alike. Assuming we were under attack, everyone threw themselves to the ground.

The firing was incessant. I thought I was going to die. In the chaos, I followed others to the only exit. Like them, I threw myself to the ground and started crawling. After a couple of metres I got up and ran. My slops hindered my speed, so I kicked them off and ran barefoot.

Only the next day did we find out that the little boy had told his parents, who called the police. Expecting to be outgunned, the police had called in the army, who triggered an explosion to startle us, and then started firing rubber bullets. Only a few of us had managed to escape. Scores were caught and arrested while our hostages disappeared into the darkness.

A fellow ANC member told me he had realised I was crying during the interrogation, but didn't consider me weak. He didn't want to participate in killing those people either, he told me. Suddenly I realised I hadn't been alone in struggling with my conscience during the marathon torture. My mate said he had managed to run home, which was nearby, and had hidden behind an iron stove until the firing stopped.

As a result of this incident, school was closed for about a week. So I returned to Pevensey. There I found that Khulu and the extended family knew everything. They said it was too dangerous for me to go back to school.

I was devastated. For the next few days, I barely ate. I thought about the girls. I reminisced about the good times I'd had with them. When school reopened, I felt even worse. I couldn't stop thinking about my mates and my latest sweetheart. In that high school and that village I was somebody. Here in Pevensey I was just a herd boy.

I had to do something. I had to get back to where there were people who cared about me. Something inside me also said I could still pass the year. It was already September, and I had failed miserably in the mid-year exams. I wrote Khulu a letter explaining and apologising to her and the extended family. I left it on a toilet seat, and slipped back to Dala's house. The next day, I was back at school. Tensions were still running high, but I slept better living away from the enemy stronghold.

Though I tried to take my studies seriously, I couldn't shake off my ANC mates or give up my loyalty to the party. And revenge was still high on their agenda. At the next meeting we talked constantly about finding weapons. Guns. I decided to take up the challenge. I told some of my mates that I could make a few guns and supply them with weapons.

Making my first homemade gun wasn't difficult at all, and the end result was a small but beautiful piece. I polished it several times a day until it shone. Finally I raised the three rand for a bullet to test it out. I went off to a field well away from the village, cocked my gun, pointed it into the air and pulled the trigger. There was a loud bang as the steel struck the back of the bullet. It worked like a charm.

I was proud. I had a spring in my step on my way back. This gun wasn't going anywhere, I decided. This was the piece with which my father would meet his end. I flaunted it to my mates. They were mesmerised. I had even cut a side chamber in which the trigger could rest. This meant that with a simple flick of the thumb to the right, the trigger quickly found the bullet. This was a big step from having to pull the trigger and let it go.

My mates asked me to make more. I was now a supplier, and gaining more status in the group. I was valuable. I felt important. Finding the raw materials wasn't hard. There were plenty of iron pipes and clamps in the dumpsite back in Pevensey. I simply went back there every weekend to replenish the parts.

People who know about this part of my life often ask if any of my weapons ever killed anyone. I don't know. I never shot anyone myself. I didn't have the guts. But as far as I was concerned back then, we were fighting an enemy that didn't think twice about shooting at us. In such a state of violence, you don't have time to reason.

At the time, I didn't realise that I had strayed and lost my way. I was like a ship headed for the rocks. What I was doing was like running through a raging fire with a container full of petrol. It was suicidal. I was heading for disaster, and I needed to take a new path. But back then I was desperate to feel I belonged.

Until then I had spent my life as a hermit, ashamed of my poverty. I never felt accepted in Pevensey. My clothes were too ragged. I didn't go to church because I didn't have decent clothes to wear. I was angry at society. But becoming part of the ANC had finally allowed me to belong somewhere, make friends and do something of value.

When the exams came that year, I knew there was little chance that I would pass. I tried to study, but it felt as if I was seeing every page for the first time. I didn't know where to start. I was lost. For the first time in my life, I failed a year.

In failing, I lost the one thing that had given me a sense of self-respect back home in Underberg. Though I had grown up with so little, I could always rely on being somewhere near the top of the class. It was my one source of credibility in the village while I was growing up.

The violence was intensifying. I knew there was no chance of returning to the rural village in Bulwer when the year ended. It was clear that school was over for me.

When I failed, my world ended. I stopped caring. Since I knew I wasn't returning to this village, I hardly cared about the girls anymore. I didn't even care about the next day.

Khulu had even more bad news for me when I got home. She would do nothing more for me. I could live under her roof, but I could expect nothing from her. I was on my own. I had disgraced her, and wasted her hard-earned money on girls and politics. I was effectively disowned. I was back to herding cattle.

Now I had no future, no prospects. My habit of getting into trouble had also created strain with the McNamaras. I now barely saw them or my sister. Eugenia reprimanded me about my ANC activities whenever she saw me. I hated it. I felt I was right and everyone else was wrong.

It crossed my mind that Eugenia reprimanded me because she cared for me. She loved my sister and didn't want to see her hurt by what I was getting up to. Eugenia was growing frustrated with me after trying so hard to win my trust. But still, I spurned her every attempt.

Seventeen

When the schools reopened in January 1993, I watched the students in their grey-and-white uniforms pass by on the dust road outside. I woke up in the mornings and just gazed at the mountains, watching the sun drift from east to west. Doing nothing.

I hardly cared about girls now. Those I tried my luck with looked down on me. I didn't go to school, my clothes were tattered and I lived in a dilapidated house. On top of it, the community hated me for the guns I had made. I was a bum. I had no hope.

Meanwhile, the violence in Gqumeni village was intensifying. First came the story of a former classmate who was attacked while he sat with friends in a thatched house at night. Realising his house was surrounded, he came out with a gun in each hand and opened fire into the darkness.

They mowed him down within seconds, and then set the hut alight. His friends were hit as they clambered out of the tiny windows, but they managed to escape. The police collected my classmate's charred remains in the morning. Then an ANC boy I knew attended another meeting where sympathisers were to receive floggings and then be forgiven. His father watched in horror as he was instead clobbered to death with knobkerries. The father, who had convinced his boy to come to the meeting, told the mob he now had nothing left to live for. He, too, was clubbed to death.

I thought back to the moment I had turned back from a previous meeting. I was lucky to be alive. These deaths of former friends made me angry, and intensified my hatred for the IFP.

With little to do, I turned to the one thing I knew: making more guns. On occasional weekends I would take the bus to Bulwer, where friends were eagerly waiting to inspect my bag, filled with my latest consignment of homemade guns. My gunmaking was now an open secret in Pevensey. Parents didn't want their teenagers near me. Not that I cared. I was back to the person I had been before I left Pevensey. I had retreated into myself. I was a hermit again.

I watched in dismay as my clothes deteriorated. My shirts, pants and jackets were getting old. There was no one I could ask for anything. Those who had donated secondhand clothing to Zinhle and I now looked right past me. They detested me for my activities. Elders in the community feared I would bring political violence to this small Catholic community, where no one gave a damn about politics.

Although many villagers knew that I made guns, I made a point of not showing them to anyone. When a local boy offered to buy one, I refused. For weeks he pestered me, offering money. Every time he came the offer grew. I badly needed money. Eventually I relented, under strict instructions that he never tell anyone where he got it, especially if the police caught him. If they interrogated him so that he couldn't keep quiet, he could only say that I gave him bullets. If he dared talk about my guns, I told him, I'd shoot him. Having scared him enough, we did the deal.

When I spotted two police vans on top of the hill one day soon afterwards, I had a hunch that it had something to do with me. It was around midday, and I was busy with my gunmaking. I rushed into the house to stash my freshly made weapons behind the wardrobe.

Then I dashed at full speed across the mealie field to where I always kept blank bullets in the undergrowth. I had always planned to use them as a decoy in case I was caught. I was relieved to find them still there. I watched as the police vehicles sped to the homestead of the boy who had bought the gun from me days earlier. Now I knew I was in trouble.

I waited for them to come after me. It didn't take long. When they arrived, a tall Afrikaans policeman spoke to me in strongly accented English. The boy had apparently used the gun to threaten his brother-in-law, who called the police. The policeman asked for the bullets the boy said I had. I was relieved. It seemed he had kept our agreement.

As I led the police towards my decoy, my mom's younger brother Malan yelled at me. "Your hardheadedness has paid off, hasn't it? I hope they lock you up, to teach you a lesson." My extended family knew about my gunmaking and vigorously disapproved. But I listened to no one. I thought I was cleverer than any of them. I led the police to the spot where my blanks were stashed. After a moment of pretending to look for them, I pointed out the ammunition.

"How old are you?" the tall policeman asked.

"Sixteen, sir."

"We're taking you in. You're going to jail."

I was scared, but managed to smile at him. "You have nothing on me, sir. You don't have enough evidence to arrest me."

He was annoyed by my arrogance. "Those bullets in your hand are harmless, sir. Collecting blanks is my hobby." The bullets by now were damp, and some had gone rusty. "They're 9-millimetre bullets, and that's a 9-millimetre pistol in your holster, sir. Why don't you test them, and then leave me alone?"

"What the hell do you know about guns?" he demanded, failing to conceal his anger.

"Only a fool wouldn't know that police carry either a .38 or a 9-millimetre pistol sir. That's how I know. Why don't you test the bullets. I assure you they're useless. You're wasting your time. You have nothing on me, sir."

"Shut up. You're coming with us."

They walked me across the field and shoved me into the back of the police van. My entire extended family gathered to watch. I could see residents of other homesteads standing outside, watching in disbelief. Like my uncle, they were probably happy I was getting arrested.

The police drove as fast as they could along the bumpy dust roads. They cornered so sharply that I was flung from side to side in the back of the van. I suspected they were angry, having found nothing strong enough to take me in. After a few minutes the van stopped, and they dumped me in the middle of the village without a word.

Those few minutes in the back of the police van started me reflecting on the direction my life was headed. After being shot at twice the previous year, I still hadn't shown any caution. The adrenalin of youth had kept me from realising that I was caught up in a deadly game. What I was doing was far from heroic. It was sheer stupidity. These warnings started ringing loudly as I walked back home after my shake-up in the police van.

I had thought about death. I had doubted that I would live past the age of eighteen. But it had never occurred to me that I could end up incarcerated. I had believed that I was making guns for a worthy cause. But the thought of what this might lead to finally began to get through to me. Why were the people I was supplying with guns still fighting? It was 1993. Our political leaders were negotiating a date for South Africa's first democratic elections.

I had managed to fool the police by using those bullets as a decoy. I should have been proud that they hadn't managed to find my guns. Instead, I began soul searching. I started to think about what I was doing to my sister, the McNamaras and myself, the people who cared about me. Slowly I began to think about what I wanted in life. The answer was there. I had no prospect of a better future, but I definitely didn't want it to get even worse. I didn't want to land up in prison. Life was miserable enough; I didn't need to ruin it further.

Later that night my uncle Malan and his cousin came into my bedroom as I sat on the bed, still reflecting. For a moment, no one said a word. I knew they wanted to talk to me about what had happened hours earlier. They wanted me to change my ways. To advise me to stop making guns. Still, they said nothing. They sat there, staring at me. Deep down inside, I knew they cared about me. Wordlessly I got up, probed for my suitcase in the back of the wardrobe, and gave them my weapons. Some were still unfinished. They included one I was still experimenting with, which I hoped would shoot six bullets.

"Here," I said. "Destroy them. I quit."

They took the guns and walked out.

But I hadn't given them everything. The original well-polished gun I had dedicated to the killing of my father was still there, safely hidden. I wasn't parting with it just yet. My mission for revenge against my father was still very much alive. I would only discard that gun when I had fulfilled my mission.

Eighteen

I was gazing at the mountains a couple of days later. The incessant boredom had returned. I decided to take a walk, an insignificant decision that was to completely change my life. I walked along the road that separated the village from the vast grazing pastures. The sun seemed to follow me, as it does in this vast open space. Far in the distance I watched the sunlight glimmering off the railway tracks.

A voice from behind caught my attention. It was a nun, dressed in a white habit like the angels that decorated the walls of the church in my village.

"Hi there, young man. I'm looking for the school."

"Morning, Sister. Just keep walking, you can't miss it. It'll be on your left about two kilometres down the road."

She was looking for the Catholic school I had left just over a year earlier, to study in Bulwer.

"Please, won't you escort me there?"

"Okay, it'll be a pleasure."

As the two of us walked, she asked why a young man like me wasn't going to school.

"I can't afford the fees," I told her.

This made her curious. "Tell me a bit about your background," she asked.

"I briefly laid out the story of my life, and she listened patiently. Occasionally she interrupted me to ask a question.

"Your English is very good," she said. She had a strong German accent herself.

I managed to smile. I couldn't remember being told I was good at anything. I had grown up being called names, and resigned myself to believing I was inferior. It made me feel good to hear a compliment.

It took us roughly ten minutes to reach the school yard. I said goodbye and turned to go.

"Wait a moment," she said. I stopped, waiting under a row of trees for her to speak.

"Are you aware that this school is expanding from next year?" she asked. "They're adding a further grade next year. Another grade will be added each year, until the final year."

"Yes, Sister, I've heard."

"I want you to come back to school on Monday. You can do all the grades, and graduate from high school in your final year. Please, come with me now." She took me to the principal, and told him she wanted me to start at school the following Monday. Then she sent me to speak to the Grade 9 teacher.

"*Bakucoshaphi?*" the teacher asked. Where did the nun find me?

"I was on the road, sir, and she asked directions."

"*Ubuphelelwe ulayini*," he replied. "You're a drifter."

But Sister Von Ohr was moved by my life story. She wanted me to go back to school. In return for paying my school fees, she asked me to varnish and paint the school windows and cupboards after school hours. In the meantime, she said, she would try to organise me a more permanent weekend job.

I had passed Grade 9 back in 1991, and failed Grade 10 the previous year after wasting my time on girls and politics. Other local teenagers had also run from the political violence, and gone back a grade instead of staying home. From here they were going to go on as the school expanded each year until they graduated.

By offering me a chance to go back to class, Sister Von Ohr had just given me a second chance in life. But I didn't see it this way initially. I simply went to class because there was nothing else to do. I had quit making guns, and there was nothing else to keep me busy. I was seated on my own, at the desk at the back of the class the morning I returned to school. The teacher stood in front of the classroom, surveying every student in the room. Then his eyes settled on me.

"*Kubuye isigebengu manje,*" he announced to the class. The criminal is back at school.

This was the teacher who had flogged me a couple of years earlier when the parents' meeting found me guilty of bringing a sword to school. It was he who had called me a drifter, a couple of days earlier when I arrived with Sister Von Ohr. He knew I had been making guns.

I wished I could tell him I had quit making guns. I wished he would support me, instead of putting me down. But I sat stony-faced as the class turned to look at me and snigger. I wanted to hide. Yet I had no choice but to sit there and take it.

It was May by now, so I was already behind with my schoolwork. I began by trying to catch up, and ended up obsessed with my books. I did more than just read and write notes to catch up. Armed with a dictionary, I never read any word I didn't understand without stopping to look it up and write down its meaning. As I went through the school notes, I created my own questions. I formulated my own tests and exams. Every night I sat on my bed by candlelight, absorbing information.

But even as I concentrated on my books and tried to turn my fortune around, I felt a void inside me. I had left all my ANC friends, who had made me feel like I belonged. Now I had no friends. I was lonely.

The people I lived with looked right past me as if they didn't see me at all. They all knew Khulu had disowned me. Hardly anyone spoke to me. I was the outcast. We were like strangers under one roof. I only entered the kitchen where everyone gathered around the stove to get a plate of food. The lounge was no place for me to sit and relax; I only passed through it to get to my bedroom. I was part of the family, and yet totally alone.

But I did nothing to reach out to the people I lived with. I didn't care. I was young and rebellious. In my bedroom, I often drifted into my imaginary world when I was tired of studying. I started dreaming of the future, of getting out of this house, this village. I wanted to be free. But reality dictated that I stay in this situation for a few more years, until I graduated from school.

To lessen my loneliness, I domesticated eight pigeons and dedicated my free time to them. I fed them on corn and water, and treated them like my children. During study breaks, I would sit on the veranda watching them walk around in the huge wire net sanctuary I had built them. I enjoyed hearing them coo. I would let them out in my bedroom while I cleaned their cage.

My pigeons brought me such inner calm. Each time I looked at them and stroked their feathers, it put a smile on my face. They became my best friends, my escape from the painful reality of life. Sometimes I let them fly away. I would watch them soar into the air, knowing they would return after stretching their wings.

One day I was wearing rollerskates when I decided to replenish my birds' water. As I was busy with the water container, one of the pigeons flew off. I turned to watch it soar into the air, and then noticed two eagles starting to chase it. In a panic, I started running across the field to protect it, but my rollerskates slowed me down.

The eagles caught my pigeon and started to feed on it at the edge of the field. I shooed them away, and was gutted to find my pigeon dying. I started crying, and realised just how close I had become to my feathered friends. But tending pigeons alone could not provide solutions to my youthful anxieties.

I was still grappling with who I was. I felt good about doing well at school. But I still felt hollow inside. Anger boiled inside me. I hated my father, and often wondered what life would have been like if Mom had been alive. To try to block such thoughts, I spent a lot of time listening to music. Lots of it.

The men of the extended family had always returned from the mines with the latest pop, country, reggae and popular South African music. I already knew every song by Bob Marley and Peter Tosh.

Meanwhile, Sister Von Ohr made regular school visits. She and I spent a lot of time chatting while I varnished cupboards and painted window frames after school. She always encouraged me to speak as much English as I could. It would be to my advantage in future, she told me.

That was exactly what the McNamaras kept telling me when I visited Zinhle. They also heightened my interest in learning. I now frequently read books. And music became more than just entertainment. I also used it to learn new English words and phrases.

At the end of the school year, the whole school gathered for the results, and the top ten students were announced in front of the entire school. Ten, nine, eight ... I watched my fellow Grade 9 students proudly walk to the front to rapturous applause. Second place was announced and still my name wasn't called. Yet I had worked so hard. I had expected to come in the top five.

It was time for first place, and at last I heard my name called. There was total silence. No one could believe it, including me. I had never imagined I could be good enough to displace the students who were respected by the entire community as the best at the school. The teacher who handed over my report was the same one who had called me a returning criminal.

"Well done," he said. I shook his hand.

In that moment my life changed. People who had always looked past me now took the time to stop and talk to me. The word was out: everyone in the village knew I had topped the class. Some simply couldn't believe it, and kept asking me again and again if it was true. I remained a hermit, but parents were now happy to let their kids talk to me. When I passed by, I stood tall. For the first time in my life, I started to think that I could win this fight; I could go on to lead a better life.

This drastic change highlighted a new challenge. It was time to adopt the good tools and jettison the bad. I started to discard my political loyalties. I no longer cared if my former ANC mates had a supply of guns. I no longer saw the IFP as my enemy. I just wanted to get on with my new life. Given the panoply of rewards, this process was easy enough to embrace. The new me wasn't difficult to accept.

The change in my life also rekindled my relationship with the

McNamaras, which had almost broken down. They were proud that I had changed. Every time I went to the shop to buy a couple of items, Eugenia always put in something extra for me. She developed a habit of throwing me a gift over the counter, just to see me jump and reach out to catch it. By now I was back to visiting the McNamaras and my sister regularly. But I was still uncomfortable treating them as parents. I still irked them by calling them sir and ma'am.

Nineteen

Auntie Zinto had recently retired from her job in Durban. A week after school broke up, she asked me to accompany her to meet a priest at the Catholic mission. I sat on the veranda outside the priest's office until they finished their meeting.

As they came out and we prepared to leave, Father Madela asked if I wanted to earn some money over the holidays. Construction of the new high school had just begun, he told me. He said he would speak to the construction manager, and that I should come back the next day.

The next day I met the construction foreman, an eccentric man missing many front teeth.

"*Ubuye ngoMvulo*," he said. "Come to work on Monday."

When I arrived there were already many local men looking for work at the site. As I walked past them to fetch a spade and shovel and join those preparing to start digging, they looked incredulous. "Why are they employing this boy instead of us?" said one impatiently. "This is a job for men."

It made me feel like a real man. Here I was, still in my teens, doing manual labour. But as the day wore on, I felt pain gathering in my shoulders and arms from the constant digging. I hated what I was doing. Surely there were better things to do in life than this, I kept thinking. But I hadn't had new clothes for a while. I also needed new candles to get me through another year of studies.

I didn't know how much I was going to earn for the month's work, yet there were so many other things I wanted to do. The following week, the work got even more intense. The foundations were dug, and it was time to fill the trenches with cement. There were endless trips pushing a heavy wheelbarrow filled with wet cement. It needed balancing as I negotiated the planks laid across the trenches. The men who filled the wheelbarrows didn't let up when it was my turn. They treated me as an equal. I had to transport the same amount of cement as everyone else.

I hated every minute of the work. I started to think that an education would help me stay clear of such backbreaking labour.

At one point the foreman came over to me. "*Uyangizonda yini mfana wami. Yini ungibuke kabi?* Do you hate me, my boy? Why do you always look at me like that?"

"Sorry, sir; I don't hate you at all. It's just that this work makes me think about my miserable life." Not interested in my problems, he walked away.

After a fortnight, I queued with the men to receive our wage envelopes. When my turn came, the foreman asked me to sit in a chair. This was strange. Everyone else had simply walked in, received their envelopes and left.

"I understand this is hard for you, my boy," he said. "But you've done well these past two weeks. I'm proud of you."

"Thank you, sir. I'm sorry you thought I hated you. I really don't. Not at all."

"Don't worry, son. I just want to tell you that I see a good man in you. You don't have to do this work all your life, you know. You're helping to build your own school. But work hard on your books, and get to university. Do that, and you'll get yourself a very nice job."

"Thank you, sir." I got up to leave, deeply impressed by his words.

"Aren't you going to take your pay?" he laughed. "If you don't want it, I'm happy to spend it," he joked. He shook my hand as he gave me my pay. I got two hundred and fifty rand for my two weeks' work. The next day, I took a taxi to the nearest town and spent the bulk of my cash on secondhand clothes, bought a couple of English books to read, and saved the rest.

Until this moment I had never thought of going to university. Only a couple of people from Pevensey had managed that, and they had come from reasonably well-off families. Since meeting Sister Von Ohr, I had thought I would finish the final year of school and then look for work. I hadn't contemplated studying further than high school.

I spent another fortnight pushing wheelbarrows full of cement and bricks. My palms were grazed and burning from the wheelbarrow handles. In the evenings I went home exhausted. The aching in my body and the weariness made me vow to follow the foreman's advice: to work hard to extricate myself from my hardships; to do all I could to avoid landing up with such jobs after high school.

I had long since forgotten the prayers I had learnt as a kid in the Catholic church, except for the Lord's Prayer. Whenever I recited it, I looked up to the heavens with tears in my eyes. "Lead me, Lord, and I will follow, even though I don't know where. You alone, Lord, know my destiny." I had now come to believe that divine intervention had something better in store for me than a lifetime of suffering.

I watched as fit and able youngsters in Pevensey got sucked into a life of heavy drinking soon after leaving school. It was depressing to see some of the men I worked with on the construction site blowing their meagre earnings on alcohol. I hated the smell of the alcohol and the way they behaved when they were drunk. It was like looking at sewage. There had to be more to life. I spent my earnings after the second fortnight on more clothes and a stock of candles.

By January I had already exhausted my money, and didn't have any left to pay my school fees. Sister Von Ohr had left the village suddenly, without even saying goodbye. I hadn't even had a chance to show her my results. I was heartbroken. I was so keen to thank her for saving me from the streets. Apart from which, I also loved talking to her.

When the other kids went to pay their school fees, I went straight to Father Madela, who by now was manager of the school. When I told him I didn't have a hundred and forty rand to pay my year's school fees, he never asked why I hadn't I saved my money from the job he had organised for me.

"Go to class," was all he said. "I'll sort it out."

That year, a nun took over as principal of the school. She was a disciplinarian, and wanted nothing but conformity to the rules of the school and the church. Most students feared her and her new rules. Like many schools in townships and rural areas, our school had a serious problem with teenage pregnancy. Without warning, girls would drop out to become young mothers.

The nun introduced a rule that made both guys and girls shudder at the consequences of teenage pregnancy. If a girl got pregnant, she could never return to school, even if her parents looked after the baby. She was banished from school forever. If the baby's father was at the school, he too would be barred forever.

Most boys were becoming sexually active. While in the past they had got away with impregnating girls, the nun was unstinting in punishing both parties. The year the rule was introduced, I saw several couples kicked out of school. Each time, it brought home the reality that my plan to finish school could go up in smoke if I became reckless and focused too much on girls. I would be playing Russian roulette. I was determined to finish school.

In a very short time the nun and Father Madela turned this once poorly managed public school into one of the most sought-after schools in the area. It also became a safe destination for youngsters running away from the villages, which were now torn apart by political violence. I became reunited with some of the ex-schoolmates I had marched with over two years earlier.

I was the only one from the village who joined a football team made up exclusively of boys from outside the village. The team members were mostly my former ANC mates. Although I continued to study hard, it was not with the same intensity as the previous year. At home I was still an outcast, and spent most of my time in my bedroom. But here, at least, I now had friends I could hang out with and play football.

At the same time, my dire financial situation eased. Father Madela gave me a job as a gardener at the Catholic mission during school holidays for seventy rand a week, more than some farm labourers were paid. I was convinced I was being overpaid. I suspected Father Madela did so because he wanted me to concentrate on my studies, and not worry too much about other challenges.

My Guidance and Biology teacher, Mr Khathi, liked to encourage the class to work harder by announcing the names of those who had done well in tests. Suddenly all the students longed for their names to be announced after a Biology test. I always did well in Biology, but with more students coveting good marks, I worked even harder. When my classmates got ninety per cent, I scored a hundred. This habit cascaded to other subjects.

The ease with which Mr Khathi got us to work harder endeared him to most students. For me, it changed the way I looked at teachers. Before I was rescued by Sister Von Ohr, I had always seen them as enemies. I was always rebellious and got caned a lot. But instead of being shamed and learning from this, I had always viewed caning as an honour.

In Mr Khathi I found my first role model. In the community in which I was growing up, there were hardly any. I had never admired the men around me. Most had no education and many drank heavily. I didn't want to be like them. I didn't know what I wanted to be like. In Mr Khathi I began to see who I could become in the future: a modest man with a stable family; a person who always wore a smile and didn't need to rely on force to exert his authority. He earned our respect.

During one of our Guidance classes he wanted to know what we planned to do when we finished school. If he had asked me the previous year, I would have told him I didn't know. But now I had started to think about going to university. I didn't know where the money was to come from, but it didn't feel bad to dream about it. I told him I wanted to be a politician or a journalist.

"A politician?" I knew he was thinking of the stories he had heard about my involvement in the ANC and my gun making. He needn't have worried. I had changed. The kind of politics I meant was working within the corridors of power.

Two of us had mentioned a desire to be journalists. The other was a boy named Sihle. We had attended some classes together, but never paid attention to one another. He had a group of friends he hung around with, and was popular with the girls, unlike me. Mr Khathi promised to bring a video to give us an idea of what journalism entailed. He said no more about politics.

A couple of days later, Mr Khathi, Sihle and I sat after school watching an hour-long documentary on journalism, while our teacher waited patiently. By the time he removed the tape from the video machine, we were both hooked. From that day on, Sihle and I started having regular conversations, although we didn't immediately become close friends.

At the end of the year when the top ten students were announced, I came second. I was dejected. What had gone wrong? I put the blame on all the time spent playing football and hanging out with the boys who had come to study in the village.

The following January, I told my football team to find a new goalkeeper. I was quitting. They were disappointed, and reminded me that we'd won the previous season and made enough money to throw a big party. But no matter how hard they tried to convince me to reconsider, I was unmoved. My mind was made up. I wanted nothing else but to be top of the class again. Other teams tried to recruit me, but I had retired from football.

Twenty

One afternoon in early 1995, as the Grade 11 students assembled in the school's brand new library, a lady walked in and introduced herself as Cheryl Wood. She asked each of us to introduce ourselves and tell her a bit about our background. Most of my classmates, having barely had a full conversation in English before, were extremely awkward. Mrs Wood nodded constantly and encouraged them every time they stumbled over their words.

When my turn came, I stood up and spoke confidently. After class, she called me over to ask where I had learnt my English. I explained about the McNamaras' English rule, my conversations with Sister Von Ohr and the books I read.

Mrs Wood became our new English teacher, and apart from being in charge of the library, she was also my class teacher. She nominated me and another student to help her run the library.

We got several new white teachers that year. Mr Wood, my class teacher's husband, became the Geography teacher. He was full of jokes and spoke a bit of Zulu. We all liked him. He used to bring packets of sweets to class to reward those who got answers right. Sometimes he simply threw the sweets unexpectedly, one at a time. One day he threw something into the air, and we leaped to catch it, assuming it was a sweet. I was the lucky one to land the catch, but this time it was just a piece of chalk. Instinctively I pretended to hurl it back and hit him with it, and he ducked playfully behind his desk to roars of laughter.

But when Mr Wood was angry, his cheeks turned red. Our class always stayed late to catch up the work we had missed before we had a Geography teacher. Once, as the rest of the school was leaving, a boy from a lower class came to mock us by making goat noises at one of our windows. When Mr Wood rushed out to challenge him, he ran off.

The next day, Mr Wood brought the boy into our classroom to teach him a lesson. Not taking his offence seriously, the boy kept grinning. Mr Wood was enraged. "You cry like an *imbuzi* (goat)," he shouted, "and when I run after you, you run like an *imbuzi*! *Hamba phumula mthunzini*," he ordered as punishment. "Go rest under a tree." It was midwinter and bitterly cold. Being banished to sit outside in the shade of a tree was punishment indeed.

In History I always sat in the front, and took time to chat to our beautiful young teacher, Mrs Muir. Many of us had a crush on her.

Our new Biology teacher, Mrs Grantham, was a strict no-nonsense type. In one of her first lessons, as she explained the intricacies of the liver's functions, a boy from the back of the class called out "*Unamanga!*". You lie.

"I never *namanga*!" she glared dangerously at the class. From then on, students stopped using Zulu for dissent in class, realising it could land them in trouble. Although we still took Zulu as a first language subject, the arrival of the white teachers had changed our medium of education to English.

While on duty at the library, I had plenty of time to talk to Mrs Wood. She put me in a reading programme, which she promised would improve my English rapidly. She started me on level 2 English novels, and took me a step up each time she felt I was ready. After level 5, she introduced me to the famous Western author Louis L'Amour.

It was a good choice. I was instantly hooked on L'Amour. I fell in love with Westerns in general, and there were plenty on the library shelves. Having retreated back into myself after quitting football, Mrs Wood helped me to see the characters in the books as friends. Her Western genre allowed me to travel to the times of cowboys and Red Indians, and I lived through the American gold rush and the formation of the United States.

But when I got caught up in the True Romance books, she discouraged me. I loved the happy endings when the couples kissed and made love after barely noticing each other throughout the book. "Those won't improve your English," she warned, realising that I was being drawn to matters of love. "They'll just teach you a superficial interest in girls. You're not ready for that."

But I'm eighteen, I thought indignantly. Yet her advice prevailed.

One day Mrs Wood asked me to stay behind after school. I was puzzled. I kept speculating about what I might have done to get into trouble. As I walked into her classroom she had her back to me, looking at the trees outside. Then she turned to look at me.

"I've been meaning to talk to you for some time," she said. It was difficult to read her face, to determine if I was in trouble.

"You're a bright young man. But I realise something is troubling you. You don't have friends. I also find it strange that you always sit on your own at the back of the class when your schoolwork is always good."

She looked right into my eyes, a sort of signal that she expected an honest reply.

"It's nothing. I just want to concentrate on my books. And I like the back of the class."

"I've taught long enough to know when there's something troubling a student. There's a lot of anger inside you." I tried to deny it, but she held my gaze evenly. "I know you're angry. And if there is anyone you can trust and confide in, I am that person."

The anger I nursed about the events of my early childhood was still churning inside me. I had managed to suppress it because my life was improving. By now there was reason to be hopeful about a better life. I had a gardening job every holiday through Father Madela, and I could buy secondhand clothes and other necessities fairly regularly. I had even managed to purchase a brand new camera, and the pictures I took at school and in the community gave me a steady stream of income. Sometimes Mr Wood took the negatives and paid for them to be developed so I could make a hundred per cent profit. Mrs Wood had started bringing me lunch at school, because she felt my diet wasn't healthy enough.

"I'm aware of what happened to your mother," she said, leaning against the desk. "Does it still make you angry?"

"No!" I insisted. I told her I had long since accepted that I had no parents.

"Please tell me, then. Why is there such anger in your eyes?"

I had never before realised that the undercurrent of hate inside me was visible in my eyes for all to see. I hated my father, but I had suppressed it all my life. No one but my sister and I ever talked about it. I wasn't comfortable discussing this with the McNamaras or anyone other than Zinhle.

Now I realised there was no avoiding the truth. I admitted to Mrs Wood how every time things got tough, I thought about how life would have been if Mom was around. I *was* angry. But my studies had helped me deal with my anger by pushing it to the back of my mind. My thoughts of revenge against my father were less frequent now. But when I did think of revenge, I still fantasised about the most brutal way to make him pay for what he had done. These dark thoughts had receded as more strangers came forward to help me. But they were still there.

Mrs Wood listened attentively. Finally she spoke.

"I know how hard this is for you," she said. "But you have to accept that your mother isn't coming back. That you will never see her again."

As her words sank in, I started to shake. I had never once thought this way. I still reminisced about being with Mom. I still ventured into my imaginary world, my Utopia where I lived in plenty, where things were less complicated than in real life. Mrs Wood's words were like a knife through my flesh.

She went on to give me a long lecture about forgiveness. "You're only hurting yourself by being angry. You're poisoning yourself. You have to try to put a stop to your anger." She told me that revenge against my father would not help me. It would simply complicate my life even more. "Once you've learnt to accept that your mother isn't coming back, you need to go on and forgive your father. This way you free yourself from the emotional burden. You cannot fully progress in life with so much anger boiling inside."

I kept shaking my head as she spoke. I couldn't answer because of the lump blocking my throat as I relived my pain. Vivid memories of my pain and Zinhle's pain came flooding back with such clarity. I was thinking so many things all at the same time. Zinhle having to put her hands on a red-hot stove; being sprayed with insect killer and burnt. All so long ago, and yet it suddenly felt like yesterday. I was shaking my head to repel what Mrs Wood was saying. I couldn't accept that I would never see my mom again. I couldn't forgive my father.

"Please think about it," she said. "And at least try. For your own sake. Try to forgive."

About two weeks later, Mrs Wood brought a newspaper cutting to class. She asked the students to use their imagination to write a full page about what we saw in the picture. It was a photograph of a tombstone shot at close range, but with every other gravestone still visible in the background. I wrote a full page about my father's violent death and about his funeral. And that no one cared to clean his grave because he had been a bad person.

The next day Mrs Wood asked me to remain after school. We sat at a table and shared a meal she had cooked. "Do you know how good you are?" she asked repeatedly. "You can lose it all if you constantly occupy your mind with thoughts of revenge." I just shrugged. She went on to tell me that failing to let my anger go was leaving crevasses in my soul. "These cracks will continue to widen as your anger multiplies. Slowly, they will shred your self-esteem, leaving you with nothing but a sense of inferiority and self-hate."

"I already hate myself," I told her.

"No, you don't have to do that. Don't blame yourself. What happened to your mom wasn't your fault. You didn't do it. You were just a little boy. You need not suffer from this. You need to look to the future. You are good, and capable of making a very good future for yourself."

"It's not that easy, Mrs Wood."

"Yes, I know. But you're going to work hard for it. I know you will."

Mrs Wood took it upon herself to counsel and guide me through my pain and hate. Slowly, as time went on, she taught me about the power of forgiveness. She was patient with me. She assured me I was going to be better off if I let go. Sometimes she would make use of a brief moment in the library. Or during lunchtime when she shared her meals with me. Or when we happened to bump into each other on the veranda at school.

One day Mrs Wood said she wouldn't be at school the next day, and she left me a videotape to play for the class. I did as I was told. The video was by Leo Buscaglia, an Italian-American philosopher and motivational speaker. The other students were bored watching this strange man preaching about lessons in life. One boy got up, took out the videotape and popped in a movie starring Jean Claude van Damme.

The next day, Mrs Wood was angry and punished the culprit. Then she asked me to remain behind to watch the tape. It carried an important message for me, she said. It was long and drawn out, but I also laughed a lot at the jokes Buscaglia cracked during his lecture. He taught me a great deal about love, forgiveness and other lessons in life.

As I sat alone and reflected at night, Mrs Wood's words started to ring in my ears. I began to trust her. Slowly, through my private tears in the darkness of those nights, I started to accept that Mom was never coming back.

One afternoon Mrs Wood and I met after school at my request. Her kindness and words of forgiveness had grown in me, and slowly I had learnt to start letting go. My sister hadn't forgiven my father; nor had my extended family. But now I realised that each of us had to deal with our anger in our own way. Each of us had to shape our own destiny. After months of soul searching, I was finally trying to forgive my father.

Mrs Wood was in her usual spot, staring out of the window. I took my time before telling her what our meeting was about. After a few minutes of small talk I put her out of her misery. "I'm willing to work on forgiving my father," I announced. I could see the smile on her face as she realised that her words and hard work were beginning to pay off. But more than anything, I realised, she was happy that I was eventually going to be free of hate.

"It's going to take time, Mrs Wood. But I'll work at it. There's just one condition, though."

She wanted to know what my condition was. I told her I would need plently of time before I'd be willing to meet my father. I had feared that she would suggest that we immediately try tracing him.

"That's understandable," she reassured me. "But remember that you want to be a journalist. It won't take your father long to find you once he hears you on radio."

I hadn't thought of that. Although I was now convinced that I was born for a career in radio, it hadn't occurred to me that my dream might one day become reality.

"What are you going to do, then, to make sure you meet him when you're ready, and on your own terms?"

"I don't know," I admitted.

"Well, we'll have to think of something."

A few days later I had a solution. I could change my identity. Then I could work on radio and continue my life without my father realising who I was. Mrs Wood thought it was a good idea. But I needed to work out who I was going to become. At night, I started looking through books to choose a name I could use to disguise myself. It was fun.

It felt good to think I could outwit my father. Within a few years, he would listen to the radio and not know he was listening to his own son. This way he couldn't bother me by seeking a meeting. Or call me to try to talk things over. Although I was working on forgiving him, I wasn't prepared to meet him. I didn't want to. I wanted to be left alone to move on with my life. I still kept my homemade gun stashed safely at home. I didn't know how I was going to feel about meeting him.

The chance of me even realising my dream of working on radio was extremely remote. But I wasn't taking any chances. I wanted to be free of my father until such time as I was ready to look him in the eye and tell him I forgave him. But I doubted there was going to be such a day. Forgiving him would take a long time. It wouldn't be easy to erase years of hatred and hurt, years in which my mind was dominated by nothing but revenge. For now, I was happy to dig a hole and bury my pain.

Cheryl Wood taught me that I could trust people. I didn't always have to push them away if they showed signs of love. By now I had also grown a lot closer to the McNamaras. I had convinced myself it wasn't such a bad idea to have a family. I now addressed their daughter Laurelle as my sister. It felt good to have people to call Mom and Dad. In a way, I regretted that it had taken me so long to warm to my new parents.

But McNamara didn't sound right as a surname. I wasn't European. Days passed without finding a new identity. I was growing frustrated. What had started out as fun was turning into a monumental challenge. Louis L'Amour's Westerns didn't trigger any names. I found nothing in the True Romance books I sneaked from the library. And no name or surname I could think of was suitable.

One afternoon as I was listening to Peter Tosh's *No Nuclear War* album, I began reading about his history. I discovered that his real name was Winston Hubert McIntosh. Right then I knew that I wanted McIntosh as my name.

"Perfect," said Mrs Wood. "It will never occur to your father that it's you. But what surname are you going to use?"

"I haven't found one."

"What surname would your father expect you to use?"

"The one I'm using. My mom's surname."

We then had a long conversation about the possibility of using my father's surname. Mrs Wood felt it was perfect because my father would never expect me to use it. But I doubted that my mom's family would accept it. They hated my father, and wanted their revenge. Besides, I didn't want to use it. But I finally yielded when I could find no other suitable surname, knowing that it would not go down well with my mom's family. I was also unsure if Zinhle would accept it. She wasn't willing to forgive our father.

Mrs Wood wasted no time familiarising the school with my new identity. The next day she told my class that a student had an announcement to make.

"Go on," she said, "tell them what we all have to call you now."

I got up, looked at everyone and told them that my name was McIntosh Nzimande.

"Why did you change it?" asked a boy from the back.

I was still trying to think of something to say when Mrs Wood said, "It's a long story. McIntosh doesn't need to explain."

From then on, my new identity caught on quickly at school. Soon it was as if I'd never had another name.

Twenty-one

It was a Friday, a week before school closed for the midyear holidays in 1995. When Father Madela called me into his office, I assumed he wanted to discuss my gardening job at the Catholic mission. Instead, he told me he had paid for a winter course at Hillcrest for me and two girls. "You leave next Friday," he told me.

I was ecstatic. I had hardly been beyond Underberg. In my imagination, Hillcrest was a faraway place. I kept trying to create a mental picture of what it would look like: traffic lights, lots of cars, skyscrapers, rows of shops ...

The following Friday we set off for Hillcrest in the back of a van. As we passed through Pietermaritzburg the driver stopped to buy fast food, and we spent much of the rest of the journey trying to figure out what KFC stood for. After two hours, we stopped at a beautiful place surrounded by trees and lots of flowers.

Koinonia was to be our home for the next two weeks. We walked into the hall to find many other young people. "Oh my God, none of them speak Zulu!" whispered one of the girls. Our fellow students were English speaking.

We had grown up in an isolated society. Only my teachers, my parents and handful of others were from outside the village culture. Koinonia was exciting; this was the first time I had mixed with people who saw life from a perspective very different from my own.

When the instructor showed a picture of women carrying

buckets of water on their heads, one student shouted, "That's so rural!" He was unaware that the three of us were from a rural area where this was perfectly normal.

It was the first time I had slept in a comfortable bed in a room with electricity. Here I also learnt to play cricket and rugby. The motivational speakers taught us about leading a successful life. Most days we were bunched together for English classes and pronunciation lessons. These were followed by basketball, cricket and rugby, and much fooling around in the vast yards of Koinonia. I took it all in with great excitement.

A few weeks later, I was back on the busy motorway, this time with Father Madela. He didn't tell me where we were going. Only when we reached our destination did I discover that it was the University of Natal in Pietermaritzburg.

I was settled in the upstairs part of the university's sports centre. Moments later, I watched students enter wearing funny-looking black gowns and square hats. A man went up to the podium to speak. He looked and sounded very familiar, but I coudn't work out who he was. Later I figured out that he was the Nobel Laureate Archbishop Desmond Tutu. I was elated. I had only seen him on television; and there he had been right in front of me.

Finally, the students were called to the front, one by one, to receive their graduation certificates. Later I saw Father Madela walk up to the front in a black gown. He hadn't told me he would be graduating.

That night I ate good food and slept in a hotel room. It made me feel very important.

Thanks to Father Madela, I began to see that there was more to life than the hills and mountains that made Underberg and Pevensey so beautiful. There was a more exciting life beyond those mountains. And if I wanted to get out of my current situation badly enough, it was up to me to take the steps. Seeing so many things I had barely dreamt of made me think a lot harder about going to university, about a better life. I wanted to get out of Underberg, but now I wasn't merely occupied by the desire to escape. I was starting to figure out how.

The answers were there for me to see. Only through an education was I going to get out. Only hard work provided the possibility of changing my fortune. The good food I had always craved, the big house, the car, these were not going to come easily. But now I had an idea of what it would take to achieve these things. It would be a long, hard road, a daunting challenge with lots of gritting and grinding of teeth. But ultimately, I now knew that I didn't want to settle for less. I was more motivated than ever to work on my studies.

One Sunday later that year, the entire community gathered in the local Catholic church. Not a space was left unoccupied anywhere, and many people had to stand. After the sermon, the school principal and Father Madela got up to tell the community the reason they had all been invited. They had decided to introduce an awards programme to encourage excellence among students.

One by one, students were called out to receive subject prizes. Sihle, the other hopeful journalist, received a Geography prize. I received a prize for English. Sihle was called a second time, and I received two more subject awards. Finally there was just one prize left, the Principal's Award for the student who had set the best example to others. We all waited.

After a drawn-out suspense, I heard the principal call my name. This time, a man from the community came over to me, lifted me up and carried me to the front like a champion to receive my award. The principal handed me a silver trophy. The sight of my own name engraved into the gleaming silver brought tears to my eyes. It was the proudest moment of my life.

After the ceremony, an old lady grabbed me by the arm.

"When did you change from an animal into such a wonderful person?" she asked with a big smile on her face.

It was true. In just a couple of years I had changed from being the naughtiest, most loathed boy in the community to being honoured as a fine example to other students. I now taught English and History to lower grades; I wrote and recited poetry for every important gathering at the school. I had changed from a rebel and a gun maker into a literature snob and a nerd. A fuzzy mental picture of Mom came, and quickly disappeared. I thought of Auntie Zinto, who had constantly lectured me to ignore the bad things in my life and focus on my studies. Now I was well on my way to shaking off my miseries. University was beckoning. I was on my way to freedom.

Inspecting my prizes later at home, I discovered that one was *Long Walk to Freedom* by Nelson Mandela, and another was a book by Desmond Tutu. It was Tutu's book I read first, having recently had the privilege of listening to his address.

During the awards ceremony, the family and the entire community learnt of my changed identity. In the initial excitement no one asked any questions; they were too proud of me. But when the excitement wore off, they wanted to know what had led me to take such a drastic step.

They listened to my explanation, but one of my aunts told me it was a big mistake. "Once you find your father, we expect you to change your surname back."

Others were unhappy that I had dropped my Christian name. "Your mother gave you that name," they reminded me. That very issue had nagged me ever since I took on my new identity. But I also loved the name McIntosh, and felt an instant connection with it. It was as if I had been born to the name.

I had serious problems with my surname, though. It was hard to connect with it. I even got annoyed when people used the praise names that go along with it when they called me. Although I was working on forgiving my father, the pain he had put me through was still etched in my mind. But in the end, my extended family accepted the surname.

"For now," they said. "But once you meet him, we will only accept you still using it if he apologises for what he did to this family." I was comfortable with that. I said it was a deal.

Twenty-two

It was my last day of Grade 11 before the long Christmas holiday, and the school was half empty. Exams were over and many students were just having fun in the school grounds. Boys played football while the girls cheered them on or played their own game of netball. A few students had probably sneaked behind the trees to smooch.

As I wandered towards the library to find a book to borrow, I saw Mr and Mrs Wood chatting outside a classroom. They called me over and led me into the classroom. They couldn't stop smiling.

"We shouldn't be telling you yet," Mr Wood said, "but we're so happy we can't wait."

Mrs Wood threw her arms open and I landed in her embrace. "Oh McIntosh, I'm so proud! You came top of the class!" The three of us embraced, Mr Wood looking behind to ensure that no one else heard.

I stepped out of the classroom elated. When I got home, I couldn't concentrate on anything. I kept thinking about the next day. I was even prouder because everyone expected the quiet girl I always competed with to take the number one spot.

The next day I stood at the back, just to make sure I didn't let the secret out by appearing too cocky. When Annamaria was called up for second place, everyone started shuffling around to see where I was. They knew what was coming. As I received my report from Mr Wood, he whispered: "Congratulations, my boy, I know you savoured the news the whole night." I smiled broadly.

A couple of months into my final year at school, I received a letter of invitation from Technikon Natal, now the Durban University of Technology, to write an entrance test. Two of us in the class received these pink letters. I was aiming to study journalism the following year, and my classmate wanted to do public relations.

We grew excited as the day drew closer. My fellow classmate kept talking about the big house and car he would buy after he got his diploma. The excitement I felt was quickly dampened whenever I thought about the tuition fees. I just couldn't figure out where the money might come from. When I considered accommodation and travel costs, the situation looked bleak. Hopeless.

I started writing letters to the addresses I found on the packaging of moisturising creams and toothpaste tubes. Like most people in my community, I used Vaseline on my skin, so I wrote to the address on the container and asked for a bursary to take me through university.

Dawn cream was more of a luxury. Sometimes it was among the items Mrs Wood bought me from her home town when she commuted to school. I collected dozens of different containers and built up a list of addresses. Not one of them was spared in my quest for a bursary.

Soon I had written to more than fify companies. Weeks passed without a single reply, not even to acknowledge my application, or to say no. I was growing more and more anxious. But I didn't stop writing letters. One of my targets was the shoe manufacturer where Khulu's sons worked.

When I came across a fan club address on the cover of a cassette of reggae icon Lucky Dube, I wrote to him too. After a couple of anxious weeks I received a reply from the shoe company. They didn't have the funds to offer me a bursary, but wished me the best of luck. I later discovered that it was a tiny business operating out of a double garage with just five employees.

A couple of days later I received another letter. I knew instantly from the green, yellow and red letterhead that Lucky Dube had taken the time to reply to me.

"I am most impressed by your beautiful command of English,"

the letter began. However, he didn't give bursaries directly to individuals, but donated to charities instead. Still, he encouraged me to enrol at technikon. As long as I had the money for a deposit, he said, I was likely to get a loan or a bursary from the institution itself.

I was disappointed that Lucky Dube didn't offer a bursary, but it impressed me that he had taken time from his international music career to write to a boy from a corner of South Africa he'd probably never heard of. I was encouraged by his advice to try to secure enough for a deposit and then let the rest take care of itself, and I heeded his call to study even harder. The number of people who believed in me was growing. Here was Lucky Dube, my radio and TV idol, telling me he believed I could make it!

After a two-hour journey in Father Madela's red Toyota Corolla, we arrived at the Mariannhill Catholic mission outside Durban. Not only had he offered my classmate and me a lift to Technikon Natal to write the entrance exam, he had also organised us rooms at the mission's guesthouse to spend the night.

I had a restless night. I thought constantly about how close I was to freeing myself from the dusty streets of Pevensey. My classmate and I woke to a delicious big breakfast from one of the nuns. We gobbled up cereal, eggs, toast, fruit and pastries. Meanwhile, the nun gave us advice about the upcoming tests and interviews: keep your answers short and to the point, she said. Then she gave us sandwiches and walked us to the car.

Father Madela wished us luck as he dropped us at Gate Four of the technikon. We found hundreds of other students queuing for places in Journalism and Public Relations. The waiting seemed to take forever: a few steps forward every few minutes, more waiting, then a few steps more. Finally I made it to the door of a huge room where the tests were taking place.

I sat down in the middle of a row for my English test. It lasted an hour. After more waiting outside, a loudspeaker announced that the results were now posted on the wall. Soon I was sandwiched among pushing students, peering to find out if I had made it for the next test. Next to each name was either Yes or No.

I felt a wave of panic as I saw No beside the name of my classmate. My heart beat faster and faster as I scanned each page on the wall. Finally I found my name. Everyone could see the relief on my face as I pushed my way out again. I had made it.

I found my classmate under a tree, looking understandably dejected. "It's all over for me," he said. I patted him on the shoulder, telling him things would be okay, though I couldn't see how. But I had to leave him. I had only a few minutes before writing my next test. This time there was no queue. Half the students hadn't made the next round.

My paper was already waiting as I sat down to my second test. A moment later a lecturer read the rules and told us we had an hour to answer just one question. The question was, how would you report on pornography? *Pornography?* I started thinking back to all the books I had read, the Westerns, True Romance, any book in which I might have come across such a word.

My head started spinning. I had no idea what the word meant. I was about to raise my hand and ask when I overhead a lecturer telling a student that she couldn't tell her what the word meant. "You should know," she told the poor girl.

I spent an hour writing the answer I thought the question was looking for. In the back of my mind I knew there was a slim chance that my guess was right. I had a bad feeling that my dream of enrolling at technikon was about to go up in smoke.

The wait for the results was excruciating. I sat under a tree, and kept painting the same optimistic scenario. Again and again I pictured myself walking up the stairs to find a Yes next to my name. Moments later, I saw myself sitting in a chair, back in the class, across from a desk. I pictured a lecturer taking me through the day's final hurdle: the interview that would give me the ticket to enrol the following year.

A loudspeaker snapped me out of my reverie. The results were up. "Good luck," said my classmate.

My legs felt heavy as I climbed the stairs to join the throng already pushing to find out if they had made it through. This time I hung back, and watched as each sullen face walked quietly down the stairs. I saw others jumping with joy. Some hugged each other before disappearing into the venue for their interview. As the students left one by one and created space, I moved steadily forward.

The moment of truth had arrived. There was the A4 sheet with the list of names, all that stood between me and going to the technikon; between a life of misery and my escape from Pevensey; between getting an interview or going home with my dreams shattered. The first paper didn't have my name. My eyes leapt to the next. Still I couldn't find it.

Each time I didn't find my name, my heart beat even faster. My thoughts kept jumping from a glimmer of hope to total hopelessness. I shifted a couple of steps to the right to check if the third and final page had news for me. It did. It was a No.

I couldn't feel my legs. I walked slowly down the stairs. My whole body was numb. I walked over to find a spot under a tree. Thoughts swirled through my brain, thoughts of living in that same house the following year. Of waking up to gaze at the same mountains, and walk the same dusty streets. I was devastated.

"How did it go?" asked Father Madela as we sped back along the motorway that evening. I think he already knew. Neither of us had said a word. He must have just been trying to break the ice. Finally I summoned the courage to tell him that we both hadn't made it.

"Don't you worry yourselves too much about it," he said. "Just take it as a lesson, and keep on applying. Other opportunities will come." A part of me badly wanted to believe what Father Madela was saying. But Technikon Natal was one of only two institutions that offered Journalism in the province at the time. The other still hadn't acknowledged my application.

Twenty-three

I was still living in the same world that had brought me so much pain. But pain was no longer my constant friend. My hate was starting to fade because of the counselling Mrs Wood offered. I celebrated more victories, savoured more successes. Angels lined up to nurture me and try to guide me to another world, a better world; a place filled with hope.

Mrs Wood still brought me lunch. The pay from Father Madela for working at the Catholic mission ensured that I could catch a taxi to the market town of Underberg to buy more clothes. And although I was reluctant to admit it, I was a golden boy at school.

Years of conquering seemingly insurmountable challenges made it hard for me to now accept that I had failed to make it to university. For days I found it hard to concentrate. I thought of nothing else. I kept replaying the day I had spent at the technikon. I daydreamed about a happy ending. In my virtual world, I rolled the clock forward to the following year, 1997. I saw myself walking on freshly trimmed lawns at the university. I walked into a class filled with smiling students in casual dress. I saw myself in the dead silence of a library filled with countless rows of cabinets, each containing endless pages of knowledge. As I ventured outside after a fruitful day, I imagined passing young couples smooching under trees in the yard.

I pictured myself walking through the streets of Durban clutching my books, dwarfed by tall buildings, absorbed by the chaos and energy amid hooting traffic, lost among the endless streams of people striding along the pavements. I marvelled at items in the shop windows. Then I would snap back to reality, back to 1996. In Pevensey, still lost. It was going to take a miracle to reach my dream.

But I knew that only an education could deliver me from the dusty streets of Pevensey, deliver me to a life of success. I longed to have the one thing no one could ever take from me: a university degree. I longed to be educated.

My setback at the technikon brought home to me the enormity of the challenge I faced. The harsh truth was that I'd probably never make it. Like so many others before me, I was probably going to end up on the street corner, watching the days go by with no prospect of a meaningful existence.

What I dreaded most was ending up working the following year. I dreaded having to do manual labour on a farm, a construction site or in a shop in Underberg. I remembered my stint digging trenches and pushing wheelbarrows of cement.

I wasn't cut out for such backbreaking work. I wanted something less physically demanding. I wanted to use my brain. My gardening job at the Catholic mission had taught me that I didn't want to work under the burning sun. I wanted an air-conditioned office and a revolving chair in front of a computer. I wanted to travel the length and breadth of South Africa; to see the world; to use my voice to share news from across the globe. I was certain I had been born for a career on radio. And now my dream had gone up in smoke. It was over.

I was still downcast several days later when Mr Khathi walked over. I had already told him about my setback. About the word "pornography" that had cost me my dream. He had just shrugged. "You're a good student," he'd said. "Something will come up for you." His words had been kind, but not much consolation.

"I've got news for you," he said now. He had phoned the technikon and convinced them to reserve a place for me in the Journalism class. I broke into a grin.

"There is a catch, though." My smile quickly faded. "You have to score five C symbols in your final exams."

"*Five Cs?*" I asked incredulously.

"You can do it."

Mr Khathi's news shifted my mood from total misery to simply feeling daunted. That night I sat on my creaky iron bed, thinking of the subjects that would possibly give me a chance.

Knowing that I was aiming at Journalism, I had chosen my subjects carefully. I had been sad to give up Physics because I was good at it. But I was fine about abandoning Mathematics, because I was only average at numbers. Now I had to decide where my chances lay. English? No problem. History? I should get a C, even a B if I worked harder. Geography? Yes definitely. Biblical Studies? I still didn't see the point of it, but it was easy enough. If I just concentrated, I could do it.

So four Cs were possible. But where would the other C come from? I thought about Zulu. I was so average at it; I had even asked to do it as a second-language subject, but I was turned down. I hated phonetics and idioms. Biology? This was a definite no.

I started to join study groups to improve my marks in Zulu. I targeted students who were good in areas where I struggled, and convinced them to teach me. They were only too happy to, because in return I taught them English, History and Geography. I spent every night creating my own exam questions. I worked at them and studied as if someone was holding a gun to my head. Having to get five C symbols felt like being given one shot at life. Just one shot. If I messed up, I knew that would be it.

I understood that if I didn't succeed at this, I would be trapped in this village forever. My life would be meaningless, aimless. I was tired of gazing at the Drakensberg, day in and day out, of watching the Polela River meander past my village. I was tired of the dry summer heat and the burning soil beneath my feet.

I hated the deafening thunder and lightning; I was weary of the heavy rains that cascaded down like nails. I was bored with the dullness of winter when the vegetation wilted. I wanted to live somewhere else. I cursed the frost in May, the snow in June, the July winds that thickened the air and filled my mouth with dust. I loathed the house I lived in and its people who treated me as if I didn't exist. I was tired of Pevensey and everything it represented. It seemed too much like hell.

I longed for freedom. I wanted to get out. I had to, even though I had no clue what this imaginary freedom had in store for me. I had almost forgotten that I still didn't know where the money might come from. There were still no replies from the toothpaste and lotion companies. No one had even promised enough for a deposit. Even so, I wanted to go to technikon.

The final-year exams went well. Now it was down to waiting for the results, to find out if my life would change forever or remain the same. Had I done enough? Or was I condemned to a life sentence in this godforsaken village? The wait went on.

Just days before Christmas of 1996, I visited Auntie Zinto. I told her of my plans. As always, she encouraged me, even though I saw despair in her eyes. "*uNkulunkulu akahlulwa lutho mfana wami.* The Lord never fails, my boy," she would constantly say, "*Kuzolunga.* All will be fine." Then she would ask, "*Kodwa imali izovelaphi?* Where will the money come from?"

"I don't know, Auntie. Something will come up." I had no answer, but I had come too far to fail. I had begun to put my trust in humanity, to believe in the selflessness of my angels, in the kindness of strangers.

I thought of the neighbours who had given us oversized secondhand clothing to make sure Zinhle and I had some semblance of dignity. And of the McNamaras who had given Zinhle shelter, and now looked after her as their own. I thought of their kindness towards me. And so I believed my dreams were possible to achieve.

All I needed from my aunt was to organise me a place to stay in Durban. I would take care of the rest. Or, more likely, the rest would take care of itself. Even if I had to work on weekends to earn money for transport. She said she would speak to her son, my cousin Musa. He had recently bought a house, and she was sure he would be happy to host me. I was excited.

I couldn't stop smiling as I took off my shoes and rolled up my trousers to cross the river on the way back home. I knew my cousin would welcome me with open arms. Now I just had to wait a few more days for my results.

Christmas passed, and the day of the results neared. The tiny village was all pent up with anticipation. Pevensey had never experienced anything like this. My class was the first to carry the pride of the small community. The pressure was telling. I started to shed my aloofness a little, to come out of my shell. I began joining other final-year students on street corners to chat about the future. To ease the pressure of expectation in this tiny community.

Young boys started gathering tyres and showing off with firecrackers in preparation for New Year's Eve. But I hardly noticed. I was too tense. The moment of truth was approaching. On the radio, on the street corners, everyone, even the heaviest drinkers, spoke of only one thing: the final-year results. The air quivered with it.

On the day of the results most of my fellow students made their way to the bus stop. I stayed home to avoid the pressure. I knew many people would look up my name in the newspaper. After all, I was the school's Dux student and a golden boy. I waited at the street corners with the few others who were too scared to make the trip to town, too terrified that they would be disappointed.

It was still morning when hordes of people returned from the market town of Underberg armed with newspapers. The mood was palpable. The announcement they brought back was a complete surprise. Our first ever final-year students had achieved a one hundred per cent pass rate. No one at all, not even the teachers, had imagined this possible.

Many of us had passed with distinction. But for me it was still not enough. Even with an A pass I was still nervous. It would be another couple of days before the teachers received our subject symbols; before I knew if I had achieved my five Cs. My long-cherished dream of escaping this village hung in the balance: my escape, the start of a new life in Durban, a proud new destiny. A brand new chapter as a technikon student.

Mom and Zinhle

Mom wearing what must have been a fashionable outfit at the time

As a child at an unknown place. I can't remember where this was

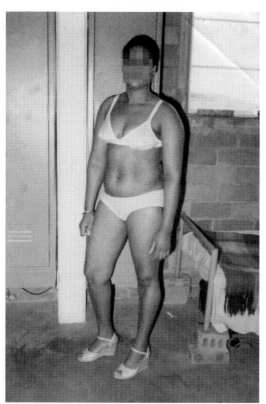

My mother sent this picture to my stepmother, to explain that all my father's money went to floozies

My sister Zinhle and me with mom in the background keeping an eye on us

My sister Zinhle with a Coca Cola, a source of so many memories when I was growing up in Pevensey

A letter that Mom wrote to my father. I will probably never read it

Another picture that rekindles memories of the time Zinhle and I spent with Mom

Mom, unknown woman and kids

On my father's bike

My reunion with Sister Margaret Von Ohr

Gogo as she looked a couple of years ago

After several more days, we got wind that the results had arrived. I made the ten-minute walk to school. Final-year students were coming and going. In the staff room I found Mr Wood carefully shuffling through the result papers. Each student waited anxiously to find out how well, or badly, they had passed. I waited my turn impatiently.

Mr Wood gave me his usual smile before handing over my results. Biology was a D. I had three Cs. And there were two Bs. I had been praying for five Cs. I was slightly confused, so fixated had I been on the need for five Cs.

I found Mr Khathi next door making photocopies. He beamed at me. "You've got your place at the technikon, now! You did even better than they asked."

Until he said it, it hadn't yet struck me that I had actually surpassed what was expected of me. But he gave me the reassurance I needed. I *was* going to technikon.

I was free! I was going to live in Durban! I was going to technikon, on my way to achieving what no one could ever take away from me. I was going to get an education.

But another voice in my head was warning me that it wasn't quite that clear cut. Not yet. I still hadn't worked out how I was going to raise the one thousand rand tuition deposit. Worse still, I didn't know where the other six thousand rand for the year was coming from. And I had no idea how I would pay the transport from Umlazi township to the technikon every day.

The excitement of living in a big city and going to university dissipated as soon as the enormity of the task ahead dawned on me. I could still fail. I could still end up trapped in this village, doing backbreaking labour. But the more I thought this, the more determined I was to make sure it didn't happen. It simply wasn't an option. I needed to find the cash, and fast.

Who could help with that amount of money? A thousand rand was an awful lot of cash. The Woods came to mind first. But they had done so much for me already. What about the McNamaras? They were very good to me. And they were my parents. But again I realised how much they had already done, especially for Zinhle.

My list wasn't long, and I quickly ruled out all the people I could think of. I had already knocked on their doors, and they had given selflessly. I didn't want to be a nuisance by asking them over and over.

I felt the same when I thought about Father Madela. He had done so much. He had found me a job and got me my first wages. He had taken me to so many places to extend my horizons and open my eyes to the world. Asking any more would be unfair. It was going to be selfish. But as my small list of possibilities shrank, I saw no other choice. I had to return to my same pool of angels for help.

Twenty-four

Father Madela had recently been transferred to the Mariannhill mission outside Durban. Plagued with mixed feelings, both excited and daunted, I took the taxi along the busy motorway. I felt as if a weight was finally lifting off my shoulders now that I was leaving my dusty village. But this was quickly replaced by the weight of not knowing what would happen next.

In my pocket, I was armed with a piece of paper from Mr Khathi, with the names of two ladies I was to seek out when I reached the technikon, Gugu Mji and Gugu Ngcobo. "They work in the counselling department, and they know about you," he explained. "They were the ones who told me the symbols you needed to enrol." Still, I had no way of knowing if Father Madela would sponsor me with the deposit money.

My first stop was Hillcrest, where my mom's two half-brothers worked in the little shoe factory. From here I could easily get to Mariannhill to meet Father Madela. I also needed one of my uncles to accompany me to Musa's house in Umlazi township. There were so many challenges to face. I still had to figure out my way around the big city. The thought of it terrified me.

That evening, my uncles and I discussed the daily transport money I would need. They got paid every Friday, but both were quick to point out that their weekly wages were scant. "But when we can, we'll give you some transport money." The words were music to my ears. It was far from a guarantee, but it was good enough under the circumstances.

The next day, I caught two taxis to reach Mariannhill. In each I prayed silently. "Lead me, Lord, and I will follow, even though I don't know where. You alone, Lord, know my destiny."

I hardly noticed as the taxi stopped to load and unload passengers. Father Madela had never once shut the door on me. But this was the biggest favour I had ever asked. Did he even have that much to just hand over to me?

My nerves grew tighter with each unanswered question. I felt overwhelmed with helplessness. I had come so far. The thought that I could still fail was too much to contemplate. I had no plan for anything else if my quest to go to technikon failed. I had nothing to fall back on. I couldn't think of any alternative I could live with.

I got off exactly where Father Madela had told me on the phone when I called him the previous day. I had told him I needed to speak to him, but I didn't have the nerve to tell him why.

Father Madela's house was the last one along the dirt road, about half a kilometre's walk. It was an old house surrounded by gum trees. The paint was peeling off the walls. The doorbell rang noisily. Then out came Father Madela with his usual smile. It had been months since I'd last seen him.

Nervously I shook his hand, and he led me up a few stairs to the lounge. I was still settling on the couch when the housekeeper brought me a glass of juice. My hand trembled as I took it and put it on the coffee table.

"*Unjani* McIntosh? How are you?" he asked, probably aware that I was nervous.

We talked at length about the year's results. He said how good he felt that my whole class had passed. It was an important achievement for him. It was on his watch that the school had expanded. He had earned the respect of the community for establishing the football and netball pitches, erecting the new brick building, and introducing the first-language English teachers who had helped mould the school into a formidable academic institution. We indulged in a lengthy reminiscence about our past together.

"So," he eventually asked, "what's brought you here today?"

I squirmed for a moment, trying to find a way to tell him the purpose of my visit. I told him about the required symbols to get into technikon. He was happy that I had achieved them. He looked at me curiously as I recounted my desire to study further. I could sense that he had an idea what I was after.

Only right at the end did I mention the deposit money.

"I came here to ask you to help me, Father." By this time I was fighting back tears. I was embarrassed to be asking him for another favour. "You're the only person I can ask."

I felt so emotional. I was also scared. Frightened that he was going to tell me he didn't have that kind of money.

And that is exactly what he told me. He made it clear that he was prepared to help in any way he could. But the kind of money I was asking for was out of his reach. I had suspected that Catholic priests didn't get paid an awful lot. I figured that they probably relied on tithing for their income. But Father Madela was the only person I could think of to ask.

As I sat there with my thoughts racing, Father Madela started to get up. I felt a tsunami of despair wash over me. This was the end. Our conversation was clearly over. He was signalling that there was nothing more to say. I got up and followed him outside. There he turned towards his car. For a moment I didn't know whether I was supposed to follow him or say goodbye and leave.

Instead he gestured for me to get into the car. Without a word, he drove towards the main building of the Marianhill mission. He led me up the stairs and knocked on a large wooden door. Then he entered and introduced me to an elderly bishop.

As if I wasn't there, Father Madela related to the bishop the story of how he knew me. He told the bishop about how well I had done at school. I was too stressed to understand why he was doing this. Finally, Father Madela told him I needed money to register at the technikon. He took pains to emphasise that if the mission didn't help me, no one would.

The bishop had hardly glanced at me since we were introduced. Now he nodded and stood up. He opened a drawer and fished out a pink cheque book. Clearly a man of few words, he signed the cheque and handed it to me. Before I could muster a word, he said,

"May God bless you and guide you in your studies."

I was still trying to thank him when he spoke again. "When you complete your studies," he looked at me solemnly, "I expect you to repay this money, so that others who need similar help can receive it."

"Thank you, Father!" I gushed. "I am more than prepared to work hard and pay back this money."

"That's what everyone says who comes through that door. But when they finish their studies, they forget us."

I couldn't find enough words to thank Father Madela as I said goodbye moments later. As the taxi sped back to my uncle's place; I couldn't stop touching my back pocket. I kept checking that my wallet with the thousand-rand cheque hadn't somehow vanished.

I hardly slept that night. I could already see myself in class, smiling ear to ear. Now no one could take it away from me. Not even my father. He might have taken my mother, but he could never take this from me.

I could see right into my future. In my imagination I was standing tall in a black gown to receive my diploma, just as I had seen at the graduation ceremony in Pietermaritzburg. I pictured myself clutching my certificate and stepping out into a world of endless possibility.

I pictured my first job on radio. I was in a revolving chair, trawling the Internet on my computer for the latest news updates, just as I had witnessed in the Guidance teacher's documentary of journalists at work. I pictured myself surrounded by countless ringing phones, typing on a keyboard to produce the latest news bulletins. I pictured myself in the studio presenting the hourly news bulletin ... I had my own apartment, I drove my own car ...

But all this still had to be achieved. For now I had to get some sleep.

The next day, Uncle Zozi, my mom's half-brother, had promised to help me through my first challenge in Durban: finding my way to my cousin Musa's place in the township, where I was going to stay while I studied. By now Zozi had grown up to be a man, and was no longer the bully Zinhle and I had feared as kids.

The two of us set off in the early morning, as Uncle Zozi had to be back in time for work. The city appeared like a sea of chaos. People walked fast, stopped for the traffic lights, then charged off again. Others didn't bother to wait and just ducked between the moving cars. Cars hooted madly. It was confusing. I felt like a total misfit. It was going to take a lot to adapt to the noise and pace of the city.

It was nervewracking. I tried to observe landmarks and memorise the route. We made our way to the M&R taxi rank. This was a landmark to memorise, I told myself. I assumed I would take the same route between the technikon and my accommodation.

But instead of going straight to where I would stay, we first went to Musa's place of work. The route I was trying to memorise was practically useless. I grew even more nervous. It didn't even occur to me that I could just ask around, and I would be okay.

I eventually ended up at Musa's house later in the day. He had prepared the spare room for me in his two-bedroomed house. The cupboard was empty and the threequarter bed nicely made. I could hardly concentrate as he and I sat reminiscing about the old days. My mind was fixated on the trip I was to make the next day. My twenty-minute ride to the technikon.

Twenty-five

Technikon was a huge step for someone from Pevensey, and anyone who managed it earned a lot of respect in the community. But it wasn't respect I was after, it was escape.

I waited just metres from Musa's house for barely a couple of minutes before a taxi came into view. I raised my index finger. I was almost paralysed from nerves, so scared was I of getting lost in the chaos of the city. I never thought to ask the taxi conductor to drop me at the technikon.

I had assumed that all taxis from Umlazi township ended up at the same taxi rank. From there I would ask directions to the technikon. But people were all disembarking at different points as the taxi made its way through the busy streets. Somewhere on Queen Street the driver parked on the side of the road and looked at me. I looked back at him.

"This is the last stop," he told me after an awkward silence.

"Could you drop me at the taxi rank, please?"

"This is it." Y was a new section of Umlazi township. Taxi owners hadn't yet found a spot in the M&R taxi rank. But as a fresher from a rural area, I had no way of knowing this.

The taxi driver noticed my confusion, and suggested I board one of the passing buses. "Ask directions!" he yelled as I jumped into a bus that didn't bother to come to a full stop, so I quite literally had to jump in as it moved. There were coins strewn beside the driver, who asked a fifty-cent fare. "Please move to the back," he asked.

I ignored him, clutched the handle overhead and yelled over the loud music to please drop me close to the technikon. "Okay. Get off at the market."

"Thanks. Please tell me when we're there. I'm new in the city."

Soon I was walking through the vast grounds of the technikon's Berea campus. I had to ask directions twice. This was nothing like the cosy atmosphere I had romanticised about. The tall buildings made me nervous. I wondered if I would ever learn my way around.

Eventually, I made it to the counselling department, where the receptionist gave me a form to fill in. I guess I took too long over it, because a lady soon called me impatiently.

"I can see you're finding the form difficult. What do you need?" Her name was Gugu Mji, one of the two Mr Khathi had told me to speak to. I was relieved.

I explained that she'd told my teacher I needed five Cs to get into Journalism. "I got them," I said confidently.

She looked puzzled. She had no idea who Mr Khathi was, and didn't recall telling anyone to get those symbols. My heart sank.

She asked to see my results, and looked them over. Then she looked back at me. "Where are you from?"

"Underberg, ma'am, in the southern Drakensberg."

"You've done well," she said. "Let me see what I can do. We're trying to increase our numbers of rural students."

She picked up the phone. "Hello, Mike. I have a student who's done very well ... They're learning subjects ... I think he'll do well in Journalism ..." A short pause.

"Mike, I really recommend you consider this student. He's from a rural area. He's done too well for us to turn him down ... At least look at his results. Please." Pause.

"I urge you to at least see him."

Things were clearly not too hopeful. "Is there really nothing you can do?" Another pause. Then she hung up.

She gave me the look of a caring mother. She could probably see my dejection. I was gutted.

By now Gugu Ngcobo had overheard and left what she was doing to come over. The two Gugus had a serious conversation. I couldn't follow what they were saying. I couldn't concentrate. I didn't know what to do next, where to go, what the immediate future held, what would become of me.

Then the two ladies turned to me. I tried to compose myself. "Relax," they said. "We're calling the Student Representative Council to try to help."

I sat there, frozen, waiting. My heart was thumping. Students came and went. Everyone seemed to be smiling. Things seemed to be going well for them. It appeared that I was the only one whose dreams had been dashed.

Eventually, the SRC president and a colleague arrived. They were young and confident, but a little too energetic, too loud. Their demeanor did nothing to lift my spirits. They took me on a technikon bus to the city campus, to find Mike Maxwell in the Journalism department. I kept quiet, and followed them upstairs into an office where we found a lady with a distinct Irish accent.

"Where's Mike?" they demanded. Their approach was a little too aggressive, and the lady was clearly taken aback. She politely asked what it was about. They told her my story. I stood by blankly, not knowing what to say. I wasn't sure if I should say something to calm the situation. It seemed to be getting out of hand.

She told us Mike was busy with student registration at S Block at Berea campus. As I followed the two SRC leaders out to return to the Berea campus, I saw her hastily grab the phone. I sensed trouble.

We arrived at the fourth floor of the looming S Block building, where a long queue of students was standing. As we strode towards the head of the queue, a tall, well-built man looked up, and I saw anger on his face. I hung back.

It was Mike Maxwell. He looked fearsome, his face almost completely covered in facial hair. He came towards us, pointing his finger in our direction. "You're disturbing me!" he blurted. "I'm extremely busy. And you had no right to go to the city campus and be rude to Janet. Please leave right now!"

Far from backing off, the student leaders pressed forward, and a confrontation erupted. In between the shouting Mike looked at me, seething with anger. It appeared we had now blown any remaining chance I might have had of registering at this technikon. Everyone in the queue was staring.

Eventually the shouting died down, and Mike asked for a copy of my results and my phone number. I handed them over with trembling hands.

"I'll put you on the waiting list in case a student doesn't show up," he told me. "I'm afraid that's all I can do."

I thanked him.

The student leaders and Mike shook hands, and we quickly departed. I suspected their wry smiles and handshakes were an attempt to lessen the tension, as the queuing students had been shuffling uncomfortably during the yelling. They seemed to relax as we left.

I went back to my cousin's house, not knowing whether to be hopeful or give up altogether. So I prayed.

I had nothing to do the next day. I watched Musa leave for work, and just sat there. I wasn't used to the Durban heat and humidity. It was unbearable. I stripped to my underwear to try to keep cool. I walked around the house. I walked back and forth, trying to contemplate what was to become of me. Hoping that Mike would call. He didn't.

The next day I took a walk through the township. I was astounded at the pace of life. It was totally different from my village in Underberg. Buses roared by. Taxis hooted to alert prospective passengers. There was so much life and so much noise.

"*Sanibona*," I greeted the strangers I bumped into. They didn't respond. I thought it strange and rather rude. But I quickly realised that people were too busy with their own lives to greet a young man. They probably found it strange that I greeted them. In Underberg you greeted, especially the elderly, as a sign of respect. But this was the city.

Days passed. Several times the phone rang, and I rushed to grab it with a beating heart. But each time it was for Musa. And once it was Musa to check if I was all right.

What was I going to do? My spirits sank. I couldn't sleep at night. He's never going to call, I thought. It gradually dawned on me that he had only agreed to put me on the waiting list to fob us off and stop us causing trouble. His handshake and smile were just a way to get rid of me.

The phone rang again the next day. I answered again, knowing it was for my cousin.

"Hello. Mike Maxwell here. I have a place for you."

"Oh God, Mr Maxwell! Thank you!"

His voice was cool. "Come in tomorrow. It's the last day of registration, so you need to be there."

I put the phone down and started crying and praying at the same time. I wasn't going back to Pevensey! It was the best news I'd ever had.

The queue to the finance office snaked across the manicured lawn around trees and buildings under a blazing sun. The students were all beautifully dressed. Some must have bought new clothes just to look the part. It seemed that making a fashion statement was probably a part of technikon life. I was embarrassed in my plaid shirt, faded jeans and hiking boots.

But the excitement of just being able to stand in this queue quickly dimmed my concerns about fashion. A part of me still couldn't believe that I was finally about to enrol at technikon, to start living my dream. I wondered if something else could still go wrong.

I kept reaching for my back pocket to check that my pink cheque was still there. I asked a couple of times just to make sure that the registration fee really was a thousand rand. I had barely any cash apart from this cheque. If they asked for any more money, I'd be in big trouble. The thought unsettled me.

It took several hours to reach the counter. The cashier took the cheque, gave me a form to fill in, and waved me to another queue going up the stairs. I was processed in moments. It was such a relief.

I was hungry now, and my stomach growled constantly to

remind me I hadn't eaten. After another hour I was finally at the front of the queue to register. I was impatient. I kept peeping through the door to see if the student ahead of me was finished yet. Finally the lady doing the registratons asked her colleague to tell me to be patient. Embarrassed, I stayed meekly outside the door until my turn came.

Twenty-six

From the first few lectures it was clear that there was a lot I didn't know. There was so much to learn. My first class was in Practice of Journalism, which entailed writing newspaper articles.

Marc Caldwell, our superintelligent lecturer, wore his shirt sleeves rolled up, over black Levis and brown trainers. He constantly modulated his voice, starting loud and then gradually lowering his voice until he was barely audible. "Not all of you will graduate from this class," he began ominously. "Three years ago we started with a group of forty, but only a dozen graduated."

Needless to say, this made me nervous. I started wondering what my chances were of being among the dozen or so who would make it. It didn't look good. I had a lot of adapting to do. This environment was so foreign.

Hanging out with fellow students on the benches under the trees or on the lawns presented its own challenges. I didn't speak their language. At first I was confused when they used the word "cool" to describe nice things.

While walking on Smith Street, we saw a group of people gathering around a fellow I didn't recognise. My classmate pushed his way in, and then came back beaming. "I got Zulu's autograph!" he said, waving his notebook. "Man, that's cool!" I didn't know what he was on about. It turned out to be the famous cricketer, Lance Klusener, whose nickname was Zulu because he spoke the language fluently.

I certainly wasn't looking for autographs. I was still learning my way around, and grateful that my classmate was taking me along as he looked for a cool T-shirt for himself.

When I got a chance to say something, there was eye rolling about the way I spoke. When I spoke English, they'd say "What kind of accent is that?" or "You sound like a nerd!" When I spoke Zulu, they'd say, "You're such a Zulu. You sound so tribal!" I felt such a misfit.

Sport dominated every conversation among guys. To survive, I started watching sports on weekends. Slowly I learnt the players' names. Football was easy to grasp. I had played goalie at high school. It took longer to understand the rules of rugby and cricket. But in no time I was hooked. And I became a fan of the Ferrari team. Michael Schumacher was my favourite Formula One driver, and I got quite involved in his rivalries with Jaque Villeneuve and later Mika Hakkinen.

It was exciting to finally have strong opinions when the lads discussed sport. There were always debates between fans of the McLaren Mercedes and Ferrari teams. We discussed each race at length, and predicting who would win the Formula One season drew passionate debates. It was exciting to be part of the club.

But sometimes I just didn't have the transport money to get to the technikon. The little money my uncles managed to give me wasn't enough. Sometimes I hogged books from the library for a couple of days while I stayed at home. I needed to make sure I was prepared for my tests and could complete my assignments.

In my first few weeks at the technikon, I went to the financial aid office to apply for a bursary or a loan to cover my tuition fees. After that I made regular trips to the office. I would brave the long queues only to find each time that my application had not been finalised. There was no satisfactory explanation as to why this was the case, and no clear answer when I asked about my chances of receiving funding.

It was another long, hot day on the streets of Durban. I had stopped bothering to wipe the sweat off my face, and was trying hard to ignore the growling in my stomach. I'd had neither breakfast nor lunch, and had no money to buy anything to eat. As usual, supper was going to be my only meal.

The pain in my feet was becoming unbearable. I had been up since before five a.m. to collect items to sell to anyone who cared to listen to my latest promotions. And I had been walking incessantly, climbing stairs and crossing roads, trying to earn the transport money to get me to the technikon next term.

Sometimes it was cheap food processors. Other days it was a set of knives, or something as ridiculous as a hand-held, battery-powered massager. Every few days the items changed. I had hardly got used to the payoff line when another product was introduced. Few people stopped to listen to my payoff line. "Would you like to take a look at our latest promotion, sir? Ma'am?"

Most people had already turned their backs by the time I'd finished the first sentence. Others glared wordlessly, letting me know I was a nuisance.

I had found the job through a newspaper advert earlier that month. We were required to dress smartly and start the day early with a briefing on how to sell the latest product. I was often enthusiastic at the start of the day. But by the end I was drained from so much walking carrying heavy bags. The company kept any commission I made until the end of the month.

Often dogs chased us from homes. Train passengers didn't give us a second glance. Shopping centre staff reminded us as we entered that we were trespassing on private property. I ignored them and did my best to sell my wares. But after I got manhandled and roughly evicted, I became more cautious.

Residential flats usually had signs saying No Hawkers. I often ignored them, and sometimes got lucky and made a sale. Mostly I guessed it was out of pity for this nicely dressed youngster. I doubt anyone ever used what I sold.

I knocked several times at the door of an old lady in Amanzimtoti, south of Durban, hoping that at least once she would be interested in my ever-changing stock of products. But she always gave the same response. "I don't buy anything at the door."

At the end of the month I went to the finance office to collect my commission. It was time to say my goodbyes. For some reason the staff had taken quite a liking to me. The boss said I would make a successful consultant one day. I shared a few polite embraces with colleagues, received exactly fourteen rand for the months' work, and then left.

In a few days, I would resume my studies at the technikon, having made hardly any transport money.

The atmosphere at my cousin's house began to sour. His younger brother Ferdi and his girlfriend had moved in and taken over my room, so I slept on the couch in the lounge. I didn't mind. But Ferdi's girlfriend disliked me.

She saw me as a nerd, and never understood why I spent so much time on my books. The house had no ceiling, so at night a light in one room penetrated to the other rooms. This became her first source of disagreement with me.

I often had to study and write assignments late into the night, using the ironing board as my desk. She complained that the light kept her awake, so I bought candles. It worked for a time.

But Ferdi had a car and worked at a petrol station just five minutes' walk from the city campus where I had most of my classes. So I started catching a lift with him. For the first time I didn't need to skip any classes. I even managed to save some money. I wasn't as close to him as to his older brother, but we got on okay and he seemed happy to give me a lift.

Then one night when we got home, I found a note on the kitchen wall from his girlfriend, declaring that I had to wash the dishes every day when I returned from class. So I did. But soon she stopped talking to me. Increasingly hostile notes appeared on the wall. Sometimes she said the pots weren't washed properly; other times that I'd burnt the food while warming it. So now I was instructed to eat my food cold, in case I damaged the pots.

Finally I wrote an angry note back, saying that the latest instruction was ridiculous. Soon our pen-and-paper arguments escalated into full-blown conflict. I heard her yelling to Ferdi about me. It seemed I had crossed a line.

A few days later, I arrived at the petrol station to catch my lift home, only to find that Ferdi had left without me. Fortunately, that day I had enough money on me to catch the bus. When I got home his girlfriend was smiling. She told me it was her doing, and that he was no longer allowed to give me a lift.

I just couldn't understand why he was allowing his girlfriend to come between us and make my life miserable. He had only recently met her. What had happened to the lifetime we'd spent together in Underberg? We were blood relatives, for goodness sake. Musa and Ferdi had been like brothers to me. Zinhle and I once spent an entire summer holiday at Auntie Zinto's, and he and I had been inseparable. Ferdi was five years older than me, but we were always very close. We would tend cattle together in the pastures, and spend the whole day playing together until it was time to drive the cattle home. After Musa moved to the city I would regularly cross the river to visit him.

Having worked so hard to escape the hostile home environment in Pevensey, here I was caught up in yet another ugly situation. I started to doubt if I could put up with this for the three years needed to complete my diploma. Musa now stayed at his girlfriend's home most of the time, rarely coming to the house. So I was isolated, with Ferdi avoiding me as much as possible.

Twenty-seven

My problems seemed to multiply with each passing day. Now that I was banished from catching a lift with my cousin, I was back to worrying about transport money again. It was a constant struggle to attend classes. The stress became unbearable. My motivation and confidence plummeted, and my studies were severely affected.

I spent a lot of time churning over my problems and trying to find solutions. But nothing seemed to work. I became severely stressed. I started getting tremendous headaches, and developed a swelling on my face. I found myself in the counselling department with a psychologist, trying to get help. But she couldn't provide a solution. I was past the point where anyone could help me.

Giving up was something I had vowed never to do. But I couldn't continue like this. I didn't see how I could possibly concentrate on my studies and pass at the end of the year while I was under so much stress.

I had failed only once in my academic history, during my first year at high school. It had devastated me. I didn't want to repeat the experience.

I understood that it if I failed this time it wouldn't be my fault. But it was no consolation. I couldn't just sit back and let it happen. I didn't have the strength to soldier through the pain of failure once again. I had to do something. I had to act, and fast, to prevent disaster. I started thinking about a way out, plotting shortcuts to a more forgiving life than this.

I thought of finding a job. But where would I start? I'd already had a taste of working from dawn till dusk only to walk away with just fourteen rand. Another useless job would only make the situation even more dire. I thought of going back to Underberg to work in a shop, a resort, anything. But that was a non-starter.

One day, among the rush-hour chaos on Smith Street, a street vendor handed me a pamphlet. I normally just tossed such pamphlets in the nearest dustbin. But this one caught my eye. It advertised a six-month course at a computer college. If I could raise the thousand rand to do this course, I would be able to find work and save enough to return to technikon. It seemed the perfect shortcut out of my misery.

I stared into the darkness that night, trying to think of a way to raise the thousand-rand fee.

A few days later, I took a taxi to a village about fifty kilometres inland towards Underberg. I had phoned another Catholic priest, Father Gwacela, who was once based in Pevensey. I told him my intentions to register at a computer college. "Come over and let's talk," he had replied when I asked if he could help me with the thousand rand to pay the fee.

I prayed throughout the journey. This seemed my only chance to redeem what had been a disastrous attempt to study at technikon. My dream was in tatters, but at least this might partly salvage things.

I arrived at the priest's house by sunset. Soon the housekeeper was laying plates of food on the dinner table as Father Gwacela and I talked at length about my time at technikon. I told him what had led to my decision to give up. I was glad he understood and sympathised. But there was no talk of whether or not he would help me.

I went to bed still anxious about securing the cash. The next day I woke early, intent on leaving for Durban that morning. But Father Gwacela had plans of his own. We hit the road, running errands and visiting his friends and fellow priests. I sat with them as they drank wine and reminisced about their days at university while they were training for the priesthood.

Sunset came, and still there was no indication that I might receive help. But for some reason I was no longer frustrated, only a little anxious as I went to bed again the second night. I decided to tell Father Gwacela early the next morning that it was time I returned to Durban.

There was no need. In the morning he handed over five hundred rand in cash, as well as transport money to get me back to Durban. He told me he didn't have any more cash. "Keep in touch, and I'll let you know when I have the rest," he told me. "Then you can come and get it." He wished me luck.

A little relieved, I returned to Durban to try to resurrect my dream again.

The money would hardly have lasted more than a few weeks if I went back to technikon. My mind was made up. The shortcut I had mapped out for myself was the best way out of my troubles. I would stay on at Musa's house for the six months at the computer college. Then I would find a job and rent a place.

The computer college was an instant disappointment. The whole place seemed like a rip-off, a fly-by-night institution. I suspected that the qualification it offered wasn't worth the paper it was written on. The college was situated in a dodgy part of town where drunks ran amok throughout the day. There were so many taverns around that it was hard to imagine why anyone would put a college in such a place.

After a few lectures I started to question the direction of the course. I could hardly define what I was studying there. One moment the lecture was about PC cables and the dangers of stepping over them; the next moment we were learning to touch type. I could already type well because it was part of my course at Technikon Natal.

I was bored and already regretting taking this course. But I was committed by now, so I kept coming back. I told myself it was important to keep the dream alive. Maybe, just maybe, this was the right path to reach my goal.

Twenty-eight

One day, several weeks into my computer course, my lectures finished at midday. Not wanting to go back to the township so early, I walked to the city campus at Technikon Natal to find my ex-classmates, who I had kept in touch with.

Strangely, when I arrived at the main gate, a large crowd of students and staff was gathered outside. I discovered that the Student Representative Council had called a strike. Whenever this happened they made sure no one went to lectures. I had experienced this firsthand a couple of months earlier when a rock came flying through the library window and landed on a desk, to frighten those students who were quietly getting on with their studies.

Now as I passed through the crowd looking for my mates, I caught sight of Janet Maxwell, wife of the head of Journalism. She pushed through the crowd with her eyes on me. I stood there transfixed, wondering why.

She pulled me aside. Thoughts raced through my mind as we moved away from the noise.

"I'm relieved you decided to come by," she said. "We've been looking for you since you disappeared three weeks ago. It took us a while to realise you'd dropped out."

"Janet," I tried to explain, "I just couldn't continue studying here. I'm sorry."

"Yes, we realised you didn't have the money. Please, come with me." She led me back to the office.

"I want you to return to technikon. We can't allow you to drop out. You're so good."

Good? I asked myself. No one had said this to me since I left high school. Since starting at the technikon I had felt so mediocre. There was a stark contrast between the Dux trophy student who left high school the previous year and this first-year technikon student. The going had been so tough that I'd resigned myself to failing first year if I didn't drop out.

"You know there's an exam in two days? You need to study. Hard. Please don't drop out. I'll ask Mike to do something about your fees. Do you still have your notes?"

I nodded.

"Then go home and study. I'll see you in the exam room. Do your best, and Mike and I will take care of the rest." Then she was gone.

I had forgotten to tell her that my tuition fees weren't the only problem. I didn't have the transport money to get to the technikon; the place I was living in was hell and I was under constant stress. I was going to need a lot more help to sort myself out.

I urgently needed a quiet place to study. So I headed for my mom's cousin, Aunt Sibongile, who lived in Clermont. As always, she gave me a meal and left me alone with my books. Athough I didn't have a change of clothes with me, I had my notes. I still carried them everywhere with me, even though I had dropped out of technikon. I didn't really know why.

For the next two days I pored over my notes. It was torture having to study under such pressure. I was nervous. But I knew I had no choice. It felt like I was seeing some of the notes for the first time. It was a matter of taking in as much as I could. I planned to just go to the exam and regurgitate everything.

For those two days I managed to forget my problems. I didn't think about how I was going to continue at the technikon with so many problems still unresolved. I just tried to focus on studying for the exam as best I could.

My heart was thumping as the invigilator read out the exam rules and started handing out the question papers. Normally I would browse through the question paper before starting to write. But this time I didn't dare. I was scared there would be too many questions I couldn't answer. I was scared that seeing them would set off a panic attack.

I was also keen to regurgitate as much as I could before I forgot. I poured out as much as I could until the exam time was up. As I walked out, I prayed that I had done enough to pass. "Lead me, Lord ..." I recited my standard prayer.

There was another exam a week later, but that wasn't so bad: I'd had enough time to prepare. I was more relaxed as I went in to write it.

While waiting for the results, I decided to go back to the computer college to deregister. I hoped they would give me my five hundred rand back. I wanted to use it for transport.

"We've missed you the past few days," said the owner of the college as I stood in his office. He was a big guy, someone you wouldn't want to mess with. But I got straight to the point, and told him I had come to deregister, and was hoping he would return my five hundred rand.

"Deregister? I don't understand."

I explained that I was returning to technikon, and I wanted my money back. He wasn't having it. "I lose money every time a student leaves this institution!" he ranted. "You owe me the five hundred rand balance you would have paid to finish the course."

"But, sir, I was here only three weeks."

"Well, I wish you the best in your studies, but I expect you to pay the five hundred rand."

When I insisted I wouldn't, he assured me he would take me to court. I stormed out.

I was angry as I walked back to the technikon. Mike and Janet had given me a second chance at the technikon, and I was keen to repay their trust by attending every lecture. But I couldn't if I still couldn't afford the transport money to get to lectures.

⬇

On campus I found some classmates busy studying for the supplementary exams a few weeks later. "Why aren't you in the library studying like us?" asked one of my classmates. "Aren't you writing any supps?"

I wasn't. The results had come out, and I was relieved to have passed, if not exactly proud of my marks. I got fifty per cent for the first exam and fifty-six for the other. But not having to write a supp gave me a breather. I was lucky to have scraped through.

"Ah, so you're one of the clever ones," said my classmate.

Still, I had to catch up the three weeks' work I'd missed while at the computer college. Catching up while preparing new assignments wasn't easy. But I decided that all my stress had affected my studies. From now on I had to try to relax and enjoy my studies.

After several days of class without hearing from Janet or Mike, I started wondering if they had forgotten about me. But eventually Mike sent word that he needed to see me the following day.

I was anxious as I walked into his office. By now I had realised that Mike wasn't the hard-living roughnecked biker he looked like. In fact he was quite a softy. He always wore a smile and joked with his students between lectures or when he left on his bike in the afternoons.

I barely spoke as Mike drove me in Janet's car to the Berea campus. He tried to start a conversation by asking me a few questions, but I answered in monosyllables. "Relax," he told me. "We'll get it sorted out."

I kept saying prayers as we walked from the parking lot to an office. A well-dressed man was expecting us when we walked in. He was clearly an important person at the college. All I knew was that he was the key to getting me funding for my first year. After a brief introduction he offered us tea. I was too nervous to mention that I drank neither tea nor coffee. "How many sugars?" he asked.

"Just three," I replied.

"Only *three*?" he teased. I realised he was also trying to get me to relax. But I'd had so many doors close on me. I was terrified he would say there was no money. I just couldn't calm my nerves.

Mike made my case to him. I was a good student, he said, and he felt I couldn't be left to drop out. I barely spoke. The man asked me a bit about where I was from and my background, to assess whether I qualified for funding. For the rest, the two of them did all the talking.

As the conversation continued, I started to relax. The dreaded words "there's no money" were never spoken. All he wanted was to be certain I deserved the funding. Mike was pushing hard to ensure that I walked out with a yes.

"You said your grandmother is your guardian, right?" I agreed. "I need you to go home and get a pension slip and a copy of her identity document, okay? Then I'll take care of the rest." He wished me the best in my studies. "I can see Mike believes in you, young man. Don't disappoint him."

"See, it wasn't so hard," Mike said as we walked back to the car.

Twenty-nine

I wasted no time getting back to Pevensey, where I found Khulu cleaning the yard. She was surprised to see me.

"*Ubekwa yini la ekuseni kangaka*? What brings you here so soon?" she asked. I was only expected at Christmas. I explained that the technikon required her documents in order to give me funding for the year.

She gave me a cold look. "Why do you bother with technikon? What are you trying to prove? Quit and look for a job." She went back to sweeping the yard as if I wasn't there.

I took a breath. I had to stay calm and polite. "My future depends on this," I started. "I need a copy of your identity document. Please could I borrow the original? I'll go to town and make a copy, and then bring it straight back. Please."

"*Uzoyilahla*," she said. "You'll just lose it."

It quickly became clear that she wasn't going to give me the document. I walked away, and she yelled once more that I mustn't waste my time, but go and look for work instead.

I was devastated. My life was crumbling before my very eyes. Tears ran down my face as I stormed out of the gate. I couldn't control myself as I walked along the grassy passage. I started crying out loud like a baby. Not even the stares of curious neighbours could stop my shameless wailing. My future was in jeopardy because Khulu just wanted me to work so I could send her money every month.

I understood that she barely had an education, and thought

graduating from high school was enough to get me a decent job. But this was no time for reasoning. I was so angry with her. I was still crying uncontrollably when I arrived at Gogo's homestead a short while later. She stood motionless when she saw me. I couldn't talk. I just cried.

She took my hand and led me into the kitchen, where she handed me a glass of water. "*Ungakhali mtanomtanami*. Please don't cry, my grandchild." She was fighting back her own tears from seeing me in such a state. "*Kwenzenjani?*" she asked. "What's going on?"

Out of breath and through my sobbing, I explained what had just happened.

Without a word, Gogo left the kitchen, and soon emerged in fresh clothes. "Come," she said. We walked to the gravel road about fifteen minutes away, and flagged down a taxi to Underberg.

It was typically chilly as Gogo and I waited in a long queue at Social Services. I was freezing in only a shirt and no jacket. But Gogo made sure I ignored the cold. She kept asking me questions about technikon. She had never gone to school, and could neither read nor write. But somehow she understood and appreciated my determination to get an education.

After explaining my story, we emerged from Social Services with a copy of her ID and two of her pension slips.

"May God be with you, my grandchild," she said as she boarded the taxi back to Pevensey.

I was going straight back to Durban.

"Thank you, Gogo!" I said, fighting back tears. "You have no idea what this means to me. I'll never forget what you've just done for me."

"Good luck in your studies," she answered. "May God protect you and shower you with blessings."

Back at technikon I studied hard. The mood in Musa's house hadn't changed. But I was happy that my tuition fees for the year were covered. This gave me something to work for. I stayed at the library till late, and only went home to sleep. I knew I couldn't bear another year in Musa's house. But I blocked any thought of what was going to happen when I started my second year at technikon. It was important for me to pass. Not only for myself, but to repay the faith shown by the people who were helping me through a difficult year.

It was a huge relief at the end of the year when I discovered that I had passed, even though my marks were no cause for celebration. I had done well in a few subjects, but most of my scores were mediocre. But after such a tough year and all the stress and misery I had endured, even to the point of giving up at one stage, it was exciting to have at least passed.

I had so looked forward to the long summer holidays back in Pevensey before returning to technikon for second year. But I couldn't get into the spirit of Christmas and New Year's Eve. Everyone around me was celebrating. Instead I was worried sick about what 1998 had in store for me. My anxiety heightened with each day that passed.

I had no money to pay for second year. Not even the deposit money, which had increased for the new year. The days kept ticking by. As registration week approached I began having sleepless nights trying to think where the deposit money could possibly come from. The Maxwells had helped me secure financial aid for the first year. But I barely had the strength to go through another year without transport money. And I dreaded returning to class with an empty stomach, day in and day out. I felt drained at the thought of going through the same strain as the previous year. I wasn't sure I could bear it.

A few days before the technikon opened, I went to Durban to stay at Aunt Sibongile's in Clermont while I figured out how I was going to raise the money to register. I wasn't sure where I was going to stay, either. I couldn't go back to Musa's house. But Aunt Sibongile's place was barely big enough for her own family, and I slept on a foam mattress on the lounge floor when I was there. The day the technikon opened, I hung around her place all morning, unsure what to do. I had hoped a solution would have presented itself by now. But still I had no money for the deposit.

I watched cartoons on television as the clock on the living-room wall ticked the minutes and hours away. My thoughts kept shifting to what was happening at the technikon: the students all lining up to pay their deposits and go back to class while catching up with each other's news. Without me. I probably wasn't going to make it back.

Almost noon and still no solution. Nothing. I just sat on the couch, waiting for I don't know what. Then Aunt Sibongile answered a phonecall.

"It's for you," she said.

For me? It was Mrs Davis, the receptionist at the Journalism department. "Why aren't you at university?" she wanted to know. I told her I had no money for the deposit. "Well then," she replied, "you'd better come to my office. Can you get here today?" I assured her I could.

I didn't know what to make of her call, but I was there within an hour. She beckoned me into the office and offered me tea. This was extremely unusual; normally she spoke to students across the counter. I asked for a glass of water.

Then she handed me an envelope with my name in type on the front of it. "It's yours," she said, noticing my hesitation. "Read it." Puzzled, I opened the letter. I couldn't believe my eyes.

The Konrad Adenauer Stiftung Foundation is pleased to inform you that you have been awarded a scholarship for your studies at Technikon Natal.

My eyes blurred as I continued to read. Not only did the scholarship cover my fees, it even took care of accommodation. I would also receive a stipend of two thousand rand a month.

"Oh my God!" I said. "Thank you, Mrs Davis. The Lord has answered my prayers."

"Congratulations," she smiled. "Now take that letter with you and go and register!"

I had actually applied to the Konrad Adenauer Stiftung

Foundation in Germany during my first year. At some stage Mike Maxwell had told several of us that this Foundation was looking to sponsor Journalism students. All applicants were required to have a bank account, so Mrs Davis had given me enough money to open an account, and then recorded my banking details. But my interview with the Foundation hadn't seemed to go well, and I had promptly forgotten the whole episode. It never occurred to me that anything might come of it. I couldn't imagine getting such a generous gift without a struggle.

I felt like I was dreamwalking as I made my way through the chaos of Smith Street to the offices of the Konrad Adenauer Stiftung Foundation. There a smiling receptionist greeted me.

"I'm here to see Lynn Schmitz," I told her.

"Morning, McIntosh, I've been expecting you," said Lynn, appearing from a small office. "Congratulations on the scholarship, we're very happy to award it to you."

"Ma'am," I replied, choking back tears, "you don't know how much this means to me."

"Don't you worry about anything now," Lynn reassured me. "Focus on your studies, and we'll take care of you." Then she handed me a document that served as a financial guarantee which I needed to register and apply for accommodation at the technikon.

I couldn't contain myself. I rushed straight to the counselling department to share the good news with the two Gugus who had pushed for me to get a place in the Journalism department. They quickly spread the news through the whole department.

A few days later I moved into the Cromer Residence. As I looked out of the window of number fifty, my small room on the fifth floor, I thought back over all the struggles of the previous year, over the whole journey that had led me, at last, to this little room with a single bed, a table and a cupboard. For the first time in my life I had a space of my own, a place where I could study, finally, on my own terms, and work towards my goal.

Thirty

Towards the end of my second year, Mrs Davis summoned me to the office one day. "I just got a call from the SABC," she smiled. "They want you for an interview." I had written to the South African Broadcasting Corporation applying for holiday work at the end of the year.

A few days after the interview, I got a call. I had my holiday job! I paced around in a state of ecstacy. For years I had wanted to be a radio journalist, and I had convinced myself that I was born to it. Now I was close to realising my dream.

I spent the first day working with one of the experienced journalists. That afternoon he took me into the studio and introduced me to his colleagues, who were in the midst of a current affairs show at Ukhozi FM. The news presenter glanced up, shook my hand, and asked me to sit opposite him and put on the headphones. Instantly I realised I was about to go live on radio. I was so nervous that the microphone in front of me seemed like a boulder.

"Stand by," he said as a jingle neared its end.

"In the studio we have our newest recruit," he announced, "a young lad who'll be helping us with the news for the next two months. McIntosh, say hello to our listeners!"

"Hello, all you Ukhozi FM listeners." My heart was beating so hard I felt it would leap out of my chest. "It's very exciting to be with you."

Fortunately there was nothing else for me to say that day.

The presenter invited me to pop by whenever I had time in the afternoons. He wanted to teach me everything I needed to know about radio.

I took his invitation very seriously. Within days I had become a co-presenter on his show. It took me no time to learn to read current affairs scripts live in the studio without any problem. I also went out on stories, and reported for different SABC radio stations. It was such an exciting time. Sometimes I looked in the mirror and reminded myself that I wasn't dreaming. This was real. I had achieved my goal.

But at the same time I was worried. It seemed such a privilege to be talking to millions of people every day. Part of me didn't feel worthy of such a privilege. My upbringing had taught me not to expect such excitement, such success. I didn't feel I deserved it. I kept thinking I'd gone too high too fast. I was scared I'd come crashing down and my life's dream would be snatched away.

But this was only a two-month internship. The following January I would be back at technikon to complete my final year of studies. What would happen after that? Would these people take me back? Or would I sit at home trying to find a job? I spent sleepless nights. This was too good; it couldn't last.

It was painful to have to leave the job to return to technikon. But registration went without a hitch, and by the end of the day I had moved into Room 5 at the Student Village. I had struggled with the noise in the Cromer Building the previous year. Student Village was a flashy new residence with the beautiful yellow-brick walls, reserved for senior students only. Here the noise of partying and misbehaving students would not be tolerated.

My new room was also slightly bigger. The fridge made life a lot easier. This was my chance to say goodbye to tinned food, which I had grown to hate after a whole year of it. Now, I could cook real food in a shared kitchen, and more importantly, I could study in my room, thanks to the strict rules about noise.

In just five months, all third-year students were expected to secure themselves six months' practical training in order to graduate. As I got stuck into my studies, I worried about whether the SABC would give me another opportunity at the end of June that year. As the weeks and months marched on, I started sending in applications and making phone calls to try to secure my spot at the SABC. Nothing came of it. I sent dozens of letters to media companies, but none came back with positive news. As the May exams approached, I started to panic. My monthly allowance from my scholarship was due to end in a month. In just a few weeks I would have to fend for myself. I worried about a place to stay, and dreaded the prospect of life without a job.

But there were no problems with my studies. The exams were going smoothly. Despite my anxiety I had managed to study hard. Each day, my classmates and I crowded out the computer room, sending emails and searching the Internet for training opportunities. We shared our fears for the future, but sharing them didn't make me feel any better. Most of the others had parents or at least somewhere to stay at the end of their studies. I didn't.

When a post came up for a computer laboratory assistant in the Journalism department, most of us applied. The job entailed teaching newspaper design and helping students with computer problems. It wasn't an ideal position for someone eager to be part of the buzz of a newsroom. But I figured I didn't have the luxury of being choosy.

The interviews took a couple of hours. Everyone, including myself, was surprised when it was announced that I had the job. I had no doubts about my abilities, but I couldn't help wondering if Janet and Mike Maxwell had felt obliged to intervene to help me once again, after helping me out of trouble during my first year.

With a job secured, I now needed a place to stay. Before the end of the week I had moved into a two-bedroomed flat with four fellow students, just a ten-minute walk from the technikon.

The job at the technikon wasn't what I had romanticised about while spending every ounce of my energy securing my a place at technikon. The salary was less than my allowance from the Konrad Adenauer Stiftung scholarship. After paying rent and buying food for the month, I could barely afford anything.

Life was miserable. Moving into my own flat, as I had hoped when I started technikon, was not going to happen for a while, let alone buying a home. Owning a car was out of the question. At nights I wallowed in grief about what was to become of me. My internship was to last a year. But I knew I couldn't spend a whole year like this. After all that hard work getting into technikon and struggling through the first year, I was starting to feel disillusioned about life. I felt unworthy.

Graduation day came. I hired a black gown, put on my jeans and a plaid shirt and joined the happy faces in the hall. I could hear Aunt Sibongile cheering when my turn came to receive my certificate. But despite the effort I'd put in to obtaining my diploma, I had little to celebrate. I had too many problems to care about wearing a silly gown. I joined a group of happy students to take photos for posterity later, but couldn't wait to get out of my clothes. I was proud of what I had achieved, but I felt no joy. I never even bothered to collect my graduation pictures, so I have no record of that day other than my memories.

Almost a year later, I got a lucky break when P4 Radio, a privately owned independent radio station, gave me an opportunity. It was the break I had always dreamt of. But by then my self-confidence had been badly eroded. I was wracked with uncertainty about my worthiness.

On my first day on P4 Radio, I was asked to read live sports bulletins in the afternoons. It started well. When I walked into the studio for my final bulletin, the deejay starting his shift told me he was impressed. "I was listening on my way in to work. You're doing well!" he said. I thanked him.

But from there on it went downhill. Doubts about my worthiness kept me nervy. I was so full of self-doubt that it was distracting. I was quickly taken off live sports and put on the news desk to be trained. Occasionally, I got to read the news. But by now I was terribly nervous and had absolutely no self-confidence. Being taken off reading sports had hit me hard, and shattered what little remained of my self-esteem.

I didn't know if I would manage to keep the job after the three-month probation period. I kept telling myself to mellow out every time I walked into the studio. Slowly, I coaxed myself to life. I needed to work hard to impress my new employers. Either this, or abandon my dream. Three months later, the station boss walked into the newsroom as I finished the afternoon bulletin.

"McIntosh," he said. "I was wrong about you." I just looked at him. "Shortly after you started, I called the editor in. I said I don't want this guy. She told me to be patient and give you time. This bulletin you just read has made it clear. She was right. You *are* good. *Very* good. Keep it up!"

From there on, my self-confidence began to recover. My job was guaranteed and I now felt accepted as a member of the team at P4 Radio. The salary wasn't the best, but it went a long way towards paying my bills. With the little I had left every month I could now go to movies and even help the McNamaras with Zinhle's tertiary education. By now Zinhle had moved to Durban and was doing computer studies.

I decided that the time had come to fulfil the promise I had made years earlier to the Catholic bishop who gave me the cheque for my deposit at technikon. I had promised him I would repay it so that others could benefit. His words still rang in my ears whenever I thought back to that day. "That's what everyone says," he had replied, "but when they finish their studies, they forget us."

I had my diploma now, and I would keep my word. That pink cheque had opened the door to technikon for me. Paying it back was the right thing to do, and I also wanted to thank the bishop for what he had done for me.

So one bright Saturday afternoon at the end of a political press conference, I drove out to Mariannhill in the company car. That day four years earlier was as fresh as if it were yesterday. I remembered how nervous I had been back then, how the fear of failure had almost paralysed me as I walked to Father Madela's house. Now I was a proud young man with an education, the one thing no one could ever take from me. The future was in my hands, and part of the reason I could now drive to Mariannhill in this company car was the generosity of Father Madela and the bishop.

I didn't even know the bishop's name. But what he had done for me was so significant, so profound, that it would stay with me as long as I lived. Now was my chance to ask him his name. I felt emotional as I parked the car and made my way up the steps. I was about to knock at the door of a small office when a much younger man appeared.

"Good afternoon, young man. How can I help you?" he asked.

"My name is McIntosh," I said. "I'm here to see the Bishop."

"You're looking at him," he smiled. "I am the Bishop," he added, seeing my confusion.

I found my tongue. "There was an older bishop here several years ago, an old white man. I've come to see him," I said.

"I know who you're talking about," said the bishop. "He's retired now, but I'm not sure where he lives. Can I help, perhaps?"

"No thanks, father. Sorry to trouble you."

He stood and watched me drive off.

I was overwhelmed with disappointment. I realised I was probably never going to get a chance to thank the bishop. The money in my pocket didn't seem as important as the act of shaking his hand, sitting down with him and relating how his act of kindness had changed my life. I felt deprived of that chance.

But I was clear what I was going to do with the money. It was the beginning of the year, and Sihle, my former high-school mate who had wanted to do Journalism, had been accepted at the Durban University of Technology, but didn't have the cash for the deposit.

I would now do for Sihle what the bishop had done for me.

By now the deposit had gone up a few hundred rand, but I made sure Sihle had enough. I wondered if I should perhaps have handed the money to the new bishop at Mariannhill, but I had been too stunned to think straight at the time. Giving Sihle the money didn't feel as satisfying as if I had met the bishop, but it felt like the right thing to do.

Back at work, my radio career was going fine, but it wasn't what I had pictured back at high school. P4 Radio was a music radio station, and news wasn't a priority. I did go out on stories, but it wasn't enough. Most of my time was spent in the news booth phoning around and recording interviews.

As the job gradually became easier, something imperceptible began to change. I was starting to grow bored. Two years after starting out as a radio journalist, I was sitting in the recording studio one day when it suddenly struck me that perhaps I wasn't born for a career in radio after all.

I needed a new challenge. I picked up the phone, and called eTV, an independent television station. "Guess what," I said in a cocky voice. "I want to work for you."

A few days later I received a call from Aakash Bramdeo, the bureau chief. "Did you read my email?" he asked.

"No, sir, I haven't checked my emails."

"I asked you to come through to my office today. Can you still make it?"

"Yes, sir! I'm on my way."

When I walked in, the chief pointed to a thick file. "The résumés of people who've applied to work here," he said. "I'm not going to employ any of them." I wasn't sure where this conversation was going.

"How soon can you start working here?" he asked.

"Excuse me?"

"You're hired. When can you start?"

I was startled. I had come to the eTV offices expecting to be grilled with questions.

"I've seen you a couple of times out on stories. I've always been struck by your professionalism. I don't know why it didn't occur to me to ask you to work here. I listened to you on radio after you called a couple of days ago, and I knew straight away that I wanted you to join us."

By now my confidence was on a high. I wasn't nervous as I counted the weeks and days before I joined eTV. Sometimes I wrote scripts at home, memorised them, and stood in front of the mirror pretending I was reporting. I was keen to know how I would come across on television. This was new territory for me, but I was excited.

On my second day at eTV I was already in front of the camera, reporting on a fourteen-day conference. Politicians and heads of state from around Africa had gathered in Durban for the launch of the African Union.

The cameraman did his best to keep me calm, but it didn't help. I was very nervous. Thank goodness this isn't live, I kept saying to myself. I finally got it right after several takes. Watching myself reporting on the evening bulletin on television was one of the proudest moments of my life.

A few weeks later, I walked into a clothing shop. It was time to change into a more camera-friendly wardrobe. I was browsing through the shirts in the shop when I noticed people staring at me. They walked straight up to me and asked to shake my hand. I was blown away. My job was exciting, but I hadn't bargained on this kind of attention.

On the streets, total strangers were suddenly greeting me. "Do you know them?" my friends would ask. I didn't, but by now I was getting used to returning greetings from people as if I knew them. I understood that they greeted me because they'd seen me on screen. Yet I hated it. I especially hated going to parties, picnics or simple gatherings. Most of the time, the conversation would turn to a story I had done.

Although I was on television, I was still an introvert. I struggled with all the attention directed at me. One Sunday a friend of mine called to say I was in a tabloid paper.

"That's impossible," I told him. "I haven't been interviewed."

"Go buy the paper."

I did. I'd never bothered to read the *Sunday World* before. But there it was. "McIntosh speaks with such a nasal accent. We find it difficult to determine what his indigenous language is."

Why didn't they just call me and ask, I thought, tossing the paper on the table. I would have told them about my background, the McNamaras, my teachers. I was annoyed. But as long as I was on television, I realised, this was going to be part of my life. I needed to stay calm and rise above such pettiness.

A year later I won Vodacom's Regional Journalist of the Year Award for my television work. By now my name had become synonymous with controversial stories. Politicians from both of the main political parties in the province now viewed me with suspicion. To them I was a menace. There was a price to be paid for the work I was doing.

I took on a story in which a civil servant in a small municipality in Greytown had allegedly defrauded a pensioner of his brand new house, sold it, and bought two brand new cars with the profit. Determined to expose this civil servant, I went to her parents' house. There the cameraman and I were confronted by an angry family, and I was mometarily concussed by a blow from a pick handle.

"Did you get the shots?" were the first words I yelled to Sibusiso Miya when I regained my senses. Luckily he had. Despite receiving blows to his arms, he had bravely kept the camera rolling, and found time amid the chaos to film me while I was down.

A local doctor was kind enough to examine me for free, and recommended an overnight stay at hospital. I watched myself on TV while nursing my pain from a bed in Durban's St Augustine Hospital that night.

But this attack wasn't the worst of my experiences during my television career. One of the things I found hardest was seeing human corpses. With so much violent crime in South Africa, there were plenty to see. I often reported on gun battles between the police and criminals. I learnt to deal with the horror of death by commenting casually on what the dead criminal was wearing. Nice shoes, or wow, a nice leather jacket. The cops taught me that trick. But no trick could overcome the shock of seeing a criminal with his brains blown out by a high-calibre rifle. It was difficult to sleep afterwards.

It was even worse when I reported on the victims of a serial killer. The first few crime scenes we filmed were all right, because the victims were already skeletons. But the last drove me close to breaking point. She had just started decomposing, and the smell was stomach turning. That night I kept picturing her in her pink floral vest with her hands bound behind her back.

Reporting on such incidents taught me the ugly reality of death. When we view our loved ones who have passed on they usually look dignified, as if in a deep sleep. But now I witnessed the grim reality before the undertakers have created that look of peace.

I was often reminded of my mother. I wondered how she had been found and what had gone through the minds of those who found her. Did it affect them? I had no answers. I knew so little about what had actually happened.

Despite the grisly side, I loved my job. In between stories I completed a degree in Journalism, and won a second Vodacom regional award for my work.

Thirty-one

Three years had passed since I started working in television, and yet, inexplicably, I still wasn't satisfied. I was living my dream, but I still didn't feel complete. There had to be something more, I started to think, something else to do, somewhere else to go.

There was.

At six a.m. one morning, I stepped out of a plane into the International Arrivals hall at Heathrow Airport. Although exhausted after an eleven-hour flight, anticipation and excitement overcame my fatigue. An official at the British Council back in South Africa had apologised in advance for the rough welcome I would receive from Immigration employees at the airport. With this in mind I was a little nervous as I handed over my passport, medical documents and other documentation explaining why I was here. Surprisingly, I was allowed into the UK within minutes. Following the instructions I had brought with me, I collected my eight hundred pound allowance in traveller's cheques and walked towards the exit.

I was struck by the vastness of the airport. Although I knew that Heathrow was the busiest airport in the world, I didn't imagine it would be quite that busy. There were people from everywhere coming and going. But among the many accents, the dominant British accent made it clear that I was now in the land of the

English. Everyone seemed busy doing something, and no one paid me much attention as I stood gawking at one thing after another.

My instructions offered several transport options, but the underground and the buses seemed confusing. I opted for a cab.

"First time in England, is it?" asked the driver as we drove along the motorway. It must have been obvious the way I was peering around, sizing up my new surroundings.

"What brings you here?"

"A twelve-month study scholarship," I told him.

I couldn't contain my excitement as I stepped out of the taxi outside 159 Great Dover Street. You're in *London*, I kept telling myself. I felt like yelling it out loud. Moments later, I dragged my luggage into the Sidney Webb House residence, my home for the duration of my stay in the UK.

It was a year since I had responded to an advert in the *Mail & Guardian* by the British Council, offering to sponsor professionals to do a Master's degree in the UK in a course of their choice. I applied and forgotten about it until they called me for an interview in Johannesburg.

I felt pretty confident after the interview. But when months passed without feedback, I assumed I'd failed to impress the interview panel. Then one day a parcel arrived by courier. It was a confirmation that I had been awarded a twelve-month postgraduate Chevening Scholarship, starting September 2005.

I spent my first day in the residence making new friends. The next day, I took bus 172 to Aldwych to register at the London School of Economics. I was going to spend a year studying towards a Master's degree in Media and Communications. But I was also determined to have fun. Lots of it.

Before long, London was home. I grew familiar with the coins so that I no longer had to ask the cashiers to count out what I owed them. When people spoke with hot potatoes in their mouths I could understand them. I loved buying fresh food at Borough market on Saturdays, wandering around Covent Garden with friends, and having fun at the Guena Bara nightclub. Most of my friends were South Americans. On Thursdays we would line up for mojitos during happy hour. In spring and summer we played football in Regent's Park. I even paid a visit to Northern Ireland to visit Janet and Mike Maxwell, who had now settled there in Janet's home country.

As the end of my studies approached, I realised that London had become an important part of me. I mulled over the possibility of staying forever. But when my year of fun and study came to an end, I decided return to South Africa.

Back at work, the desk I had left a year earlier was still waiting for me. My colleagues were happy to have me back. But was I happy to be back?

I wasn't so sure. I missed London and the friends I had made there. But, I told myself, I would soon settle back in and move on with my life.

After a couple of months I received a mail from the London School of Economics. There it was in front of me.

McIntosh Nzimande, having completed the approved course of study and passed the examinations, has this day been admitted by the London School of Economics and Political Science to the University of London Degree of Master of Science in Media and Communications.

I had officially earned my Master's degree at LSE, one of the universities under the umbrella of the University of London.

By now I had been moved to the television station's main offices in Johannesburg. I had achieved more than I had hoped for in my wildest dreams. And still I felt empty.

At last it began to occur to me what the problem was.

I had spent over a dozen years running. I had pushed myself hard to tackle a new challenge every few years. I was constantly trying to distract myself, to shift my focus away from something. It dawned on me that I had left my job on radio not because I was bored, but because I had settled into it. Being settled in any job didn't feel good. It gave me time to think, which forced me to face the things I was running from. Things I was trying hard to avoid.

I realised that not even a Master's degree from the London School of Economics could fill the emptiness in my soul. Being a famous journalist meant nothing if I didn't do what I needed to do. I had to find closure. I needed to face this person if I was to find peace.

Thirty-two

It was time to do the one thing I hadn't had the strength to face. It was time to find my father. I had to find a way to look him in the eye and tell him that I forgave him for taking my mom's life. I needed to try to build some sort of relationship with him at last. And I knew it wouldn't be easy.

I had spent years using his surname, yet still I felt no attachment to it. I needed to know who I was and where and with whom I belonged. And I needed, finally, to accept my name.

I had long since forgiven my father. And often I had thought of looking for him. But each time I postponed it. Instead, I spent years trying to forget all that had happened. I was scared to test my resolve. Most of all, I was scared to face the past. At times I wasn't even sure if my forgiveness was genuine. I felt especially confused whenever I cried about my mom. Even at just over thirty, I still cried like a baby when I thought about her. I still missed her, and thought about all the things I could have done for her. By now I would have long gotten her to retire from working as a housekeeper; I would have made it my responsibility to look after her.

Like many around me had done for their parents, I would have built her a decent house at a place of her choosing and sent her money every month. I pictured those moments over and over. And every time, tears rolled down my face. My father had taken more than just her life. He had taken a piece of my soul. These thoughts tested my forgiveness, and made me scared about how I would react to meeting him again. I had grown up with too much

168

pain. Awakening the past would bring it all back. I dreaded being reminded of all that had happened to me and my sister.

I still felt I should have done more to protect her. I still blamed myself for allowing her to go through that pain and humiliation, and for not telling enough people. Yes, I had tried telling Father Sebastian, but I should have kept on trying, called a meeting and informed him of what was happening. But back then I was a terrified little boy, small for my age and fearful of adults.

Approaching my father now would force me to revisit all that pain. I didn't know if I had the strength. I was terrified that it might be too vivid and overwhelm me. But now I began to see that I couldn't actually avoid it any longer. I couldn't outrun the voice in my head telling me to face the truth and make my peace with it. I'd run out of escape routes. If I kept on running I would be stuck in my painful childhood forever.

The time had come to do what I had always dreaded: to confront my past. I had to look my biological father in the eyes and tell him that I forgave him. By now I had started to put my life story, this book, into words. Through doing this, I started for the first time to venture into my upbringing in a meaningful way. I began to revisit not just the horrors of my past, but also the moments of fun I'd had as a kid.

Although I had forgiven my father, there were still moments when I felt my rage coming back. I felt strongly that the only way I could deal with the anger and the unanswered questions was to find out what actually happened to Mom. I needed to know if my father really was the monster I had come to believe, whether the snippets of information I had pieced together over the years were correct.

As I continued to pen my life story, I realised how tied it was to both my biological parents. No matter how hard I wanted to ignore this fact, my story was never going to be complete without finding out more about them both. Cheryl Wood and the McNamaras had been right. I needed to find my father.

Putting my story into words showed me just how little I knew about what had happened to my mom. Even after accomplishing so much in my life, I hadn't yet found the strength to investigate. And apart from what I could remember from my early childhood, I knew little about my father, except that he was a monster who had murdered my mom.

This was what I had been told while growing up. And I knew for sure that he had abandoned us. He had left Zinhle and me with almost no prospect of a future. I was proud that we had proved him wrong. We had grown up to be better people than he would have expected. As hard as it was for some of my extended family to accept, I had learnt to forgive him. A part of me, even to my own surprise, wanted to embrace him, to try to build some sort of relationship.

So I set out to find the truth, no matter how difficult or hurtful it might be. I decided to start by speaking to those who were closest to my mom before she died. Hopefully they had also met my father. I hoped they would have the answers I needed about my parents. Good or bad, I needed to know.

I planned it all out. First I would speak to members of my mom's extended family to try to establish how and why she was killed. This, I felt, would somehow lead me eventually to my father. I knew it would be a long, hard and emotional journey. But I was going to walk it.

First, I phoned the McNamaras to tell them my decision. Edward was now in his eighties but still tough as nails, despite a health scare years earlier that had left him with a limp.

"It's important that you do this while your mom and I are still alive," he told me. "We're here to support you." Then he passed the phone to Eugenia.

She was as cheerful as ever. "I bet he's ugly and still doesn't shave his scruffy beard," she said of my biological father. With the blessing of both my adopted parents, I was all set to begin.

The next day Eugenia called again. "Edward's had a heart attack. We're taking him to Albert Luthuli Hospital in Durban."

I asked her if I should drive to Durban to be by his side. "Don't worry, son. He's going to be fine. We'll let you know if the situation changes."

She sounded relaxed. After all, Edward had had what seemed like a crippling stroke a couple of years earlier, but recovered and continued his normal life, running his small shop as well as fixing cars, his favorite hobby. Of course he'll be fine, I told myself.

That afternoon I went to a movie in Sandton to relax and digest the news. It had been a rough week. Days earlier I had resigned from my job as a senior television journalist at eTV, and an ugly scene had ensued. One of the bosses felt betrayed by my decision because they had held my position for me while I studied in London. I ended up being marched off the work premises. The news of Dad's heart attack had added to an emotional week.

I sat at the movies and managed to forget reality for a while. I stopped worrying about the uncertainty that came with leaving a job after five and half years; and I stopped wondering if Dad was going to be fine, and whether I should have driven to Durban to be with him.

As I stepped out of the theatre my cell phone rang. It was my sister, Laurelle. Our Dad had passed away.

I felt my world falling apart. I didn't cry. I couldn't, not because I was in the midst of a crowded lobby, but because the news had struck like an avalanche. I was angry at myself for resisting the urge to take the five-hour drive to be by Dad's side in his final hours. I wondered what his last words to me would have been. I was utterly devastated.

Only when I got home did I give vent to my despair. The moment I had dreaded for so long had come. After a lifetime trying to deal with the loss of my biological mom, I never wanted to go through that again. Perhaps it was one reason I had resisted getting close to the McNamaras for so long after they adopted my sister. But now here I was, reliving that experience again.

A couple of days later we prepared for Dad's cremation. I learnt that Dad was still his usual self just hours before his last breath, stubborn and abrasive as ever. When he overheard a nurse being sarcastic about his command of Zulu, he had summoned her to his bedside. "*Ingakho ningashadile nje anihloniphi*," he apparently told her. "You have no respect, no wonder you can't find a husband."

I spent a couple of days in Pevensey following my Dad's passing. At one point Eugenia called me for a private chat. "Who would have guessed that your dad would leave us so suddenly? You must realise that I won't live forever, either. You need to find your biological father, and tell him you forgive him so you can find closure," she said. Her kindness touched me. She made it her responsibility to be there for me while I undertook that journey, knowing it would be difficult for me. She had only just lost my dad, and instead of being preoccupied with her own loss, she was still doing her best to help me through my emotions.

"You're only fifty-six, Mom!" was all I could manage to say. "You'll still be with us for a long time."

I returned to Johannesburg a couple of days later, in mourning for my dad's passing, which drew all my thoughts away from the issue of my biological father.

Five months later, Eugenia was admitted to hospital. Doctors had discovered gallstones, and she told me they were going to operate to remove them. I shouted at her for using a state hospital. Mom was now Mayor of Underberg. I just couldn't understand why she would use such a hospital when her medical aid entitled her to go to a private one.

"It's not right, Mom. I don't think they'll look after you properly," I said. But she was so humble. As Mayor, she had refused to emulate her fellow politicians by having bodyguards. She lived just as she had always done, and always said God would protect her from political enemies.

A couple of days later, I phoned to find out how her operation had gone. She was fine, she told me, and we had a long chat about the usual topics. She was keen to get back home, where she still looked after numerous orphaned children, just as she had when she took in Zinhle years earlier. But now the situation was different. A German couple that had visited her orphanage in the pigsty had raised enough money for a proper building in the village, and the children now had proper beds, and woke to a hot meal prepared on stoves the couple had donated.

Mom was going to stay home and recuperate for a couple of weeks. We chattered about the politics of the small town of Underberg, and said many a loving goodbye, only to start chatting again about something else.

The next morning my phone rang in the early hours. From the sound of Laurelle's voice I knew something was wrong. "Mom has passed on ..." she began.

"Why?" I blurted, completely stunned. It wasn't possible. It couldn't be true. Just hours earlier, we'd had such a long conversation and she'd sounded so well.

At fifty-six Eugenia had looked and sounded so youthful. She was full of energy, and was kept constantly busy by the many orphaned and poor kids she looked after, who needed to be woken each morning, washed, fed and prepared for school. Some were noisy and ran around, some were naughty, and others got sick and needed attention. There was constant noise at home, but Mom's voice was always the loudest. She was in charge and it was clear she knew how to control things. But more importantly, she acted from the bottom of her heart, and never seemed too tired from so many kids competing for her attention. She had done this for years. Even when she became Mayor, she never stopped giving her love to the kids.

Mom's passing brought back her words of warning to me that she would not live forever. It was as if somehow she'd known her time was near. Her death made me realise that it was no longer right to postpone things.

It was due to this realisation that I was in Durban the day after my mom's cremation. It was a typically warm Durban afternoon as I sat down with Aunt Sibongile, my biological mom's cousin, in the lounge of her large new house in New Germany. I had my laptop ready to record every word she said.

During the five-hour drive from Johannesburg to Durban I had stopped to pray beside the Lions River. I said the Lord's Prayer and asked for guidance, then spoke to my mom's soul to keep me strong. I don't believe in ancestors the way many African people do, but I do subscribe to the Catholic beliefs bred into me as a child, that the souls of the dead live on in some form, and that God allows them to watch over us.

Aunt Sibongile sat fidgeting uncomfortably at the edge of the couch. We looked at one another in silence, and I saw her eyes fill with tears. But I was determined to record an accurate account of what she was about to relate.

"Your mom and I both worked in Westville as housekeepers," she began. "We were very close, and we visited each other whenever we could. We would walk out on the streets or sit under a tree and catch up with each other's news. But we didn't always find time. Sometimes weeks passed without seeing each other."

I typed away frantically on my laptop, trying not to interrupt her flow. But with each word my heart seemed to beat faster.

"Sometime around mid-1982, a couple of weeks went by without your mom calling or visiting. As more weeks passed, I should have started to feel uneasy. But I just assumed your mom needed a bit of space after yet another bitter break-up with your father," Aunt Sibongile continued.

"One day your father came to my place of work. He wanted to know if I'd been in touch with *sisi* recently. I thought it very strange that he would come to my place to ask about your mom. After he left, I decided to go to her work, to find out why she'd been so quiet.

"Something about your mom's employers made me uneasy. I could tell something wasn't right. They sat me down and offered me a glass of water. Then they said they'd arrived home a couple of weeks earlier to find the door of the main house open. Smoke was coming out of the kitchen. Pots were cooking on the stove, but the food was burning.

"There were cookies in the oven that were already black. They said it wasn't like your mom to leave food burning. They were upset that she was so careless that their home could have gone up in flames. They went looking for her, shouting her name. But there was silence. After a while, they realised your mom had vanished.

"But she hadn't taken anything with her. The door of her room wasn't locked. The radio was still on. Her bed was neatly made and all her clothes still there. So she hadn't run away to another job. She had just vanished."

My ears were ringing from the horror of her words, but I forced my fingers to keep tapping on my keyboard.

"They reported your mom missing. It was a terrible time for the family. We tried to imagine where she could have gone. I thought she was just tired of being hounded by your father to take him back. That she probably needed time alone. But then why hadn't she taken leave? Other family members had different theories and speculations, but nothing added up.

"The days dragged by so slowly, without any word. Months later, the police came to see me. They told me your mother's body had been found almost two months earlier in Lions River, more than a hundred kilometres from Westville. She was still in her housekeeper's outfit. Police had taken fingerprints from the body, and sent them to the main office in Pretoria. They had been waiting for the fingerprint results. Meanwhile they made announcements on the radio and in local newspapers about the body of an unknown woman. But no one came forward to claim her. So she got a pauper's burial," said Aunt Sibongile.

By now I could barely see, my eyes were so full of tears. I had known it was going to be difficult to listen to Aunt Sibongile's account. But I was determined to be strong. Auntie Zinto had already told me about it in my early teens. But this was the first time I was getting such a complete account. Listening to these details about my mom was unbearable. I couldn't take it. The way Aunt Sibongile spoke made it feel like it happened just days ago. Yet it had been twenty-six years.

Aunt Sibongile and I cried together. The rules I had set for the interview were forgotten. I couldn't remain a detached interviewer any more. I was caught up in the horror of it. This was my own life story, and the pictures her words conjured in my mind were difficult to ignore and just continue typing. I kept asking myself what kind of person was capable of doing such a thing. Somehow I had to accept that this person was my own father, my own flesh and blood.

"Shortly after the police reported this grim news to me, I learnt that your father was in custody. That's when I started putting things together. I remembered the day your father came to ask if I had seen or heard from your mom. I realised he was just trying to find out if anyone in the family knew she was missing. He was fishing to see if I knew that he'd killed her."

"But why? Why would he kill my mom?" I finally asked.

"He was a very jealous man. His jealousy would make him mad with rage. After your mother had been with him eleven years, she found out that he was actually married under customary law. His wife lived near Ladysmith.

"At that time, it was common for men to leave their wives at home and work in the cities. The big cities like Durban and Johannesburg were full of migrant labourers like your father: young men who had left their wives and homes in search of a better life. And he ended up meeting your mom.

"Your mother was also a migrant worker. It was common for women to leave their homes to work as housekeepers for white families. But your father never told her that he was married. Even after they had a little boy together."

"Me?"

She nodded. "When she found out, she dumped him. But when your father said he would take her as his second wife, they got back together again. Then Zinhle was born, and your father still hadn't kept his promise.

"Your mom eventually realised that he was wasting her time. She dumped him again. I knew it was for real when your mom met another man and decided to move on with her life. After a few months her new boyfriend asked her to marry him.

"Your father heard the news that a man was paying *lobola* and preparing to marry your mom. He was enraged with jealousy. Maybe he decided that if he was going to lose your mother, no other man was going to have her. I think that's why he decided to kill her."

I was reeling from her words. But Aunt Sibongile had more to tell.

"I don't believe he did it all on his own. He killed her here in Durban, but he must have needed someone to help carry the body to his car. Your father was a small man. I don't think he had the strength to carry your mom's body alone. I believe she was already dead when she was taken to where her body was found. She would never have agreed to go so far with him if she was alive."

The more Aunt Sibongile told me, the more questions tumbled through my mind.

"How long did my father spend in prison for her murder?" Auntie Zinto had already told me years earlier. But somehow I longed to hear that it had been longer.

"A couple of weeks at most. Just while he was waiting for the trial."

I asked why she thought my father had got away with the murder.

"In the family we feel it was because a black person's life didn't matter under apartheid. This was the eighties, remember. Our lives were cheap."

I had hardly experienced apartheid, so it was hard to relate to Aunt Sibongile's words. But by now I understood politics and South African history. Yet it was hard to believe that the police would have gone to so much trouble to identify my mom, arrest her killer and then just let him go, because her life wasn't important.

It also didn't make sense that my father was let out of prison after awaiting trial for murder. I started to think that he may have won the case, that there may have been no evidence, or that the court was convinced he wasn't the killer. Maybe what I'd been told while growing up wasn't true. Maybe my father wasn't a monster.

"Several years later," Aunt Sibongile continued, "I got onto a bus, and when the driver looked into my eyes as I paid my fare, I almost collapsed. It was your father. The terrible loss of my dearest cousin and friend came back and I cried all the way to work. Seeing that monster opened my wound all over again."

Aunt Sibongile was oddly silent when at last I got up to say goodbye. I suspected there was something she wanted to tell me. Her look made me feel uneasy. I looked back at her and waited for her to speak.

"Would you like to meet your father?" she asked slowly.

I searched her face for a clue. "What are you saying, Auntie?"

"I have a friend who was once married to one of your father's brothers. Her husband has since passed away. But she is a social worker in Clermont." That was the township we had lived in as a family when we were kids. "Would you like to go and speak to her?"

I had imagined that tracing my father would involve a long search. I was sure no one in my mom's family knew where he was. There were all sorts of stories about him. Auntie Zinto had told me she'd heard he was now a traditional doctor. Another time she'd said she didn't think he was still alive.

"I would. Thank you, Auntie."

That night thoughts whirled through my mind. How had my father avoided doing time in prison if he had murdered Mom? And what if I was just days, even hours from finding him? I didn't feel ready.

Thirty-three

I was anxious the next day as I drove through the streets of Clermont. I was also amazed at the speed things were going. How would I feel if I saw him now? I wasn't prepared for that meeting just yet.

At the municipal offices I was told Aunt Sibongile's friend wasn't at work that day. The news was somewhat disappointing, but also a relief. As I walked back to my car, I bumped into a man who knew me through Aunt Sibongile. He said he knew the house of my father's sister-in-law, and offered to take me there.

I was nervous as I approached the door. Here I was taking tentative but bold steps towards finding my father. I still hadn't fully convinced myself that this was the right decision. I found the lady sitting on the couch in the lounge, watching television. She looked a little uneasy when I sat down to introduce myself.

I told her I was the son of her brother-in-law, and told her my father's name. I explained that I had lost contact with my father twenty-six years ago. To my surprise she knew my story. Even though she had never met us, she knew about Zinhle and me. I made sure she understood that I didn't want anything from my father. Just to meet and talk to him.

"My husband was a very honest man," she said. "He told me what your father did to your mom. And that he had two kids who he abandoned. I know everything." She said it was good that I didn't want anything from my father or his family.

Although I was a stranger to her, she gave me some insight into my father and the family to which I was about to be introduced. She told me that he and his close family relatives were a very arrogant bunch, who treated everyone who approached them as if they were after something of theirs.

"What is he like? What does he do?" I had so many questions. She answered them all patiently.

"Your father has two wives. The same woman he was with when he dated your mom. He also has a younger wife he married just a couple of years ago."

"What about children? Do I have half-brothers and -sisters that I need to know about?"

"Your father has seven or eight children with his first wife. He also has a child about two years old with the younger wife. But I'm sure there are more I don't know about. I believe he's making plans to marry a third woman from Swaziland."

"I see." That's all I could manage to say. I was feeling overwhelmed. I had grown up in a Catholic community where polygamy was strictly forbidden. Even divorce was frowned on. And I had strong objections of my own to polygamy. Yet here I was discovering that I was part of a polygamist family.

The woman was freely sharing everything she knew. She told me there was a family feud as a result of my father taking a second wife. His kids were split. Some sided with his first wife, whom they felt was being unfairly treated since the younger wife came into the picture. Others supported his decision to marry again.

"I feel you need to know all this, so you understand what you're getting involved in."

"I just want to meet my father. I don't plan to get involved in family politics."

"You're very brave wanting to meet your father after what he did to your mom. I admire your courage."

"I don't think it's courage, ma'am. I need to do this to help me move on with my life."

She offered to take me to a family elder, my father's uncle. "Your father and his uncle are close. I think it will be easier for you to go through his uncle."

I thanked her.

As we drove to his house, she warned me that the old man was also arrogant, like the rest of them. It was possible that he would simply dismiss me as a trickster.

She advised me to make it clear that I wanted nothing from my father and his family, only to meet him and talk to him. Nothing more. It annoyed me to hear this. Here I was, after years of struggling without a father, and I now had to come across apologetic. It galled me to have to kowtow to these people. It was true that I wanted nothing. But I wasn't prepared to apologise for trying to find my father. After all, I was the one reaching out to tell him that he was forgiven. That the years Zinhle and I had spent as orphans and victims of abuse weren't being held against him, and that despite growing up with the knowledge that he'd snuffed out my mother's life, I still recognised him as my father. Why did I need to be apologetic?

We found the family elder in a brick house protected by burglar bars. The house overlooked a huge double-storey building the old man was renting out to multiple tenants. It was apparently one of many properties he owned. Perhaps this was the reason for their arrogance, I thought. They were the haves among the have-nots, the poor who use their meagre salaries to rent accommodation from them. His property was surrounded by shacks.

The old man rested his elbows on the burglar bars as he listened to my story. He didn't open the gate to let us in and allow us to sit down. As I related my story, the bars remained a barrier between us.

He asked a barrage of questions. "Who looked after you while you were growing up? What level of education do you have? How did you manage without parents? Where do you work?" Although I found some of his questions irritating, I answered them all patiently.

In the end, the old man gave me my father's cell phone number and instructed me to call him. "Sir, I don't know if I'm ready to speak to him," I said. "Please could I take his number and call him later?" I asked.

"No," he said. "Call him now."

My fingers trembled as I dialled the number on my cell phone. I didn't know if I wanted to do this, but there was no turning back. Here I was, reaching out to the person accused of killing my mom, the person possibly responsible for all the hardship I had endured growing up. Was I doing the right thing? Would my mom, wherever she was watching from, approve of this? I would never know.

The phone rang and rang. I was almost relieved that he didn't answer. Halfheartedly, I tried again. This time a male voice answered.

"Hello!" he said.

"Hello, sir, I'm trying to get hold of Mr Nzimande," I said, with my heart almost beating out of my chest.

"It's Mr Nzimande speaking, how can I help you?"

"This is Edista Shezi's son," I replied.

There was silence. It seemed to last forever.

"My sister and I would like to meet with you. We need to talk to you."

I could sense that he was stunned speechless.

But he regained his composure. "We saw a story about you in a newspaper," he said. "I suspected it was you. But that wasn't the name I knew you by."

So changing my identity had worked. Perhaps he would have looked for me if I had kept my original name.

"Has my uncle shown you his properties?" he asked.

"No, sir, I came here to ask your uncle to put me in touch with you," I replied.

His arrogance made me angry, but I contained myself. I wasn't interested in his possessions. I was interested in the truth, and in telling him that I had forgiven him. I promised to call him once Zinhle and I had agreed on the date.

I wept all the way back to Johannesburg. Talking to my father had left me with a chilly feeling. I was in turmoil. I didn't know whether to be proud that I had found him, or guilty for betraying the extended family who had kept me all those hard years of growing up.

Some of them had treated Zinhle and me badly, and they had shown us no love. Yet I was grateful for the shelter they had provided. Although they were often short of food, they had shared what they had with us. My mom's impoverished extended family might have seen us as an extra burden, but they did their best to ensure that we went to school. They helped with our upbringing, which made it easier to forgive the family members who had abused us. But I wasn't sure if meeting my father meant I had betrayed my mom's soul. And what about all the angels who had extended a helping hand as I grew up? Had I betrayed them by reaching out to one who had played no part in my upbringing?

I was suddenly wracked with guilt. So preoccupied was I with these thoughts that several times I nearly lost control on the curves. The more I thought about what I had done, the more I hit the accelerator. My inner turbulence seemed to spur my foot muscles into action. I needed to calm down.

I rang Aunt Sibongile as soon as I reached Johannesburg. I needed to talk to someone. I longed for her assurance that I had done the right thing. Although she still hadn't forgiven him, she supported me. She told me this would lift the weight off my shoulders.

"The only one who should feel guilty is your father," she told me.

She was right, I realised. I started to feel better about myself.

The woman who had introduced me to my father's uncle phoned the next morning. My father had called her in the early hours of the morning, she said. "He must have been unable to sleep after talking to you. He was on the phone for an hour, asking me questions. How you look, what car you drive. He was keen to find out if you looked successful."

Well, I thought, I don't know what his measure of success is, but I haven't done too badly.

"He sounded astonished that you drive a black American car and work in Johannesburg," she went on. "He also wanted to know if you were married and had a family."

"He said he felt guilty for abandoning you two. And it hurt him more knowing that you had grown into responsible adults."

Apparently my father hadn't expected Zinhle and I to make it in life without his help.

Now my father was eager to meet us. And he wanted the meeting to take place within days. He had decided that hearing from me was God's way of solving his problems before he died. The previous year he had thought he was dying. He was annoyed and disappointed that most of his children were not successful in life. As a result, he had bought himself a fleet of cars so that none of them would inherit anything of value.

I couldn't agree to a quick meeting. I needed to brief my mom's family and to prepare my sister. Zinhle hadn't forgiven my father. She was still very angry. I knew the meeting would be tough for her. So I began calling her regularly. I emphasised that although we needed to ask him a lot of questions, we also had to show him respect.

There would be no dignity in showing disrespect. He was the one who needed to acknowledge guilt, not us. But if we showed disrespect, we wouldn't achieve much. We were unlikely to get the answers we wanted if we approached him with anger. This was a time to be calm, however strong our emotions.

I wanted to know if my father had ever thought about us over the past twenty-six years. And what had he thought when Zinhle and I crossed his mind? Did he think we would grow up okay without him? Why had so many years passed without him reaching out? Why did it take me, not him, to arrange some kind of a reunion? Did he never think of trying to find out how we were doing?

I also needed to get to the bottom of what happened to my mom. Did he kill her? And if so, why? I had spent years haunted by what happened when I was five. I needed to find peace. But I wasn't prepared to be vindictive or seek revenge. As a teenager I had learnt that revenge was a poison that leads us astray. I wanted to make sure that Zinhle and I were agreed on this approach.

If he had killed my mom, I wanted him to share the details of how he had done it. Full disclosure was crucial. I didn't want any questions left unanswered. I needed closure, and so did my sister.

I spoke to my father on the phone several times before the

meeting. Each time, our conversation was longer. He wanted more details about me. I also asked him more questions. I wanted to get him to relax and trust that I wasn't going to harm him.

During one such conversation I asked what he'd been doing all these past years.

He told me he had worked as a bus driver until 1988. Then he had taken a payout from his employers and started his own business. He now owned five depots in two provinces, where he produced and sold cornmeal to local communities. In 1988 I had often gone hungry, I thought, while my father was supplying food to others. It hurt me.

I grew anxious as the meeting date drew closer. I kept phoning Zinhle to prepare her. I had started building a picture of what my father now looked like. The last time I had seen him, he had an unkempt beard. I wondered if he had changed his style. He might be quite frail now, I thought. I wondered what his first words might be as he saw us. Would it be a happy meeting with hugs and handshakes, or tense and awkward as we struggled to look at one another?

I also wondered how Zinhle would cope with seeing someone she still hadn't forgiven. I didn't want things to get out of hand. Would it be best to have just a one-off meeting in which I got a chance to tell him I had forgiven him? I also hoped to ask him all the questions that had troubled me. My hope was that Zinhle would get all the answers to her own questions, from which she would somehow find it in her heart to heal and forgive.

I hoped the meeting would give me a chance to cleanse myself of the demons that haunted me, especially thoughts of my mom's suffering as she died at the hand of my father. I wanted him to help me venture into the abyss, make sense of it all, and emerge a new person. A part of me hoped that the meeting would relieve me of the burden I'd been carrying all these years.

Even though I had forgiven my father, I still carried this weight on my shoulders. I still wept when I thought how proud Mom would have been to see me grow into a better person, one with an education, a professional job, a fairly comfortable life, and more than I had ever imagined possible. How wonderful for Mom to have seen all this, to have been a part of it, even to have benefited from it. Such fantasies still made me cry myself to sleep. As the weeks became days, I grew increasingly anxious.

From what I had managed to piece together about my father, I was optimistic that our meeting would be a success. He had done well for himself; he was wealthy now. I reasoned that he was now a man of dignity who cared about the feelings of others. He would sympathise and give me the information I needed. He would understand how important the meeting was for us, and help us to find closure. He would be open and forthcoming about what had happened those many years ago.

It seemed so long ago that the chain of events that had led to so much pain had been set in motion. Yet these events all came back in my final hours of preparation for the meeting, as fresh as if they had just happened. It just didn't make sense that a father who had been so devoted to me as a little boy could have done something so horrible.

Thirty-four

Zinhle and I had spent four weeks on the phone almost constantly, as I tried to prepare her for the meeting with our father. I myself was never going to be ready for the moment. But as her big brother, I felt obliged to help her through her emotions.

Two days before the scheduled meeting, I drove to Underberg to fetch Zinhle. We got Khulu and Gogo together to discuss our trip with them. For the first time ever, they started to talk about their own pain at losing our mom. "We kept hearing anouncements on the radio about a woman's body found in the Lions River area," said Khulu. "But it never occurred to us that it could be your mom."

"Are you sure you're going to be safe?" Gogo asked, concerned for our safety at meeting our mom's murderer. "I still don't trust your father."

"We'll be fine, Gogo," I assured her.

The two old ladies told us about the family's disappointment when my father walked out of the court and escaped punishment for his crime. Khulu said that my mom's youngest brother, Malan, was badly affected by Mom's death. "When your father walked free he was completely shattered," she said. By now Malan had himself passed on.

"Why didn't they tell us any of this all those years while we were growing up?" was Zinhle's first question as we drove to Durban.

"It must also have been very hard for them," was all I could manage to say.

As Zinhle and I waited together at Aunt Sibongile's house the next day, we received a call to say that my father was around the corner. Emotion suddenly surged through me, in powerful waves of sadness and pain. I began to cry. I was taken by surprise. I started to think of my mom. In my mind I told her I wasn't just doing this for the two of us, but for her too. I hoped she approved.

As I drove very slowly to the meeting venue, I asked Zinhle if she was okay. We agreed that we were hoping to hear the word "sorry" from our father's mouth.

The woman who had introduced us to his uncle had kindly offered her house for the meeting. As I pulled into the driveway, a red SUV also pulled up, a modest four-wheel-drive with a spare tyre perched at the rear. Just as Aunt Sibongile had described.

I felt unable to turn and look at my father as he got out of the car. Something in me didn't want to give him the hug I had thought about before the meeting. Something told me not to go over to offer a handshake. Spontaneously we turned our backs and disappeared into the house.

We had settled down before my father entered. He still had the same unkempt beard I remembered, but it was greying in places and the Afro was gone. He greeted us.

Then there was silence.

Sitting beside my sister, I didn't know where to begin. I guessed that my father couldn't find words either.

Then suddenly he was barking instructions. "Stand up," he told Zinhle. Abruptly he told her to sit down again. He did the same with me. I obliged. I understood that he wanted to see how tall we had grown. Elders did this with kids they hadn't seen for a couple of years, to compliment them on how they'd grown.

But we were no longer kids. It was awkward and patronising. And now my father began to chat as if we had known each other all along, about politics, business, and why he supported Robert Mugabe's twisted land reform programme in Zimbabwe.

I held my tongue. This wasn't what we came for, I thought. Why didn't he ask how we'd managed all these years and say sorry, if not for taking away our mom, then at least for abandoning us, for sentencing us to a life of suffering? I began to wonder whether our father grasped the gravity of what we had gone through.

Now he was talking about what he had achieved as a businessman, how well he had done. Had we managed to make enough money? Lots of it? How did we plan to make a fortune, then?

Zinhle replied that she just wanted a comfortable life.

"That's laziness!" he told her.

I was growing bored. The silences between us grew longer. Each time Zinhle or I tried to say what was on our minds, he interjected with more business talk, more politics.

It was becoming clear that he was in denial about the real reason for our meeting. He wanted to dominate the conversation, to scupper any chance of us asking him the real questions.

When my cell phone rang in the middle of the meeting, I answered and quickly excused myself. I went outside to chat, to get a break from this charade.

"How's the meeting going?" my friend asked. I told him I had nothing at all in common with my father.

Perhaps that was what I wanted: to have nothing in common with the person I'd grown up believing was a monster. I had sometimes told friends I was scared I might become like my father, that I might snap and do something I'd regret forever. Aware of this fear, I tried always to do the opposite: to be polite, to be humble.

When I walked back into the house, I knew that a golden opportunity had been lost. My father had failed to reconnect with us. If he had just said he was sorry, I would have been freed of all my demons. I would have breathed a sigh of relief, probably given him a hug and told him I would work on learning to love him as a father. Then I would have pleaded with Zinhle to forgive, to let go of the pain for her own sake.

Of the two of us, Zinhle had been picked on more often as a child. I could still sense her suffering despite her constant laughter. I heard oppression in the tone of her speech, felt her anger and pain when she shared it with me over the phone. I heard her sobs, and still cried with her.

It was the bond that had kept us together, that had made us who we were. Even when we laughed together, we never forgot what we'd gone through. We can never forget. Yet here we were, reaching out to our father, and he was doing his best to avoid what we had come to the meeting for.

I refused to concede defeat. I called my father aside and asked if he and I could meet again the next day. He agreed. I left feeling optimistic.

Zinhle told me I shouldn't have dragged her to the meeting. I told her I was sorry, but that I would still make our father see the light.

I felt drained as I got into bed. I lay awake thinking of ways to get my father to apologise, of words to make him realise how important this apology was. If he would just say so on the phone to Zinhle it would make her feel better, and help convince her that the trip to Durban had been worth it.

The next day my father phoned to say he would be ten minutes late for our meeting. I waited outside the boat shop where we'd agreed to meet. He had a newfound interest in commercial fishing, and was thinking of buying a fishing boat. He had grown tired of milling, and wanted something fresh and more stimulating. I hoped his fresh start would include facing the past and moving on with a clean conscience.

My father was eloquent and self-assured, just as I had been told. As we stood together outside the boat shop, I recognised that we had more in common than I had been willing to admit. He was adventurous; he didn't accept boundaries. For a black South African of his age, commercial fishing would normally have seemed out of the question. Yet, to my astonishment, he told me he loved water, loved swimming. He had decided to use water to make himself even richer.

I thought about my own adventurousness. I played sports that many considered unconventional, even pretentious, for a person of my skin colour. I liked kayaking, ice skating, ten-pin bowling and golf. Like my father, I didn't let boundaries stop me from doing what I wanted. I stepped right over obstacles when I had a goal.

My father walked proudly outside the fence, looking at the boats on display. It was a Sunday, and the shop was closed, but we examined each one through the fence, trying to figure out what size vehicle would be required to tow it. We discussed fish finders, motors and the hazards of fishing. I went along with his conversation. I was in no hurry. I wanted him to feel at ease before I tried to engage him on more serious matters.

When I eventually tired, I suggested we drive the short distance to Durban harbour, park next to the boats there and talk. He obliged.

It was windy at the harbour. I jumped into the passenger seat of his car. Gazing at the boats in front of us, I told him that being in his car reminded me of when I was a little boy, of when he used to put me on his lap and let me hold the steering wheel. He smiled.

"Did you have any idea where we were, these past twenty-six years?" I ventured. "Did you ever wonder how Zinhle and I were surviving?"

"I knew you'd eventually come looking for me," he said, evading my question.

"How did you know? Surely you couldn't have known that."

"I didn't hide from you, son."

"We were just kids, father. I'm sure you realised that the only way we could have reunited with you was if you made an effort to find us."

"I'm telling you, I didn't hide from you."

"But you knew where Zinhle and I were. There were only two places we could have been, in Bulwer with Dala, or in Underberg with Mom's extended family."

"Your mom's family knew all along where I was."

"Come on, father. They had lost their daughter. They blamed her death on you. Surely you didn't expect them to come looking for you."

"It wasn't by my hand that your mother passed away."

"Father, have you any idea how we suffered?"

"Listen, son. Your mother's family is the reason I stayed away."

"Really?"

"Your mother's uncle knows the whole truth."

"Well, he died in 1989, father. So there's no way I can find out from him. You'll have to tell me, since he's no longer able to speak."

Again he changed the subject, and avoided talking about my mom. Every time I mentioned her, he simply brushed off the matter.

Almost an hour had passed and I felt I'd achieved nothing. I'd let my sister down. I told my father that Zinhle and I needed to sit down with him and talk about the past, that this was important so that the two of us could move on with our lives.

"I don't want to go back to the past. It won't help."

"It will help Zinhle and I find closure."

The more I tried to reason with him, the more adamant he was that it was unnecessary.

"Are you scared to talk about Mom?"

"No. I just don't feel you're ready to talk about such things."

"How so?" I asked.

"You need to have your own family and your own house in the rural area to be ready for such things. You need to be a man."

"A man? I don't want to try to ask you the meaning of such a word. I just want you to understand the reason I decided to approach you in the first place. I wanted to tell you that I forgive you for taking my mom's life. I forgive you for abandoning us to suffer without parents and a proper upbringing." I paused. "I was also hoping you would say sorry."

He was quiet for a while. I hoped my words had got through to him. That he would stop avoiding the subject and apologise.

"Son, I've already told you that it was not by my hand that your mom passed away."

"Are you haunted by what you did in 1982?"

"I have no reason to be haunted."

"I'm not asking you to tell me what happened. I already know. I just wanted to let you know that I've forgiven you, and to hear you say you're sorry."

"I don't see why I should apologise. I didn't do anything."

"Okay. If you didn't kill Mom, you should at least be sorry you abandoned us."

"No. I have nothing to apologise for. I think your mom's family has told you lies, because they realise that you're successful. They're poor, and they want you to support them financially. That's why they tell you these lies."

It was clear that I was wasting my time. Still, I refused to admit defeat. Was he too arrogant or too scared to admit what he'd done? I had already assured him that all was forgiven from my side. Why was the truth so difficult to face?

"You know, father, I've used your name for over ten years. I can't continue to do so if you don't at least pick up the phone and apologise to Mom's family. Can you do that for me?"

He looked at me in silence.

"I grew up not knowing who I was. I grew up using your surname, and yet I felt no connection to it. I need you to help me connect with who I am. All you have to do is to apologise to Mom's family. They are Catholic and God-fearing people. They will forgive you."

"I will not apologise to those lowlifes. I don't care what surname you use. But I won't humiliate myself by apologising to those people."

"Father, I'll pretend I didn't hear what you just said. I'll give you time to think about it. As I said, it's important to me that you apologise to them. That way, they can accept me using your surname. Right now, they don't even know what to call me. I don't know what to call myself. If it's difficult for you to talk about what you did to my mom and say you're sorry, at least free me. Let me know and accept who I am."

"Son, you'll have to excuse me. I'm due to meet a friend on the South Coast."

I was frustrated and confused. I didn't know where I was. I was going to return to Johannesburg later that day. My father was to return to wherever he stayed. We would be hundreds of kilometres apart. Arranging another meeting would be a logistical nightmare. That's if there was ever going to be another meeting.

I had to admit that this was going to be a process. It was naïve to have hoped for a one-off meeting; to try to resolve twenty-six years over a weekend. But I needed time to convince myself that it was worth trying again in future, that my father was worth spending time on. I hoped he would eventually talk about the issues that mattered to us.

Yet it occurred to me that my sister and I might have to be satisfied with merely having met our father, though a part of me was beginning to regret meeting him. Still, at least I'd had a chance to tell him that I forgave him. But it broke my heart that Zinhle might never hear him say sorry, or get to ask about Mom.

I decided it wasn't worth pressing for information he was clearly uncomfortable about. I would ask him when he was ready, if he ever was. Like many who do terrible things, he would probably save the details for his deathbed.

To Zinhle, Mom was little more than a fantasy. All she knew of Mom was what the photos showed and what she'd been told, mostly about her tragic end. But it wasn't enough. My father could have described her best. But he refused to recall her for us, to let us relive a few moments with our mother.

Thirty-five

After the meeting with my father, my cell phone began ringing incessantly. My half-brothers and half-sister called to tell me how glad they were that Zinhle and I were back in their lives. I had heard from one of my aunts that I'd spent some time in rural Ladysmith staying with my father's first wife and my older siblings. The older siblings remembered me from then, though I barely remembered them. Those who were younger than me had heard endless stories about us, and were happy they would finally get to meet us.

I didn't share their happiness. I was confused. Should I establish a relationship with these siblings, or just get on with my life? My father's withholding didn't make it easy. I wasn't sure I wanted any further contact with him or any of his relations. When they called I was cold and non-committal. It wasn't out of arrogance, but confusion.

The eldest, Sindi, couldn't stop calling. She lived barely twenty minutes away in Johannesburg and wanted to meet right away. On the phone, Sindi told me about the times we'd shared together as kids; about a birthday we once celebrated, and about photos of us smiling as we cut the cake. I couldn't remember any of it. I apologised for sounding dumb. She understood.

Sindi told me that our family photos had been destroyed when her mother's house burnt down two years earlier. But she still had a picture of me that she'd kept all these years, even though she knew there was little chance we'd ever meet again. She was very keen to show it to me. And she wanted to tell me about my father.

195

I was curious. I thought I could probably learn some important information from her. Eventually I agreed to meet her at her house in Tembisa, a township outside Johannesburg. But each time we were due to meet, I got cold feet. A couple of times I postponed at the last minute. I could sense Sindi's frustration building. But things were moving too fast for me. I could hardly make sense of it all.

One Thursday afternoon I mustered the courage to call her and tell her I was coming. I tried to build a mental image of her, and pictured a beautiful, light-skinned lady in her thirties, a bit like Zinhle.

That was what I was expecting as she and her fiancé were on their way to pick me up near Tembisa Hospital. From our phone calls I knew she spoke a very deep colloquial Zulu.

A small white truck pulled up next to my car. I had told them how to recognise my car, so it was easy for Sindi to spot me. As she emerged I tried to match her to my mental picture. She was slightly darker, and well built with a beautiful smile. We shared a polite embrace. Then I greeted her fiancé, who was still behind the wheel of the truck.

Back at her house, a short, fit-looking lad welcomed us. He introduced himself as my half-brother Siya, and couldn't hide his delight at seeing me. I gave him a firm handshake and we bumped shoulders the way guy friends greet one another. I felt an instant connection with him.

The three of us wasted no time. We started talking. They told me they'd lost hope of ever seeing me and Zinhle again. Siya said several people had phoned him recently one morning to say that the Zulu newspaper, *Isolezwe*, had a picture of his father and a strange man on its front page. The newspaper had discovered through an aquaintance of mine who worked for them that I had found my father, and photographed our second meeting at the harbour. Siya thought his friends were joking, but after several calls he decided to buy the paper, and almost burst into tears when he saw me in the picture.

I discovered that Siya was just three months older than me. Like me, he didn't remember our time together in rural Ladysmith. But that didn't matter; he was thrilled that his long-lost brother had reappeared.

They wanted my impressions of my father. "He's very stubborn," I replied. They burst out laughing and said it was a perfect description. They knew him well and would tell me all about him. But first they wanted to hear my story.

I briefly related a few of the horrors and difficulties of my upbringing. To my astonishment, they didn't seem shocked. I was close to tears by the time I finished my story.

"You had it better," said Sindi.

"How can you say that?" I was hurt. "You don't know the pain my sister and I went through. That's just a fraction of what we endured."

Still, they seemed unfazed. They told me they envied the car I drove and were proud of the level of education I had attained. "If you'd been raised anywhere near our father, you'd never have gone to university. You'd only be driving that car in your dreams. He didn't see the value of sending any of us to university. He thought it would brainwash us into working for white people. That's something he resents."

"That's very shortsighted of him," I replied. "Being educated gives you a better chance of choosing what to do with your life. You can choose not to work for anyone, or you can use work as a stepping-stone to set up your own business. I have nothing against working."

As the eldest of all my father's children, Sindi started describing their childhood. "Our father never looked after us," she told me. "As kids, we dreamt of being taken shopping. My mother eked out a living selling cookies. She raised us with the help of our grandmother. Things only got better when my mother started rearing chickens and selling eggs. Years later she got a sawing business going.

"My father came home from Durban only once a year, in December. Later, he came home every six months. Then every three months. Then he started showing up every month."

"That must have been an improvement," I remarked.

Sindi shook her head. "We used to run and hide whenever he came home. He beat us for almost anything. When we came out of hiding, he sometimes gave us a bit of cash and sent us to buy something in a nearby shop. When we got home, all the doors would be locked. My mother would be screaming at the top of her voice as he beat her brutally. The neighbours would bang on the doors to get him to stop. Sometimes they broke down the doors to save her from being killed.

"My mother was just a punching bag to him. And he constantly insulted her. He still calls her names even now. His latest word is slut."

I wondered how any woman could possibly put up with such treatment. It reminded me of the time my father beat my mom with a sjambok. Beating women must have been his habit.

"He learnt it from his parents," Sindi told me. "His father used to beat his mother."

"That doesn't justify it," I replied. "As an adult, I'm sure he knew it was wrong."

"Yes," she said, "but he was also beaten and abused as a kid."

It sounded as if she was excusing our father's behaviour. I told her I disagreed. "I was also abused and beaten while I was growing up. That's no excuse to beat one's wife and kids."

To this day I read and know about men who beat their girlfriends and wives. I know of men who find it taboo to put their kids on their lap, play with them or show them any affection. I know of parents who dismiss their kids as nothing more than a sideshow to their own lives. The kids are always sharply dismissed to play outside or go sit with other kids. They get a backhander for the most minor mistake. Having had this happen to him, and having witnessed his own mother treated like trash, my father should have known better as an adult.

As my father came home more often, they said, he treated them like slaves. "He needed manpower to grow mealies for his milling business. Our days started in the fields in the early hours of the morning. After school he would pick us up in his truck to do more manual labour in the mealie fields."

Sindi took out a photo album, and showed me pictures of them as kids. In one they were standing next to a white truck on the edge of a field. The mealies in the photo were knee high. I assumed they were doing the backbreaking job of weeding when the photo was taken.

They told me they sometimes hid until my father went off to visit friends. "We did whatever we could to avoid any confrontation that would result in a beating."

Siya showed me the scar on his head. He was close to tears as he spoke. They had both been beaten until they were hospitalised, he said. "Even now my father and I come close to blows when we see each another. I finally got tired of his bullying, and decided to talk back when he tried it. I feel he hates me the most of all his children."

"A few years ago he pulled a gun on us," he told me. "We'd fixed a motorbike for a friend. But our father told us he didn't want the bike on his property. He thought we'd stolen it. I explained that we were fixing it to make money, but he didn't care. So we worked on it at a neighbour's place. We did a test drive after fixing it and ran into my father on the main road. He chased us in his SUV. I was scared he would kill us, or that we'd lose control at the speed we were doing to escape. He eventually ran us off the road and pulled a gun when we tried to run away."

Sindi told him that talking back to my father wouldn't get him anywhere. I thought about how I would have felt if I'd kept seeing my mom abused. I knew what it was like to get up in the early hours to drive cattle to the pastures. But it was nothing compared to what my Sindi and Siya were telling me. Their stories sounded horrific. I pictured the frosty winter mornings they had endured and the fear they must have experienced.

Perhaps my upbringing *had* been better than theirs. Perhaps it was better to have endured my hardships knowing that I didn't have parents. To have such a father must have felt like a curse. Their stories humbled me. They made me even more determined to pursue the journey I had begun, to discover who I was and find closure.

The more we talked, the more at ease I felt with them. As we shared and connected, I realised that my fears about meeting them had been misplaced. This wasn't a step too far. I was going to stay in touch with them. I was going to visit them and accept them as they had accepted me. As family.

I asked them how my father had made his money. "Our mother started it all," my sister said. "She'd seen the yields from her egg and sewing businesses. She decided to expand the business and get capital from the bank to buy milling machinery. But our parents are married in community of property, so they both had to sign for the funding at the bank. At that time my father had decided to take a financial package from work. He invested some of it in the milling business, and then took it over.

"All of us in the family had put our shoulders to the wheel to make the new venture succeed, but my father showed up only to demand the financial gains. When the family decided to open other milling depots and expand into another province, my father still demanded almost all the money they generated.

"I tried to convince my mother to open other bank accounts to stash the money away from my father. But she's a loyal, old-fashioned wife. She thought that would be stealing from her husband. To this day, our siblings do all the work, and my father demands all the profit. He uses it to feed his love of new cars and new women."

Our father was now fifty-eight, they said, but his appetite for women wasn't showing signs of slowing down. If anything, it was growing, my sister smiled. "I'll tell you how we found out about his second wife." I suspected her smile was her way of coping with the horror.

"My parents lived separately. Each time my father came home, he made my mother wash his car. One day she discovered a piece of paper in his car listing the gifts to be exchanged with a prospective wife. My mother knew his penchant for women, but she couldn't believe her eyes. When she told me our father might be taking a second wife, we decided not to say anything. It would only have given him another excuse to beat her. ·

"After a while our brother, who ran the milling depots in the

Eastern Cape, cut his arm while working. We were worried about the state of the hospitals in that province, so we brought him to be treated in Durban. My father was the closest family member to the depot, so we phoned to ask him to fetch my brother.

"On the phone we could hear people celebrating in the background. They were ululating. We tried several times, but he switched off his phone. Days earlier my father had demanded twenty-seven thousand rand from my mother.

"We realised it was probably to buy the gifts for his new wife. The celebration we heard on the phone was the exchange of the gifts. Later we discovered he'd taken a couple of trusted cousins and their wives to the ceremony."

"How did you find out he was married?" I asked.

"My father always gets caught. He left an envelope lying around the house some time later. Eventually my mother got curious and opened it. It contained an invitation to his wedding. Again, we decided not to confront him.

"Weeks later, he came home, and asked my mother to go with him to the local department of Home Affairs. There he asked an official to check if he and my mother were legally married. When they confirmed this, he told Home Affairs he wanted a divorce."

"But that's crazy!" I said. "How can you divorce someone over the counter?"

"They told him the procedure to follow. But my father just stormed out of Home Affairs, and left my mother standing there. He was desperate to get divorced so he could marry the younger wife. We met her recently. She asked me how many children my father had. She almost fainted when I told her there were eleven of us, including you and Zinhle.

"His new wife said that when she met our father, he told her he was from Swaziland. He said he had left there years earlier. He convinced her that he wanted to settle down with someone here in South Africa. He never mentioned any of his children."

Listening to these stories made me feel numb. It was just a week since I'd met my father. I had been relieved to discover that he was wealthy and more than capable of taking care of himself, and needed no financial help from me. But there was nothing good about him, I was beginning to learn. He was flawed beyond redemption.

Despite all the disappointment, I decided it was best to forgive him. I still hoped he would eventually say sorry. But my siblings shook their heads. I was expecting the impossible. They too wanted apologies from him. But they knew it would never happen.

I was shocked that they had never once seen him smile at them. On a lighter note, they advised me that if I ever wanted to buy him a gift, I needn't spend much. They suggested pliers to fix the farm fences, or a knobkerrie to sort out his enemies.

My father's first wife called during this meeting with my siblings. She sounded incredibly happy to talk to me. She also had advice for me. "Just forgive your father," she said, "and then move on with your life." She then invited me to Sindi's wedding to be held a few weeks later. Our conversation was very brief, but for a person who had endured so much abuse, she sounded remarkably self-assured. She seemed to have dealt with it very well, as if she had managed to forgive my father and find a way to be herself again.

I wanted to meet my stepmother. I felt that talking to her would help me with my own issues with my father. Perhaps she could also help Zinhle to forgive and move on. Although it didn't sound like a good idea at first, I decided to honour her invitation to Sindi's wedding.

When I got up to leave, Sindi warned me to get used to hearing grim stories about my father.

"Every family member has a story to tell," she said. "And none of them are happy ones, I'm afraid."

Thirty-six

I wasn't sure how to get my father to talk about the past. I had grown up being told that he was a monster. Now my siblings' stories of his savage treatment of his wife and children were like a sequel to a horror movie.

For weeks afterwards, I didn't call my father. I couldn't. I began to suspect that his eloquence was a facade, and that behind it lay a deep deceit and a desire to manipulate us to overlook the past. He wanted us to move on without him shouldering any responsibility. He wanted us to deal with the past and the pain all by ourselves. At times I felt deeply angry. But I still felt it best to forgive him. I felt that my purpose was to finally define myself.

My next date was Sindi's wedding. It wasn't the wedding itself I was interested in, but the chance to meet my father's first wife. I left Johannesburg for Ladysmith with mixed emotions that Saturday morning. I was late for the ceremony and sped along the motorway. My father had phoned me the previous day. "Just ask for the Nzimande homestead when you arrive at the village," he'd said. "Everyone knows me. You can't miss it."

Three hours later I arrived at a large village. I took him at his word and started asking people: schoolchildren, women coming from meetings, guys loitering around. Nobody knew the Nzimande homestead. No one knew of a wedding. But most had seen a convoy of cars going in a certain direction.

I drove endlessly over potholes and dirt roads. A young boy finally pointed to a house at the foot of a hill. He didn't know of the

Nzimande homestead or a wedding, but that was where the convoy had headed. At a distance I saw a great number of parked cars. I sped towards the home. But as I got closer, it started to feel wrong.

For a wedding, the gathering was awfully sombre and quiet. There didn't seem to be much movement. The only sign of activity was a circle of people all focused toward the centre. Some were bent over, hard at work. I thought they were slaughtering a beast. As I got closer I realised they were lowering a coffin into a grave. Embarrassed, I made a U-turn and sped off, leaving the mourners wondering what this Johannesburg car was doing disrespecting such a serious occasion.

If I were superstitious, I would have taken this as bad luck, a sign that I shouldn't have made the trip in the first place. But I laughed off the thought. It struck me that I was a fool to have believed my father's ranting about his fame in the village.

I phoned Siya for proper directions. He was thrilled that I had come, and instead of giving me directions that might further confuse me, he left the wedding to meet me.

When we reached the hall together, he introduced me to many long-lost relatives who were visibly happy to see me: aunts, uncles and many more Nzimandes. Many had stories about me as a kid, though I couldn't remember any of them. An uncle told me I used to cry and follow him when he left for school as a teenager. They were disappointed that I remembered nothing.

After the small talk, my half-brother ushered me to a seat he had saved for me next to my father. The look on my father's face suggested he hadn't expected me to come.

I was keen to meet my father's first wife. But she wasn't among the people at the wedding ceremony. I decided not to ask why. I assumed she was at home putting the final touches to the wedding feast. The ceremony finished, and later we went to the family home, where I was introduced to more family, mostly women who had stayed behind to cook and prepare to feed the guests.

One of the women I was introduced to didn't say hello like the rest, but just grabbed me in a hug and held me for what seemed like forever, tearfully thanking God and the ancestors that her son was back. I was overwhelmed and somewhat embarrassed. Here was this beautiful old lady that I didn't even know showing me so much love. It wasn't hard to figure out who she was.

After enjoying the Zulu dancing and feasting on the abundant food, my father and I sat and chatted as we watched the guests. Young men queued at a trailer tank filled with beer. Most were armed with glasses, but a few had larger plastic containers.

My father complained bitterly about the teenagers joining the queue. He wondered aloud why a trailer tank had been brought in for such a backward lot. Such things were for civilised people, he said. He wished he had bought *isiqatha*, a traditional beer allegedly made of ingredients such as rotten bread and battery powder. He reckoned this concoction would have got the people drunk much faster. Then they could be dragged away before they became a nuisance.

Eventually my father had had enough. He ordered the tank to be closed, to the disappointment of those enjoying the cold beer. He ordered his relatives to haul buckets of Zulu beer and serve it instead. But the guests still had their sights set on the tank.

The night took flight, and guests started to disappear. I finally got an opportunity to speak to my stepmother. "*Ubaba wakho uyize*," she said. "Your father is good for nothing." She told me that he had never looked after her or any of their kids. But our conversation was brief. "We need a lot of time to talk, my son. Stories about this family never end." She then disappeared to do more chores.

I was disappointed. I sensed there was a lot she wanted to tell me. But she wasn't comfortable to talk. We could hear my father's voice speaking to friends and relatives around the fire. I was impatient, but this was not the time for a lengthy conversation with my stepmother.

The next day, the family introduced me to my father's second wife. She had a little girl of about two years old, who was introduced as my half-sister. I managed a smile, but deep down I wondered if they were joking. I was over thirty, so it was strange to be told that a girl so tiny was my half-sister.

The second day of the wedding was spent at the groom's home, with more feasting, more Zulu dancing and another tank of beer, while my father cursed at the men he thought too uncivilised for such a treat.

After two days with my father's family, I got ready to leave. My stepmother gathered all my half-brothers around. She made us all kneel and started a religious song. When the singing was over, she thanked the Lord that I had finally returned. She prayed for my safe return to Johannesburg and asked the Lord to bless me. "I pray for a big house for my son, and a good wife who will worship him."

Her prayer was so indulgent towards me that I fought back tears. Then she sent me on my way with a big chunk of meat, freshly baked cookies and fizzy drinks. She paid no attention when I protested that she leave some food for her family. She smiled and told me she would call me when it was a good time to talk.

I reached the N3 freeway as the sun sank towards the mountains, still thinking about her prayer. A wife to worship me, she had said. Had she simply accepted all my father's abuse because she worshipped him? Perhaps she hadn't done enough to challenge him. I would find out in time. I put my foot on the accelerator as the mountains swallowed the remains of the sun.

Over the next three months my father's wife called regularly. But she said nothing about being ready to talk to me. I decided to be patient. My father also phoned a couple of times for a brief chat. During one of his calls he offered me some advice.

"No woman in this world is clever," he said. "Women are shrewd, but never clever."

What was his point? I nearly asked him, but he kept on talking. "Never share your plans with a woman, no matter how much you love her. Never trust them."

His words left me confused. Had he really said that? What the hell was it all about?

Through his phone calls I started to learn the kind of person my father was, especially towards women. He often berated them. I started to think he was a misogynist. His hatred was driven by power: he liked to have a string of women, yet he hated them, and regarded them as mere objects.

Thirty-seven

I was sitting beside my stepmother in a thatched hut in Ladysmith. She had invited me to visit her. Occasionally she fed wood into the fire. The smell of goat's meat was fresh. Its body was laid carefully on its skin to one side of the hut.

"I've suffered for so long with your father," she started. "I worked so hard for money, but your father took it all and left us without food. Sometimes my children begged me to hide some of it. But I was too honest. Your father's taken everything from me."

I rubbed my eyes. They were burning from the smoke.

"When he worked in Durban, he showed up only once a year, only to make babies with me. He never looked after any of them. I had to struggle with them on my own." I kept my eyes down, absorbing every word. She grew more animated and emotional. "I've endured a lot of heartache. Your father abused me very badly. Several times I woke up in hospital."

"Why didn't you leave?" I asked.

"I ran away several times," she said. "But each time my uncles and brothers sent me back to him. My mother's father was a priest and his family was very conservative. They were ashamed to have someone with children who wasn't married. It was taboo at that time. So I just kept praying for your father to change. I was young, and I thought he would eventually grow up and be a good husband. But he got worse. To this day, he still gives me so much trouble."

She told me the story of the twenty-seven thousand rand he had used to buy gifts for the relatives of his second wife. She started laughing as she told me how he came home later holding one hand behind his back. "It made me suspicious. I was keen to find out what he was hiding. When I saw the ring on his finger, I congratulated him on getting married. Before that he had never worn a wedding ring."

"How could you congratulate him?"

"What else could I do? I simply told him it would have been better if he'd told his family he was getting married. Nobody would have stopped him. I wouldn't have. Once your father makes up his mind about something, he goes ahead and does it. He doesn't care what I think."

"How did you feel about him marrying another woman?"

She giggled. "I didn't care. My love for him died long ago. I'm just here for your brothers and sisters. Your father has done so many horrible things that I can't worry about something as trivial as marrying someone else."

One of my half-brothers walked in carrying plates of food. My stepmother stopped to say grace. Afterwards she became serious.

"Twice your father almost killed me. Once he came home and demanded that I remove tons of corn I'd already put in the milling machine. I refused, and he flew into a rage. He grabbed me by the clothes and I fell to the ground. He began kicking me and yelling: 'Why don't you just die, woman?'

"I thought he was going to kill me that day. He had assaulted me many times, but not with such viciousness. One of your brothers saved me. He was a teenager at the time. I spent two weeks in hospital.

"The doctors advised me to open a case against your father. A few days after I was discharged from hospital, there was a family funeral. I had to travel with other family members in the car your father was driving. A police investigator called me while I was in the car, and asked to speak to your father. I told him to call your father's cell phone. I was in the back of the car and your father didn't hear the conversation. But his relatives did, and they must have told him.

"When I was back at my farm later that day, your father came down the driveway with a knobkerrie, yelling '*Wemfazi, usungibizele amaphoyisa*! You set the police on me, woman!' He grabbed my mother, who was old and frail and lived on my farm, threw her to the ground and told her she was no longer welcome. Then he came to me with his knobkerrie raised. I realised he was about to kill me. Somehow I managed to laugh. I covered my head and told him to go ahead and kill me. He froze. Then got into his car and sped off.

"Two days later, your brothers came to me with bad news, but they couldn't bring themselves to tell me. It turned out that my chicken farm had been burnt to the ground.

"I couldn't believe it. I thought of my contract to supply eggs to the petrol station shops. How was I going to look after the children who still depended on me? And my grandchildren? When I saw the gutted farmhouses, I realised how much I had lost. Corrugated iron, paint, brand new furniture, all the tools I'd bought with my grant from the Department of Agriculture, all the stuff from the neighbouring farm I was about to buy. It was all destroyed.

"The police told me someone had doused my property with petrol and set it alight. Your father was furious when he realised we'd laid a charge. He didn't want us to make statements to the police. He even tried to persuade me to say I'd torched my own farm. I know he did it. But I've reported him to the police countless times. They never arrest him because he's wealthy. He has money to throw around."

"Why would he burn your farm?" I asked.

"He doesn't want anyone else to succeed. He wants us all to work for him and beg him for money. Even buying and maintaining my egg farm was a struggle. He would hear nothing of it. He wanted me just to work full time in his milling business.

"The provincial Department of Agriculture had promised me a three-million-rand grant to improve my farm. After the fire, your father went to tell their officials that I'd misused the first instalment. He told them he didn't want any more of their money in his family. After that I never received another cent. It still pains me that I can't continue egg farming. And I wonder what happened to the rest of the money they were supposed to give me."

Thirty-eight

I was walking down a steep hill through the woods. The sun was out, and the air was dead still. It seemed more like a plantation than a natural forest. The trees were tall and in neat rows, but not too close together, allowing me to walk in a straight line. I was tired, and struggled to stay on my feet because of the steep gradient. Now and then I held onto the stems of the trees as I surged forward.

A voice was urging me on, asking me to say the names of the dead out loud. I obliged, although I didn't know whose names they were, or what they had to do with me. I kept walking for what seemed an eternity, overwhelmed with fatigue. I felt I was going to collapse.

Then the woods started to clear. I must be reaching the end of the forest, I thought, reaching my destiny. Finally I saw a clearing. As I paused in the shade of the last tree before braving the blazing sun, I stood transfixed. There before me was my mother.

Without hesitation, she pulled a black bag from the ground. It was covered with dust and soil that had accumulated over years. I took the bag and felt how heavy it was, as if filled with rusty coins. But before I could look inside, she said: "This is your luck. Come and fetch me."

I spent days poring over my strange dream. It was impossible, ridiculous. I hadn't dreamt of my mom since I was a teenager. But this dream was different: I remembered every detail vividly, every word she'd said. What did it mean? It seemed absurd that my mom would come to me in a dream and ask me to fetch her.

I knew about ancestors, but I didn't believe in them. Ancestor stories always seemed too far fetched. They were irrational. But this was different. My mom was asking me to fetch her. I couldn't just dismiss it as superstition. Still, I didn't dare tell anyone. They'd think I'd gone mad.

For days the dream dominated my thoughts. Had writing my life story made me dream of my mom? Was my subconscious playing with me? Maybe I was just being an idiot.

Three days later, Zinhle called. "Why didn't you give me your new cell phone number?" she scolded. She'd been trying get me for three days. "Mom came to me in a dream," she said.

"She wants us to fetch her, doesn't she?" I interjected.

"Yes."

It was unbelievable. She'd had almost the same dream on the same night.

"What should we do?" she asked. "I know how cynical you are about ancestors."

"I'll speak to one of Mom's half-brothers," I replied. "He'll probably know what to do."

"Let this be done in both our names. Mom wants us both to do it."

"I'll put together a budget. Even if you give me two hundred rand it'll be enough. Love you lots," I said.

"Love you too," she replied.

The mutual love and trust that had kept the two of us strong through our grim past was still there. I still loved Zinhle more than anything and knew she felt the same for me. Whenever we met we would share a hug and a kiss, just as Eugenia McNamara had modelled to us. Although it wasn't part of the culture we grew up in, and the community found it strange, we kept the habit going as a reminder of our eternal bond.

"How can I fetch my mom's spirit?" I asked Zozi, my mom's half-brother.

"*Ufuna ukulandwa yini usisi?* Does she want you to fetch her?"

"Yes." I told him about the dream my sister and I had.

"You need to buy a goat. I'll phone the elders for the details. We need to set a date."

At least I now had a starting point. But where was I going to find her spirit? I wondered. I didn't know where her remains were. Without that it would be impossible to conduct the ritual.

One Sunday morning a few days later, I got a call from Sindi. She said her mother was in Johannesburg and didn't want to leave without visiting me.

My stepmother came for lunch with one of her sons and a male relative. Afterwards she asked me to show her around the house. After roaming the yard, she sat down on the steps of the veranda. I sat down beside her and we chatted. I brought out my only picture of my mom. In it, she was sort of crouched and gently reaching for the grass, her right hand resting on her thigh, and her hair neatly platted. She was smiling into the camera. She looked beautiful.

My stepmother gazed at the picture for a while. Then she shook her head. I could see she was struggling with her emotions.

"Let me tell you how your mother and I met. I had three children then. My youngest was still a baby. Your father had invited me to come to Durban with the children. When we arrived at his house he was still at work. He had told me he'd leave the key under the mat.

"But it wasn't there, so I tried the door. It opened. Inside was a woman holding a baby. She was visibly startled. It was your mother and you. You looked the same age as the baby on my back. That was how we were introduced to one another. We both got the shock of our lives. I didn't know about you and your mother, and she didn't know about me and my children. She burst into tears when she realised she was a mistress. Your father and I were married under customary law.

"In those days, whenever your father came home to Ladysmith, he would leave with a live sheep to throw a party in Durban. He had just left with a sheep a couple of days earlier. As I looked around, I could see there had just been a party. There was leftover meat in the kitchen, and half-drunk cool drinks were lying around. I realised he'd asked me to come so I would clean up after his party. I felt angry seeing my kids having to lick leftovers from dirty plates.

"When he came back from work later that evening, I asked why he'd invited us for the leftovers instead of the actual party. In answer, he hit me so hard over the head that I passed out."

My stepmother showed me the scar on her temple. "When I regained consciousness, your mom was nursing me. We became instant friends."

She had stayed on in Durban with relatives before returning to Ladysmith. A couple of weeks later she decided to move to Durban. She rented a small house in the same township, and earned money sewing clothes.

"For months I sat sewing on my veranda. Across the valley I could see the township depot where your father left his bus when he got off work. But he rarely came to see me.

"Once he found me visiting your mother. He asked me to stay the night so both of us could share his bed with him, one on each side. When we refused, he threatened to beat us. Your mother was stronger than me. When he wanted to beat us, she told him to *voetsek*. Bugger off."

"Why do you think he killed her?" I asked.

"I think it was because she challenged him. I survived all these years because I was a doormat. I let him to do anything he wanted. I was scared of him. But your mother told him off. He wasn't used to people saying no to him, especially a woman. So he killed her. The last time I saw her, she had come to get her belongings. She said she was fed up with him, and that he would never stop abusing me. She was right."

My stepmother was in Ladysmith, heavily pregnant with her fourth child, when my mom died. "Many nights before I found out that your mother had passed away, she came to me in my dreams. She seemed to be telling me that she had been beaten to death. The dreams alarmed me, so I wrote her a letter.

"A few days after I posted it, I got a letter from your father saying he was in prison, under arrest for killing your mother. Then I understood what the dreams had meant. I had no doubt that he'd killed her. Instead of visiting him in prison as he asked, I decided to pack my bags and run away from him. But my family sent me back again, as always."

I told my stepmother about the dream Zinhle and I had had, and of my plans to go to the police station in Lions River to find the records of my mom's death. I wanted to see the map and pictures of the crime scene. It was my only way to find where my mom's body had been dumped.

"No," my stepmother said, appalled. "It's not right for you to see those records. Please come to Ladysmith. Ask your father to point out the spot."

I had considered asking my father, but quickly dismissed the idea. I remembered how insensitive he had been about apologising to my mom's family. Why would he empathise with me? But eventually we agreed it was worth a try.

We had been chatting on the veranda for two hours. It seemed rude to leave the others alone inside, so I got up to go back in.

"Your father still won't leave me alone," she said.

"What do you mean?" I asked, sitting down again.

She stared at the ground for a while. "He comes to my farm in the early hours of the morning. He wakes me up, and tells me to go and work in one of my farmhouses. When we get there he pulls out a gun and starts giving me trouble. Then he spits in my face and calls me a slut."

I looked at my stepmother. The hairs protruding from her *doek* were turning grey. I was speechless. I started to tremble. "You've been together more than thirty years, and all this time he's never let up?" She nodded. I tried to figure out what kind of trouble she meant. I looked up to the sky with tears in my eyes. "Please, Lord," I whispered. "Don't let it be what I'm thinking."

She told me that the reason she was in Johannesburg was to speak to Sindi and me. She was tired of enduring abuse from my father. After the latest episode she wanted to come out into the open about her plight.

"I don't care if he kills me," she said. "It can't go on." She wanted our advice on what to do. As we walked into the house I kept praying that what I was thinking wasn't happening.

A couple of days later, Sindi invited me to a party at her house. People danced; others were so drunk they could barely stand. The music was loud and everyone was in high spirits, except for the two of us. She had quietly led me to a bedroom and closed the door to drown out the noise. She confirmed my worst fears about what my father was doing to her mother.

We wept together. Sindi no longer had mixed feelings towards my father, as she had when I first met her. She was adamant about what had to be done. We agreed that he had to be put in prison. She was prepared to go through with it. I assured her I would take the lead in finding help. I would find a women's organisation to help her mother. We agreed that we couldn't trust the police from rural Ladysmith. They had always failed her.

Sindi had something else to discuss. She said her ex-boyfriend had died after being shot several years earlier. She had been ready to testify in court until she saw pictures of his body. Then she had cracked. "For a long time afterwards, I wasn't myself," she said.

"Why are you telling me this?" I asked.

"My mother said you were planning to look at the records of your mother's death. Please don't. My father must show you. It's not right that you suffer for what he did." The tone in her voice changed when she mentioned her father. I could hear her resentment.

After that I had no more doubts about my feelings for my father. I wanted to be rid of him, of everything he represented. Including his name. I wanted nothing to do with him. It was time to disown him. I thought of the many times I had looked into his hauntingly deep eyes and thought, this is the man who snuffed out my mom's life. This is her murderer.

Learning of the abuse he was still meting out to his wife was too much. I was angry. I felt helpless. Here was a woman who had endured the worst possible abuse throughout her life, and yet succeeded against all odds. She had bought a farm and asked nothing more than a chance to make something of her life and raise her kids.

She had raised them entirely on her own. All my father needed to do was just acknowledge her efforts and leave her alone. But no. Even after so many years, she was still a punching bag, a "slut", nothing but an object against which to manifest his power, to vent his hate, to spit on. This made me seethe. I found it hard to imagine what drove my father to be the monster he was. Yet even as I trembled with revulsion and felt the tears burn my face, I was still adamant that forgiving him for what he had done to my mom was the right thing.

I had to take a stand, once and for all. It was time to carve out my own identity, to free myself from him and move on. Those years of recognising and using my father's surname were a mistake. It felt like such a betrayal that after taking my mom's life, he still had no respect for women. I didn't regret having met up with him again, but I wanted nothing more to do with him and all he represented.

Meantime, I searched the Internet for women's organisations and phoned my stepmother and Sindi to give them the contact numbers. To my dismay, my stepmother didn't sound keen to make my father face the consequenses of his actions. "I've thought about it. I think it's my responsibility to help you and your sister through your journey. I'll leave my problems to the Lord to solve," she said.

"You've already done enough for me," I protested. "Whatever is left to do, I'll be able to manage on my own. We need to do something about what you told me. Please use the numbers I gave you." But she was adamant. "I have prayed for you and your sister for so long. Your mother was my friend," she said simply, "and it's important to me to help you."

I longed to help my stepmother break free of her hardships, but I wasn't sure whether I had the strength to help her through while still continuing my own journey. I didn't want to get embroiled in my father's family problems, but what was happening to my stepmother troubled me deeply. I was amazed that despite the tragedy of her own life, she still wanted to help my sister and I find closure. It was selfless of her, but it made me uncomfortable.

Thirty-nine

A couple of days later I obtained an affidavit form from a police station to begin the process of changing the surname I'd used for over ten years. Symbolically, it wasn't the surname I was parting with, but my father. I was ridding myself of a monster.

For perhaps the first time in my life, I was going to say my surname with pride. I had no doubt about the power of its symbolism. I thought of that lifechanging moment on the bridge when I had almost ended my life. The day I had chosen to live. My new surname, Polela, was the very embodiment of the meaning of my life.

What remained now was to go to Ladysmith. I didn't know how I would find the strength. But I was going to sit down with my father, possibly for the last time. To look him in the eye and ask him to drive to Lions River, to point out where he had dumped Mom's body twenty-six years earlier.

It was his responsibility to do this. His own family had told me that he needed to own up. I hoped this would be my last interaction with him before we went our separate ways.

I wasn't looking forward to the conversation, or confrontation, whichever it would be. I imagined the different scenarios that might unfold. Would he tell me he didn't want to revisit the past, just as when I requested an apology from him? Would he keep denying the murder? He would probably blame someone else. He was good at pointing fingers at everyone but himself.

I wasn't optimistic. If he dismissed my request, I would go

to Howick Police Station. I had already packed Mom's death certificate and other documents in my luggage. I would show these to the police as proof that I was related to Mom. I hoped this would be enough to convince them to hand over the crime scene records. If I was lucky, maybe the police would even escort me to the spot.

I imagined facing the pictures of my mom's bloodied and lifeless body. Aunt Mathuthu who had seen them twenty-six years earlier told me they still haunted her to this day. How would I cope? I had no answer. I would just have to go with the flow. I felt almost robotic, drifting through what I felt was expected of me. I had lost all feeling. I was doing this for my mom. I wanted to find the spot and take her spirit back home. To put her soul to rest.

Forty

A couple of days before Christmas 2008 I set out for Ladysmith. The sun was edging towards the hills in the west. I took the N3 to KwaZulu-Natal, and felt the car responding as I stepped on the accelerator. I would spend the night in Ladysmith and meet my father early the next morning. That would allow enough time to proceed to the police station to view Mom's death records if he refused to help me.

My stepmother had phoned me earlier in the day, and asked if I could come over to her farm. It was already dark when I arrived. She burst into a religious song as I entered her farmhouse. I hummed along with her song, and then joined her in prayer.

After a drink and cookies, she led me to another building. "This is where I used to breed chickens before the farm was destroyed," she said. We sat down on a bench. She had a small plastic bag on her lap.

"Your father and mother loved taking pictures. They had a big album of them. When I found out that your mother had been murdered, I knew your father would destroy the album. So I stole it and all the photos while he was in custody. For years I prayed that some day you would show up. Some of the pictures got burnt in the fire. But after I visited you in Johannesburg, I remembered I'd hidden the pictures in two separate places. These are the ones that were saved." She handed me the plastic bag.

My hands trembled as I opened it and pulled out the first picture.

"That's your mom holding you. That was the day I walked into the house and met your mom for the first time."

The next one was of Zinhle sitting on the bed with a cool drink in the background. For a moment I was transported back in time to our brief fairy-tale life as a family, when we were showered with presents and an endless supply of snacks, peanuts and cool drinks.

There were lots more pictures of us as kids and of Mom smiling. She was beautiful, I thought each time I saw a picture of her. There were happy photos of my sister and I together, and pictures of Mom holding us. Us as a family. But then it all went wrong. Why did she have to leave us so suddenly?

I struggled to hold back the tears. I was embarrassed to weep in front of my stepmother. She didn't seem to pay attention, but she could see I was crying. She had told me so much about her abuse, but never once had she cried. In fact, she'd even smiled while relating her horrendous stories. She had endured so much pain she must have become numb to it. And here I was, a man, sobbing beside her.

"That's not my mom," I said, looking at a picture of a beautiful young woman in just panties and a bra.

"Ah," she said. "Your mother and I communicated by letter after we became friends. She sent this picture in one of her letters. She found it while cleaning your father's house. She said she knew he wasn't giving me any financial support, and she wanted to assure me that she wasn't getting any either. She said he was wasting all his income on this woman in this picture. But she didn't need to explain. I knew your father never cared about his children. *Imali wayeyidla nonondindwa.* He wasted his money on floozies."

We went through the last few pictures. "I hoped you'd show up one day. I kept these because I knew you'd need them. Take them. They belong to you, you and Zinhle."

I hoped my stepmother knew how much this meant to me. These weren't just pictures. These were my life, and my mom's life. They were our history. My thank-you to my stepmother felt so inadequate.

Zinhle and I had received no more love after our mom died. No one had hugged or kissed us or taken us on walks. There were no more birthday parties, and no one to take pictures of us as kids. The only time I remembered having my picture taken was with a group of boys at our first communion. But these weren't my own pictures; they belonged to the mothers of the other boys in the picture. It meant the world to me to sit with my stepmother and hold photos of myself, Zinhle and Mom. It was like holding a piece of the love I had lost twenty-six years ago.

In one picture I was sitting on my father's bike as it leaned against a wall. My stepmother's explanation resolved the longstanding mystery of why Zinhle was living with Mom and I with my father at the time when I had tried to give Zinhle my apple.

"Your mom was determined to get your father to pay maintenance for you two. But he never did. When she got fed up trying the courts, she went to his work one morning and dropped you off with his boss. This photo was taken by one of your father's friends at his workplace just after she dropped you off. Your mom told his boss she'd fetch you when your father started contributing to your upbringing. For a week your father tried to send you back to your mom. But eventually she had to give in without getting a cent of maintenance.

"Several times your father showed up in Ladysmith unannounced. He'd drop you off with me and roar off back to Durban. Usually you had only the clothes you were wearing. It happened whenever he had a fight with your mother. At that time I made my income from sewing, so I would hastily sew you some rather funny-looking clothes just to keep you covered and warm. If I had any money, I would go to town and buy you some cheap clothes. Do you remember coming here as a kid?"

"Barely," I replied. "I remember once arriving with my father in his truck. We got stuck crossing a river, and some men tried to push us out. I must have fallen asleep. I also remember my father and a relative in a kraal loading up a sheep the next morning. I suppose it must have been for one of his parties in Durban."

My stepmother smiled as she listened. I was getting used to that smile. It was always so fleeting, and she would look down shyly each time. Then it would disappear as she began to speak again.

She also liked to laugh. No matter how painful the story she was telling, she always found something amusing in it.

As we got to the end of the pictures, she drew my attention to a neatly folded letter. Judging by the sharpness of the folds, it had been untouched for years. That's a letter your mom wrote your father. I kept many of the letters she wrote me. But they got destroyed in the fire.

I opened the letter. Deep lines had formed where it had stayed folded, and parts started to tear. I held it gently to prevent it from tearing further. I felt like I was holding a part of my mom. For a moment I just sat there, staring at it. I could remember how it felt being a little boy. It was as if I could hear my mom talking to me. My stepmother just let me sit and stare. She must have thought I was reading it. I wasn't. I couldn't.

I needed to choose the right moment to read her letter. Part of me was scared I would lose control and break down uncontrollably. Another part of me was conscious of the reason I was here in Ladysmith. I was scared the letter might reveal things that would make me very angry with my father. I didn't want to compromise my meeting with him the next morning.

I carefully refolded the letter and returned it to the plastic bag. Two half-brothers walked in just then. My stepmother smiled at them and showed them the pictures. They'd clearly never seen them before.

"*Mama uyafihla bo!* Mom, you really can keep a secret!" one said.

So my stepmother had sat with these pictures for twenty-six years and never revealed them to anyone. She'd waited a lifetime to show them to me, keeping them for me and Zinhle. I marvelled at her patience. I felt immensely proud of her bravery. She had trusted all these years that we would eventually show up. All through that night, I thought of nothing else but Mom.

It was painful being so vividly reminded of her. Yet I also felt proud that I was making such progress in my quest to find the truth about her. About my past. I stared up at the corrugated iron above my head until fatigue finally allowed me to sleep.

It was almost six a.m. when I awoke. I washed hurriedly and prepared to meet my father. My stepmother asked three of my half-brothers to accompany me to our father's farm. One took the wheel of my car. Six-twenty a.m. The deejay on the radio announced a golden oldie he was about to play. The musician's name evaporated from my mind as soon as he had announced it.

I sat in the passenger seat, staring at the horizon. Grey clouds frowned over the lush mountainside. A dull day ahead, I thought. I sensed it wouldn't be a good day for me. I still wasn't myself. The pain of the previous night had gone, but I felt joyless, numb, robotic. I lacked certainty about what I was about to do. I didn't feel ready to look him in the eye and ask what I needed to. I was simply drifting.

Six twenty-four a.m. The deejay announced that the South African cricket team had just beaten the Aussies in the first test in Australia. It was cause for great celebration. But I stared at the horizon as if nothing had happened. Six twenty-eight. The Senegalese musician Akon was singing "I Wanna Wake Up". It was still playing as we pulled over at the gate to my father's farm. One of my brothers got out, opened the gate and walked over to the farmhouse. Moments later, he was on his way back, signalling that my father wasn't there.

I was relieved. I felt unprepared. "I'll stay another night," I announced. Clearly I needed a whole day to prepare for this. It occurred to me that I was now messing with my schedule. But rather that than meet my father while I was wavering.

I needed to relax, to summon my ability to feel again. I killed time watching mindless DVDs with my half-brothers: the *Incredible Hulk*, then *Iron Man*. By lunchtime we were watching *PS I Love You*. My emotions were slowly thawing. I was starting to feel again. I was no longer numb, drifting. I had managed to relax and gather the strength I needed to confront my father.

I began to sketch the conversation we would have the next morning. I pictured his reactions and contemplated his possible responses. It wouldn't be easy, I knew. The outcome wasn't promising. I was probably wasting my time. But I would do it, and my father could make his decision.

Forty-one

I set my clock for four thirty the next morning. Even before it rang, my stepmother was knocking at my door. She had brought me a basin of water so I could wash.

"You won't find your father if you don't get to his farm immediately," she warned.

Minutes later, my half-brothers Siya and Sne and I were on our way. This time I was driving. I didn't turn on the radio or look at the clouds. I guided my car quietly, thinking about what I was about to do. I was ready.

As we pulled over at the farm gate, one brother announced that my father's SUV was in the garage. He was here. I hesitated as my brother opened the gate.

"Aren't you going to bring the car in?" he asked. Reluctantly I drove in. My mind was sketching the worst-case scenario, that my father would be so enraged he would damage my car.

Don't be stupid, McIntosh, I told myself.

It took time for my father to open the door after I knocked. When he did, he was in his work clothes. He stepped out and put on a dull cowboy hat. This isn't going to pan out as planned, I thought. My father immediately confirmed my suspicion.

"Please get the battery out of the truck and put it in the tractor, then start it. I'm going to plough," he instructed.

This is going to be a long day, I thought as the tractor's growl drowned our whispered complaints.

The sun wasn't yet up, and it was cold. We took shelter in the garage, watching my father urge his tractor on. He drove the plough through the field from one end to the other. We sat there, discussing my father's bizarre technique for avoiding me. I noticed that the front bars of his SUV were dented and the front lights damaged.

"What happened to the car?" I asked.

"A neighbour's cow got through his fence every night, and he complained to him. When the cow kept getting in, he drove his SUV into it, and shoved it all the way back to its owner's yard. He told the neighbour he'd shoot it next time."

"He's crazy," I said. They laughed. Soon my father whistled for us to come over. But when we arrived, he just carried on ploughing. "So why did he call us?" I asked.

"His girlfriend is probably at the farmhouse. He wants her to sneak out without us noticing."

"Which girlfriend? Doesn't he have a new wife and a fiancée in Swaziland?"

"*Awuyazi intshebe wena*. You don't know the bearded one," they replied.

We had been there an hour already. I was getting anxious that I wasn't going to achieve anything. I was fed up watching my father go up and down in his tractor. I walked over and signalled him to stop. "I phoned you two days ago because I need to discuss something with you," I yelled, trying to compete with the noise of the tractor. "And I still have to fetch my sister Laurelle in Durban and get to Underberg."

He handed the tractor to one of my half-brothers, and walked with me to the garage. We sat down, and I wasted no time explaining my purpose.

"Mom needs me to fetch her from the spot when the police found her body in 1982." I deliberately used direct language, implying that it was an instruction from Mom. I knew how seriously my father took cultural superstitions. Then I described my dream to him, and told him that Zinhle had had a similar dream.

"How do you want me to help you?" he asked.

"Besides the police who found her, only you know the spot."

"It wasn't by my hand that your mom died."

I pretended not to hear, and kept hammering the message that this wasn't a choice. Mom wanted it. But he went on trying to derail me. "You're not ready for such things. You need to get married. You need a proper house in the rural areas where you can take your mom's spirit."

"I don't need a home in Pevensey," I countered. "I live in Johannesburg. Mom has her home to go to. It's still there, waiting for her."

"No. You need to be a man first. Only then will you be ready to fetch her."

I was getting frustrated. Anger welled up. I thought of getting into the car and driving off. A lump was forming in my throat. I wasn't going to win this one. I was wasting my time.

"You said all this when we met in Durban, remember? I told you I forgave you. I tried to get you to tell me about my mom. But you just told me I wasn't yet a man. Is this how you avoid speaking about her?"

"No, son, I'm speaking the truth."

"Father, I'm over thirty years old. If I'm not a man in your eyes, I never will be. I'm going to do what she expects, whether you help me or not. I hope you can live with your conscience."

"When do you want to do this?"

"On Saturday, two days after Christmas. I just need you to show me the spot and walk away. That's all I need from you."

"That's not how you do it. I'll have to guide you in this. You have to do it right. You're just a kid. I need to teach you how these things are done."

"Please don't call me a kid."

I had started to feel hopeful. "Let's walk around the farm," he said.

As we walked, he repeated his boasting about how many farms he had, and then gave me a long lecture on farming. "I can tell you're not the farming type. You're a city boy."

"I'm not a boy."

"There's money in farming, and you don't need to work years to get a pension. You can determine your wealth using the size of your farm, and the amount of your yield ..."

I was bored, so bored I kept looking towards my half-brothers. By now the field was ploughed. They grinned back at me. They'd heard it all before.

After an interminably drawn-out walk around the farm, we again settled down in the garage. I looked at my watch. It was now three and half hours since I'd arrived, and I'd achieved nothing. He had said all the same things when I asked him to apologise. He wasn't going to tell me anything until I got married. Did he seriously still see me as the boy he abandoned twenty-six years earlier? My thoughts were drifting, and my anger building. I stared at the ground.

"My landmark is a bridge," he said.

I was caught completely off guard. I looked up.

"Go on," I said, quickly recovering my senses.

"After your mom passed away, she gave me a lot of trouble."

"You mean she haunted you?"

"Yes. So I know the spot very well. I had to return there twice after her body was found. To perform rituals to get her to stop, you know."

"What kind of rituals? Please tell me."

"I went and slaughtered a goat on the spot in the early hours of the morning. I followed the instructions of a traditional healer. But I still had sleepless nights. Your mom went on haunting me. The next time, I took the traditional healer with me to lead the ritual. After that the haunting stopped."

"I understand. So will you show me the spot?"

"Yes, but I have one request. Please don't fetch her on the same day I show you the spot."

"Why not?"

He didn't answer. "You must bring *impepho*, a dried plant with a strong scent to burn on the day. It is used to communicate with ancestors. While it's burning, tell your mom over the scent and smoke to get ready to come with you. Tell her to prepare herself for the journey home. Then, return a day or two later to fetch her. That's how it's done."

"Please show me on Friday. I'll come back to fetch her the next day." We agreed. I shook his hand to thank him and walked a couple of metres away. "Thank you, Lord, thank you," I prayed.

I felt a sense of triumph as I drove to Durban and then on to Underberg. I was proud that I had managed to confront my father and succeed. Although it hurt, it was important to finally hear him admit that he *did* have something to do with my mom's death. His confession was indirect. He hadn't committed to anything except knowing the spot. But that was enough for me.

Forty-two

The days leading to the fetching of Mom's spirit were frantic with preparations. I found a big female goat and made frequent trips between the market town of Underberg and Pevensey village. My uncles helped me as I walked from shop to shop, buying the long list of items prepared by Zinhle and Uncle Eric's wife.

The day before Christmas, I finally had most of the requirements: crates of booze, cool drinks and plenty of food. I decided that the goat was too small for the number of guests expected, so we also bought a sheep. Although we had invited only relatives and friends, it was common for most of the village to come, even if they weren't invited.

I planned to give myself a well-earned break on Christmas Day. But at the last minute I went to church. I couldn't be sure my father would show up. I needed some extra help; I needed to pray. The service started at ten, and the choir sang song after song, long-forgotten hymns I used to sing as a kid before I began to boycott church. I hummed along.

In between I said the Lord's Prayer over and over. I asked Him to ensure that my father made the trip to Lions River the next day. While people queued for communion, I asked my cousin to step outside with me. We walked to the large graveyard behind the church building, and located the grave of my mother's brother, Uncle Malan. I paused there to pray and reflect.

The last time I'd seen him alive was when I threw a party before leaving for London. He died before I got back. Standing over the grave I remembered the two of us dancing together at that party. His wife blamed him for my total lack of rhythm. He got your genes, she used to tease him. I mumbled to him now that I was going to fetch his sister. Then we returned to the church entrance. The service was about to finish.

I phoned my father several times to confirm our arrangement. He assured me he would be there. But still I was apprehensive. What if he just switched off his cell phone and stayed home? I wished I had gone ahead with plan B, summoned the strength to lay my eyes on the dreaded pictures. Had I been braver, I wouldn't be reliant on him now. With every hour that passed, my anxiety grew.

But a stream of calls from my stepmother gave me hope. She kept assuring me that her husband would keep his promise. "Don't worry," she told me. "He's stubborn, but he knows he has to do this."

I wished it were that simple. In the short time I'd known my father, I'd learnt not to rely on him.

After sunset on Christmas Day, I visited my two sisters at the McNamaras. Zinhle told me she wanted to come with me to see where Mom's body had been dumped. I gave her a firm no. "I regretted bringing you to see our father. Do you know how bad I felt when it turned out such a disappointment?"

But Zinhle was adamant. She refused to back down. "She was my mom too, you know."

"What do you think?" I asked Laurelle, hoping she would back me up.

"I see her point. Zinhle's very sensitive," she said.

"Exactly. That's why she shouldn't come. I don't want her hurt. She's had enough hurt already."

But Laurelle didn't agree. "If Zinhle feels strongly that she needs to go, let her. It's her decision. In the end she's the one who will have to deal with her emotions."

I gave in.

Friday came quickly. I barely slept. I was to meet my father at a petrol station near Lions River. At first light I decided to phone him to confirm one last time. "Let's meet at noon," he said, telling me he was in the Eastern Cape. I calculated that it would take him roughly three hours to get from there to Lions River.

As the hands of the clock drifted closer towards journey time, I was suddenly struck by a wave of emotion. I found myself reviewing all that had happened over the six months since I'd met up with my father. It had already been such a journey. I felt exhausted thinking about it. And I felt overwhelmed by all the recent things I'd had to do. But I had to be strong. Everyone in the Shezi family was looking to me for guidance. They were drawing their strength from me. It felt like a huge responsibility.

Three uncles stood behind me as I lit the *impepho* in the thatched house to announce our journey to the ancestors. I was trembling, and overcome with helplessness. The words I spoke to the dead were interspersed with sobs. I let the tears roll down my cheeks unchecked; I had no strength to wipe them away.

"*Ungakhali mfana, sekuyalunga*. Don't cry, my boy," said one of my uncles. "Things are falling into place now."

When I finished speaking to the unseen, I walked quickly to the car. I heard the doors slam one by one, and drove off. No one spoke. Zinhle was beside me in the passenger seat. She stared into the distance. I knew she was hurting. She was trying hard to be strong. I wished I could read her mind, reach out to her and tell her it would all be okay.

I was reminded of the hard times we had shared as kids. The terrifying abuse meted out to her. She had hardly showed any emotion back then, barely cried. She wasn't about to change now. No matter how hard she was hurting, Zinhle would not share her pain with anyone. I had tried one last time to prevent her from coming on this journey. I didn't think she was strong enough. But it was me who was struggling to cope. And we hadn't even reached the spot yet.

As we got closer to Lions River, I phoned a half-brother who was with my father in the Eastern Cape. He told me he had left about an hour earlier. That would make my father two hours late. So we decided to stop in Pietermaritzburg for lunch. After a browse through some shops at the Midlands Mall and a big lunch, we drove through fog to Lions River.

My father was already waiting outside the petrol station near Mpophomeni. I stopped and went over to him. We exchanged greetings.

"*Ngilandeleni*," he said, inviting me to follow him in my car.

My uncles Vusi and Zozi were surprised that he had come alone. "Isn't he worried we might attack him?"

"He probably has a gun with him," I said. "But I've assured him that we're a God-fearing family, and not out for revenge."

My father soon put on his hazard lights and pulled off the road. I got out of the car and went over. He rolled down his window.

"This is the place," he said. "But let's drive further up, just to be sure." We were now driving up through a forest plantation. After a couple of minutes, my father put on his hazards again and made a U-turn. I followed. As we reached the edge of the forest, he made another U-turn and stopped at the first spot.

I got out and went over to him. My uncles and Zinhle stayed in the car. "I'm sure that's the spot, over there," he said, pointing to a clearing near a small stream. He took off his hat, and walked with bowed head down an embankment to where the stream flowed under a bridge.

I surveyed the place. Above us was the plantation nearly half a kilometre away. The forest reminded me of the dream I'd had. Could these be the woods I walked through in my dream?

There were houses nearby. Was this really a place where someone would consider concealing a body? It wasn't what I had pictured. I had thought of trees and tall grass. In my dream, Mom had been resting under a tree near a clearing. Here there were only a few young trees just across the stream. Perhaps the intervening years had wiped the details from my father's memory. The plantation looked like a more likely spot.

"There were no houses back then," said my father, reading my mind. "This place was uninhabited. It's changed a lot."

He spent about ten minutes advising me on what to do the next day. I kept nodding to show him I understood.

As he prepared to leave, I shook his hand and thanked him. "I wish you luck," he said. "I forgive your mom, and I ask her to forgive me."

Then he put his hat on and walked over to my car. He shook hands and greeted Zinhle and my uncles. I watched the awkwardness. Zinhle was expressionless. My uncles didn't know what to do when he extended a hand to them. They quietly shook his hand, perhaps remembering what I had told them.

"There's no need for revenge," I'd said. "There's no dignity in disrespecting my father. We need to show him that we're different. That we're humane."

I understood that they were still hurting at the loss of my mom. Even after so many years, none of us had found closure. It was made worse by our failure to find my mom's grave. None of us had properly mourned her.

My father drove off. I quickly pulled a steel plate and the bag of *impepho* out of the boot. We all walked down the embankment to the stream. I put the *impepho* on the plate and lit it. As the smoke and the scent blew into my face, I began speaking to Mom.

"Mom, this is your son. I'm here with Zinhle and your brothers. For far too long you've stayed in this strange place. It's time for you to come home. I'm here to ask you to prepare yourself. Tomorrow we will come and fetch you, to go and live in peace with Amadlaba, the Shezi clan."

I kept staring as the small fire took its time to consume the *impepho*. I savoured the moment by picturing Mom staring at me and smiling. I let the smoke blow into my face, and inhaled the dry scent, while the smoke disappeared. I could feel myself entering this superstitious world. Still staring at the ash building up on the plate, I was interrupted by Uncle Vusi lighting a cigarette. I looked at him. "Mom didn't take kindly to smoking," I said. "Just watch. In a few seconds the cigarette will die." I had meant it as a joke. But perhaps in awe of the dead, he quickly walked away. We laughed as Uncle Vusi stumbled on the rocks and almost fell.

As we sat around the table later that night, my uncles wondered aloud how long my mom's spirit had wandered that valley. The view is that if the spirit of a dead person is not taken home from where they die, they become restless and unhappy. It must have been a difficult twenty-six years for her, I thought, sinking into the world of myth and superstition.

"Countless spirits are left to wander," my uncles said. "These forsaken souls do their best to comfort one another. But with each year that passes, they grow more restless, waiting for their living relatives to come for them. The spirits long to go home and be with other ancestors. Sometimes their longing makes them angry. So angry that they cast bad luck onto the living to get their attention. But once home, the spirits find peace and become good ancestors. After finding peace, they shower their family with good luck."

I had always been cynical about all this. But now I wasn't sure what to think. But since it was Mom who had come to me in a dream, I decided it wasn't about me or what I thought. What I believed was beside the point. I just wanted Mom to be happy. If she wanted me to walk this road to bring her peace, I was happy to walk it with her. I would do anything to appease her spirit and make her happy.

We spent the next day preparing to fetch Mom. We would leave in the afternoon and be home shortly after sunset. I spent anxious hours researching as much as I could to ensure every ritual was performed correctly. To my dismay, not even the elders knew for sure what to do. Only two elders in the family could offer a few pieces of information. My uncles just shrugged.

In the small Catholic village of Pevensey the priests were mostly German and didn't allow cultural rituals in the community. According to the Church, the souls of the dead left the flesh after death. Those who had loved and feared God went to heaven, while the souls of others who had lived a life of sin went to purgatory to repent and be purified before they were fit for heaven. Those who had sinned so badly that they couldn't be purified ended up in limbo.

Because goats were used for traditional rituals, they were forbidden in Pevensey. The few who performed such rituals did so at night. But they risked being caught by watchful village leaders, who wouldn't hesitate to report them to the priests. Those who were caught might even be exiled from the village. But by now the German priests had been replaced by black South African priests who understood cultural practices. I could now openly perform a ritual.

But decades without these rituals meant that no one knew for sure what I was meant to do. Once again my stepmother came to the rescue. I sat on my laptop, frantically typing every step as she guided me over the phone. My uncles were amused at my habit of typing up every detail. My education, they teased, had weakened my mind and robbed me of the ability to absorb and remember what I was told.

But I wanted to be sure I got everything right. I constantly repeated the information to my uncles. There would be no time to refer to my laptop when the time came.

Around sunset, I set out with uncles Zozi and Eric, and a relative who would drive on the way back. Halfway through our journey, we stopped to look for the *umlahlankosi* tree. We needed a small branch from it to carry the spirit of my mother on her journey home. The rest of the way was painfully slow because of a thick fog.

Finally I walked down the embankment, holding a plate of burning *impepho* in one hand and a branch in the other, calling out to my mother.

"Mom, I've come back to take you home, like I promised." I reached the spot beside the stream, put down the plate and continued speaking to her. "Please come home with me." Soon the *impepho* had burnt out. When I opened the car door moments later, I asked Mom to get in with me. The ritual dictated that as soon as I left the spot where I had asked Mom to come home, I wasn't to speak to anyone else, nor look around. I was to look forward and speak only to Mom.

I needed to ask her to stay with us each time we crossed a bridge. This made me nervous. I suddenly realised that I'd forgotten to note all the bridges on the way there. As we were about to cross the first bridge near where we had just lit the *impepho*, I asked her to cross over with us. We then drove more than two dozen kilometres through the fog. We were approaching Boston when my uncle whispered that we were approaching a bridge. After quickly saying okay and doing as he had said, I realised he shouldn't have spoken to me. I felt annoyed.

My neck was stiff from looking in one direction only. I couldn't wait to get home and be released from all this. I looked down at the branch I was holding and saw a white spider. It must have been on the branch when I tore it off the tree. Watching the spider brought respite from the boredom of being unable to turn my head. No one spoke. The radio was off, and the only sound was the light patter of raindrops.

A river cut across the road as we approached the villages before Bulwer. I warned Mom that we were about to cross another bridge, and urged her to stay with us. My uncle nodded his approval. I was proud that I'd remembered. Very soon afterwards he gestured with his hands, reminding me that the river meandered along and then cut across the road a second time. Again I asked Mom to stay with us as we crossed.

Hail started to fall as we climbed past the villages of Nkumba and Nkelabantwana that dotted the hills. The driver glanced back at me and gestured with his hands, trying to alert me that the pounding hail might damage the car. I ignored him. It didn't seem important. I just wanted this to go well. I could worry about my car later when this was done. The hail was soon over.

About ten kilometres from home we came to a railway bridge. Instinctively, I announced that we were about to cross. I told my mom it was the same railway track that passed our village. Uncle Eric nodded, impressed. Next, I announced that we were about to cross the Polela. Finally we turned onto the gravel road to Pevensey village. I told Mom not to be surprised at the improved roads.

"Many things have changed here, Mom. But this is where you grew up. You're home."

There was a large bucket of water mixed with herbs waiting for us at the gate. Uncle Vusi, who had stayed behind, was holding a black chicken. I stepped out of the car, still carrying the branch.

Kneeling beside the bucket, I told Mom we were about to cleanse her with the chicken and water. "*Ngifuna ungene kwaDlaba umhlophe umsulwa*," I told Mom. I wanted her to join her fellow ancestors looking bright and beautiful.

No sooner had I uttered these words that Uncle Zozi pulled a knife and cut the chicken's throat. Then he tore open its torso without removing the feathers. Squeamish, I looked away and pointed to the goat, telling Mom that I'd bought it for her to share with the ancestors. Uncle Zozi found the bile of the chicken, and sprinkled some into the bucket before handing the remainder to me to sprinkle on the branch. The cleansing process to welcome Mom home was now complete.

They handed me the live goat as I entered the gate. The party followed me as I walked around the homestead, showing Mom around her home. I showed her all the houses in the homestead. Then we entered a thatched hut. At the far end were seven candles arranged around a clay calabash filled with traditional beer.

I burnt the *impepho* once more, and asked the ancestors to welcome Mom into their fold. Then I lit the candles, telling my Mom that six of them represented the fellow ancestors she was joining, and the seventh represented her.

Uncle Vusi knelt behind me. "*Usukhululekile manje mfana*," he said, releasing me from the restriction of speaking to no one but Mom. It was a relief.

I sat down to rest on a bench. Immediately Uncle Zozi handed me a spear. "You must kill the goat." Everyone turned to look at me.

I was horrified. "No," I shook my head. "I really can't. Please do it for me."

He smiled and approached the goat as I headed for the door. I couldn't bear to watch it meet its end.

"You softy," said Uncle Vusi as I stepped out of the hut. I managed a smile. As a boy I had shot birds with a catapult, but always kept away when larger prey like buck and rabbits were finished off. With my lack of experience, the poor goat would have suffered as I fumbled to kill it. The sound of its squeals drove me even further from the house. I only returned when my cousins were removing the skin.

The goat's parts were carefully laid on its skin. Now it was time for the sheep. This wasn't part of the ritual, but to ensure enough food for all the visitors the next day. Uncle Zozi waited for me to step outside before slaughtering it. But sheep die quietly, so I didn't have to run so far this time.

Forty-three

On the morning of the feast it poured with rain. Everyone worried about where to position the fires for the three-legged pots in which the food was to be cooked. The size of the pots meant that several fires were needed to cook all the meat and dumplings. My uncles struggled to get the fires going in the thatched house. But at about 10 a.m. the rain cleared.

Later, many guests said that the rain was a sign we had successfully brought Mom home. "You're a man now," one old woman said to me. "You should be proud of yourself."

I felt enormous relief. It was as if a massive boulder had been lifted from my shoulders. In just six months I had achieved a lot. I had found my father and discovered a great deal about my mother. Most of the questions I had carried as a child were now answered. I felt spiritually relieved, and positive about life. So positive that I felt I could do anything I wanted with minimal pain and uncertainty.

"*Umama wakho uzokupha izinhlanhla*. Your mother will shower you with luck," I was told many times that day. I wasn't so sure. I was grateful to these people, because they really meant these words and wished me well. But I hadn't done this to bring luck. I had done it because Mom had asked me to. I hoped she was happy that I had honoured her request, and was now released from her years of suffering. I was happy she was now home.

I saw many happy faces that day, and shook many hands of those who had come to support me. I felt a lot of satisfaction. It's over, I kept thinking. I could now live my life knowing that I had put most pieces of the puzzle together. I now knew a great deal about what had happened to Mom. I had dug up so much information. Yet finding my father had been a great disappointment and a fresh source of heartache. On that score I was no better off than before.

Before leaving Pevensey to return to Johannesburg, I paid a visit to Auntie Zinto. At the feast she had asked me to come and see her, and I was glad to. She had been an angel while I was growing up, buying me secondhand clothes, producing a new suit for my first communion, and giving me advice when I got into difficulties as a teenager. And whenever I had strayed, she had never hidden her disappointment.

Apart from Zinhle and I, Auntie Zinto was perhaps the one most affected by our mom's death. It was clear that the pain still weighed heavily on her as she sat on the couch.

"I've kept quiet all these years," she said, "to protect you two from the pain. But it's clear that you want to know."

"For years your mom hoped your father would marry her, even after she found out that he had a common-law wife. He always promised to marry her. But his family didn't like your mom. Rural people didn't like their sons to marry city women, because they felt these women didn't respect their husbands and their families.

"I never liked your father from the start. Something about him made me uneasy. But your mom always laughed off my doubts, until he started assaulting her and cheating on her openly. But it took years of abuse and empty promises before your mom found the courage to leave him for another man.

"Your father was furious. He flew into a rage and started phoning daily, threatening to kill her if she didn't take him back. But she'd made up her mind. Nothing could sway her this time. She had left him many times before, but taken him back when he pleaded with her.

"This time was different. But the more she refused your father's advances, the more he threatened her. I was there once when she

242

received a call. She kept telling him she'd rather die than take him back. We never thought he might actually carry out his threat.

"One night when I was visiting your mom I saw a figure hiding in the trees. I warned her that it could be your father, but she laughed. I told her that the stalking might go beyond phone calls. But she was in love and too happy to be worried.

"One morning she came to me crying. She told me your father had abducted her the previous night. We went to the police to open a rape case. Your mom had to take the witness stand to relate how your father had come to her outside room at her work, bundled her into his car and kidnapped her for the night. It was harrowing to hear her story. She told the court that your father had sexually assaulted her throughout the night."

I sat listening in silence. So this was the final piece of the puzzle.

"That's why he killed her. To silence her once and for all. She vanished before she could finish testifying. Even after she vanished, your father continued attending the court dates. Several times the case was postponed because your mom failed to show up. The judge threatened to withdraw the case if your mom didn't come to court the next time.

"Meanwhile your mom's new boyfriend came to my place to say that he couldn't find her. So I went to her work, and realised that she'd gone missing. Her employers had found the food burning in the kitchen, and no sign of your mom. I knew then that she was dead. That your father had carried out his threat.

"It was nearly two months after your mom vanished when I got a call to say her body had been found in Lions River. A farm labourer had noticed what looked like a woman sleeping next to a stream. He thought she was drunk and yelled at her. When she didn't respond, he went closer to look. What he discovered horrified him. Your mother was covered in blood and wounds. She was dead.

"The police took her fingerprints and sent them to Pretoria for analysis. They decided to bury her. When the police eventually came to me, I told them about your father's threats. I then gave them the date he was next expected in court for his rape case. That's how he was arrested. I sent the police after him.

"When your father and his lawyer walked into the courtroom, it was clear they hadn't slept. They had clearly spent the whole night with a traditional healer to help him win the case.

"The magistrate nodded every time your father's lawyer spoke. Through his lawyer, your father made a full confession. He said he had used a blunt object to assault your mom. He said he had only meant to punish her. But when he realised she was dead, he panicked and bundled her body into the boot of his car. He drove towards Underberg, but when he reached Lions River he worried that he would get caught if he drove on. So he dumped her body on the side of the road near a plantation.

"The lawyer asked for leniency because it was a first offence. He asked that your father not be sent to jail, because he hadn't intended to kill her. He said that if your father went to jail, his kids would starve, because you would effectively become orphans. So he requested a suspended sentence.

"The court was convinced by your father's confession and his display of remorse, and gave him a six-year suspended sentence so he could look after you and your sister. My family members who had packed the court never even saw him leave. He was sneaked out the back. They sat there not believing their eyes.

"I had hoped to testify about the abuse, the threatening phone calls and the rape. But we were poor. We didn't have a lawyer to argue on our behalf. It was so hard to come to terms with your mom's death. But seeing your father go free was the darkest day of my life. I will never, never forgive him."

Then she began to talk about watching Zinhle and me growing up. "Sometimes I lost hope. I thought you two might never succeed in life." She shook her head. I could see the tears in her eyes. "*Unkulunkulu mkhulu*, the Lord is great," she said.

I was reminded of her advice to me when times were really tough. "Let it go in one ear and straight out the other." Those words had helped me survive. I remembered when Zinhle was forced to miss school to be a babysitter, and Auntie Zinto stormed into the yard and demanded she be allowed back to school. Auntie Zinto had saved us many times. She had been a true guardian angel.

Forty-four

Underberg had brought me nothing but misery in my childhood, but I still went back now and then, not to visit the past but to enjoy its scenic splendour. One day I had driven into the Drakensberg and was marvelling at the horizon and feeling blessed. Such peace, such beauty, what more could one ask?

Then something occurred to me. One more thing, Mr Polela. There was someone I still needed to see.

Seventeen years had passed since I had last seen Sister Von Ohr. Back then I was a disaffected teenager, disowned by the family I lived with and without any prospect of a future.

She had turned my life around by getting me back into school and giving me a gardening job to cover the fees. She set off a chain of events that eventually saw me educated.

My heart was beating as I pressed the bell at the gate of Sacred Heart, the old age home in Ixopo I had traced her to through Father Madela. Would she remember me? "She still has her senses," Father Madela had told me.

I had serious doubts that she would recollect what had happened so long ago. But it didn't matter, I told myself. What was more important was to thank her for changing my life, as inadequate as these words were. My story would have been very different if not for her.

The electric gate opened. No one asked who I was before letting me in. As my friend and I got out of the car, a smiling nun was waiting for us.

"Good afternoon, young men. How can I help you?" I explained, and she went off to look for her.

"She'll be with you shortly," she told me when she returned. She had just offered us tea and juice when Sister Von Ohr walked in. The wisp of hair protruding from her white headcover was grey. But she still looked healthy.

I stood up and she shook my hand warmly. "What can I do for you?" she asked in her German accent, as if it was the first time we had met.

I introduced myself, and reminded her of our chance meeting that had changed my life.

"Oh Lord. What a wonderful story!" she exclaimed. "And what are you doing now? Are you at university?" She wanted my whole story.

"You were the first person who told me I was good at anything," I told her. "The day we met, you told me my English was very good."

She listened intently to my tale, taking off her glasses to wipe a tear.

"This is the most beautiful Friday of my life," she said.

"Do you actually remember me, Sister?"

"Your name rings a bell. But whenever I walked from the mission to the school, I spoke to as many people as possible on the way. I put several people to work and helped them financially."

So I wasn't the only one whose life Sister Von Ohr's generosity had changed. It had meant so much to me. But she was only doing what she felt the Lord wanted.

"Why did you leave Pevensey without saying goodbye?" I wanted to know. She told me that she had been transferred, but still went back to visit occasionally. We discussed the priests who were there during her time, and the McNamaras, and reminisced about the early nineties. Then she told me her own news. She had just turned eighty, but still taught the novices and led them in prayer.

She smiled. "You've made my day, McIntosh," she said.

"You changed my life, Sister." We laughed.

As we walked outside we continued to chat while my friend took photos of us. I didn't want to leave, and she too seemed to want to prolong the moment. Then we shared a polite hug and said goodbye.

"I'll never forget you, McIntosh, even when I'm ninety. May God be with you. I'll take your name with me when I go to heaven."

She didn't stop waving until I was out of sight.

Forty-five

In June 2010, my stepmother and her family called me to Ladysmith for a "meeting". On the phone my stepmother told me that the family was particularly happy that Zinhle had finally agreed after two years to make the trip and meet the family. When I arrived that afternoon, I was surprised to see so many cars parked in the yard.

Moments later, the family led us to a thatched hut for a special ceremony. Two chairs were reserved, one for Zinhle and one for me. In front of us was a large white cake with our names written in icing, and the words "Welcome Home". A preacher led us in prayer, and then my stepmother rose tell us why we were all here.

"This is the happiest day of my life," she said emotionally. "My kids have come home. I know that the two of you were invited to a meeting, but when Zinhle agreed to come, we all decided that it was time to officially welcome you home and celebrate with you." Then she told everyone that she had invited my father to come. "But I don't think he will," she said.

What started as a formal introduction of Zinhle and me into the Nzimande family quickly turned into an opportunity for us all to express our feelings. We shared tears, and everyone decided that it was time to forgive my father. I had long since forgiven him, but for them it had taken until this moment to do so. I was the first to be asked to speak.

This was the first time I had seen my name on a cake, I told them. As a child who had never once celebrated my birthday, nor even been reminded of it or received a birthday gift, this cake meant a lot to me, even though it wasn't my birthday.

My sister never speaks much, so when she rose, I expected her to say thank you and sit down. I was in for a surprise.

"For a long time, I never accepted my father," she said. She turned to me. "I always referred to him as *your* father. But now I feel like I've been born again, and I realise there's no point living in the past. It's time to leave it behind. I accept him as my father, and by the grace of God I will learn to love him."

At this moment, I was released from my guilt for convincing Zinhle to meet our father. I was so proud that she had eventually decided to forgive him.

My eldest half-brother, Simpiwe, spoke next. "In this family, almost all the males drive trucks, because my father refused to let us go to university," he said. "When I went on trips in my truck, I always carried McIntosh's photo with me. Whenever I was in Durban, I would take out the picture and walk around the city looking at the street kids to try to find him. I thought there was no chance he would have made it in life after my father abandoned him and Zinhle. When I found street kids sleeping under a bridge near my trucking depot in Durban, I would lift the plastic bags under which they were sleeping and examine their faces. But I was always disappointed.

"Eventually I realised that you were probably a young man and looked different. I gave up looking for you, and hoped you would show up one day. When you did, I saw your car and it was like a dream. I realised I'd been wasting my time looking for you in the streets. There's no dumpster for people with the kind of childhood we've had. We can defy the odds, tear up the scripts people expect us to follow and create our own.

"I remember when I was a teenager, and I finally dared to ask my parents where you two were. I expected my father to beat me, as usual. But he just told me to leave the room. Later my mother said I had made him very angry, and he had warned her that we must never ask about you again."

Then Sindi spoke. "To this day, I can't wear high heels, because my father hit me so badly that my ankle is damaged. I rebelled against him and managed to get a teaching diploma. Even when I got married, he tried to stop me, and I had to defy him."

Sne tried to speak next, but simply burst into tears. He couldn't handle the pain.

As the night wore on, I began to reflect on this family who my sister and I had never got to spend time with growing up. Despite their own hardships, they genuinely loved and cared about us. I completely understood the horrors they had related to me, and now to my sister. Perhaps through understanding our own, they had chosen to embrace my sister and me. My father had turned out to be a bitter disappointment; but through seeking him, Zinhle and I had discovered that we'd had a loving family all along, who had always cared about us.

It was probably too late to build a close bond after so many years had passed. Each of us had to go our separate ways and carve out our own lives. But from now on, we would forever know that we had a family. In finding my father, I had also managed to say goodbye to my mom. It wasn't as good as attending her funeral and having a grave to visit or ashes to scatter. But I had got the chance to rest her soul, nonetheless.

It was thanks to this family that I could do so. I was immensely grateful to my stepmother for her honesty and braveness. Zinhle and I had come into this world because her husband had cheated on her. Yet she had embraced and loved us as her own. I will forever be indebted to her for what she has done for me. It pains me that she will probably endure terrible treatment from my father for as long as she lives, but I will always be there when she needs my help. It's the least I can do after all she's done for me.

My stepmother helped me to mourn my mom and ease the pain I have always carried at losing her. By preserving a part of my history through those photos and the letter my mom had written twenty-six years earlier, my stepmother helped me through a significant part of my journey.

I still have not summoned the strength to open or read the letter. I have decided never to do so, for fear of being gutted and disappointed by my mom's words. But I will keep it with me for as long as I live. That little blue piece of paper will forever be a reminder that Zinhle and I, at least for a couple of years of our lives, had a mom who loved and cared for us. Although she never had the chance to show just how much she did, she will forever be special in our memories.

Epilogue

Pevensey has changed little. The cocks still crow at dawn, and young boys still wake at first light to milk the cows and drive the cattle to the pastures. During school holidays, they stay in the fields to tend them. Boys still swim in the Polela and play pranks on unsuspecting newcomers. Their social horizon is as narrow as mine was back in the early eighties. They hardly know that there is life beyond the hills.

There are many such villages in South Africa and elsewhere. And there are many stories like mine, stories that are sometimes hard to believe. People who see me on television or hear me on radio assume that I grew up in a well-to-do family and went on expensive holidays. They cannot imagine me growing up in a place like Pevensey. Childhood friends encounter skepticism when they say we grew up together. But it gives me immense pleasure to know that for generations to come, my kids, their kids and their grandchildren will walk along the Polela and say: "This is where we originate. This is where we come from."

Although I have attained an education, and endless opportunities lie before me, I will never forget the long road I travelled from the small village of Pevensey all the way to the streets of London. I will forever be a country boy from Underberg. This knowledge keeps me grounded.

Zinhle, too, is now educated and has a job. In March 2009 I gave her away in marriage. In my speech I thanked the Shezi family for giving us food and shelter. I thanked the McNamaras for raising my sister, helping us through difficult times and giving us our sister, Laurelle. And I asked Zinhle's husband to take care of my beloved sister. It was one of the proudest days of my life.

My wonderful stepmother, who has done so much for me, still has stories to tell. Her tales of horror at the hands of my father never end. She still encourages me to find my mother's grave. She believes that my father must pay to have my mom's remains exhumed so that she can rest in dignity next to her relatives some day. I agree. But for now, I need to recharge. It's been a long and exhausting journey.

Nothing has assuaged my grief as effectively as writing this book. It has helped me to join the dots, dig up the truth and put the puzzle pieces together. As a teenager I made mistakes. The decisions of youth, when we are stupid and unafraid, have a major impact on our lives. Writing my life story has allowed me to examine the choices I made and the painful things I experienced. Somehow, my instincts saved me. I knew when to quit.

Some of the things that happened to my sister and me I have told no one. But as the pages of this book multiplied, we found it easier to talk and to deal with the hidden aspects of our early lives. It has become easier to accept that our pain is part of our past, a past we can neither change nor erase.

By seeking my father, I had hoped to put the past behind me. Instead, the past caught up with me. My father did not turn out as I anticipated. He turned out to be just as my extended family had described: a monster. His evil ways have torn up the script of my fantasies. I cannot change the monster that is my father. But these pages have given me the courage to gaze into my soul and cleanse the squalid thoughts I had about him; to seek him out, look into his eyes and ask for answers. Though I was deeply disappointed, I have come out a stronger person. Since the day my father pointed out where my mom's body had lain, I have been certain of his guilt. But questions still linger. Why such rage, such brutality, such evil?

Even when what I heard about my father was too much to bear, I grew stronger. I found the wisdom to know what to do. It has taken time to reassemble the pieces of my heart that were blown to smithereens by pain, anger, hate and thoughts of revenge. Slowly, piece by piece in the face of doubt, I have had some release through reaching out and forgiving.

My father has tested the limits and strength of my ability to forgive. Yet I have come through it still believing it was the right thing to do. Before I forgave him I had merely existed, wallowing in grief. Only when I forgave did I start to live. Suddenly there was purpose in my life and I could move on. Without him.

When I discarded my father's surname, I did so unhesitatingly. I knew it was right to rid myself of him once and for all, to cease to carry his sins. To become myself.

It feels strange to have twice changed my identity. But in some strange way I'm proud to have carved my own destiny. I'm proud of the entire journey that got me here. I've made my choices. I could have quit and yelled "Enough!" I could have played victim, dropped out of school and blamed everyone but myself. I certainly came perilously close to fulfilling my lust for revenge.

But I chose to overcome my appalling childhood, and turn my back on anger. I forgave, let go of my past as best I could and became a better person. I'm only lucky I was able to live through it all and overcome the odds.

Yet I have not completely shaken off my father. For a brief moment, a weight lifted off my shoulders when I told him that I forgave him. But subsequent revelations, along with the pain he still inflicts on those he is meant to love, have brought new heaviness.

My father still phones and lectures me. Sometimes he tells me he is the equivalent of a god whom I and all his children should worship. I would write him off as crazy, except that this might appear to exonerate him from all the evil he has done.

At one stage after meeting him, frustration got the better of me and I made plans to return to the UK forever. But then I realised that I could never escape him by crossing the ocean, because he remains a part of me. At the same time, I realise that I don't have to carry my father's sins and mistakes and suffer as if they were mine. And I don't have to be defined by my past.

I have defined myself. I grew up fearing I would turn out like my father. But I am not. I can never be.

Although I grew up in confusion, without knowing where I belonged, I have found a new vigour. I may not have found happiness, but at least I have the truth. Naturally, after such a difficult upbringing, some embers remain from the fire. I cannot shake off the images of my past. They will stay with me forever, and I will probably carry scars for the rest of my days.

Perhaps I may never find closure, but my journey to healing continues. Some who know my story have suggested extensive counselling to deal with my past. But where could one begin when there has been so much pain? And how could I take advice from an outsider? I have developed my own survival techniques and made it through.

I still keep to myself and have few close friends. But I am lucky to have had a few who have taught me that it's okay to be loved. I have by my side an incredible person who has stuck with me even in the hardest of times.

If I had the chance to change my upbinging, there is little I would change. For the challenges I faced have shaped my identity and my life. I've learnt that regrets are pointless. We often believe that the loss of a loved one signifies the end of a life. I clung to the loss of my mother until Cheryl Wood taught me that it was an opportunity to change, accept, forgive and become a new person. And I was reborn and began a new life.

My mom's death taught me to tackle life's challenges without the cushion of a shoulder to cry on; with no one to run to with excuses when I tripped and fell for lack of trying hard enough.

I'm convinced that she died so I could grow to be a better person. The pain of her loss and my years of suffering have made me stronger. They taught Zinhle and me to tackle seemingly insurmountable challenges and succeed.

I am grateful to all who opened their doors when I knocked, who listened to my story and took me under their wing, who felt pity and did something about the story I told. I was blessed with many people who changed my life and taught me the value of hard work.

My striving for an education made a world of a difference. I learnt that even coming from a tiny and backward village, I could be someone. I could almost conjure miracles.

Sometimes I marvel that I made it through. And then it occurs to me that my faith in the Lord saw me through. He heard my prayers and guided me through the difficult times. He gave me strength when it seemed I had reached a dead end. He gave me an ounce of extra energy when I couldn't take another step.

When hope was lost, a solution always came out of nowhere. When I was out on the dusty streets, disowned for my behaviour, Sister Von Ohr appeared to make sure I returned to school. At high school Mrs Wood picked me out and allowed me to forgive my father. Father Madela happened to transfer to Mariannhill just as I finished school, and organised the cheque that got me into technikon. And when I quit because it was impossible to study, Janet Maxwell happened to be at the gate when I visited the campus. Some nights I have tears of gratitude for Gogo, who came forward to help me get through technikon. I love her so much I wish she could live forever, and continue to give kindness to others in need. I feel I owe my very being to her and to all who contributed when I needed help. I am only sad that I never had the chance to thank many who contributed to my life. These include Dala, who died while I was at university, and the Woods who apparently now live in the United Kingdom, but whom I have been unable to trace.

I cannot explain how all these things happened, but I feel that someone looked out for me all the way. I have come to accept it all as the Lord's plan. I'm not deeply religious, and I hardly go to church, but my faith has never left me. I am convinced that the Lord has guided and looked after me all the way. I believe He is the reason I have won the battle against my demons.

I still recite the Lord's Prayer, and then say the same words from my youth: "Lead me, Lord, and I will follow, even though I don't know where. You alone, Lord, know my destiny."

What is *My Father, My Monster* about?
It's my life journey from about the age of five. As you have just found out from reading my memoir, most of it reads like a horror movie. But it was all very real for me.

Did you write this book as some form of catharsis; to rid yourself of the demons?
I had, for almost all my life, put a lid on my pain, my horrors and my demons. I decided to face all of these and hopefully rid myself of them once and for all. But more importantly, I wanted to find closure.
Facing my pain has helped me get some release. But at the same time, the past has caught up with me and made it all very real and fresh. I don't know that I will ever be free.

You and your sister were brutally abused by some members of your extended family. Have you managed to forgive them?
I have managed to forgive them and I guess this part was easier compared to forgiving my father. My extended family provided food and shelter. They barely had anything and they chose to face some of the difficulties in their life with us. Zozi and his younger brother Igbo helped with transport money while I was at university. We have been in contact as family for the rest of our lives. I guess this helped redeem the pain they inflicted. It's taken a lot longer for Zinhle to forgive, but I'm glad she has.

Did you achieve what you hoped to achieve by changing both your name and surname?
Being McIntosh has always felt great, it was like I was born with the name. I guess because it doesn't carry any baggage. Nzimande was a different story! I never accepted the surname. But almost every time I hear people call me McIntosh Polela, I feel a sense of pride. Polela gives me some sense of history. To me, this is the meaning of life itself, it's very profound. Being McIntosh Polela makes me feel complete. It's one part of my life that says I'm finally free.

To ask McIntosh more questions, follow him on Twitter @toshpolela and Facebook McIntosh Polela.

You can also view a short interview with him at www.jacana.co.za